Charles William Eliot

American contributions to civilization,

And other essays and addresses

Charles William Eliot

American contributions to civilization,
And other essays and addresses

ISBN/EAN: 9783337717056

Printed in Europe, USA, Canada, Australia, Japan

Cover: Foto ©ninafisch / pixelio.de

More available books at **www.hansebooks.com**

AMERICAN CONTRIBUTIONS TO CIVILIZATION

AND

OTHER ESSAYS AND ADDRESSES

BY

CHARLES WILLIAM ELIOT, LL.D.

PRESIDENT OF HARVARD UNIVERSITY

NEW YORK

The Century Co.

1898

THE DEVINNE PRESS.

PREFACE

THIS book contains some of the miscellaneous addresses and magazine articles which I have written during the last twenty-five years, educational addresses and papers being reserved for another volume. With the exception of trifling corrections made in revising the proofs, these papers are now printed just as they were originally published.

I beg the reader to regard the date of each address or article. Otherwise he may be surprised at some statements which have ceased to be entirely accurate.

C. W. E.

NORTH EAST HARBOR, MAINE.
August 20, 1897.

CONTENTS

FIVE AMERICAN CONTRIBUTIONS TO CIVILIZATION

AN ADDRESS

Delivered at Chautauqua, August 19, 1896

FIVE AMERICAN CONTRIBUTIONS TO CIVILIZATION

LOOKING back over forty centuries of history, we observe that many nations have made characteristic contributions to the progress of civilization, the beneficent effects of which have been permanent, although the races that made them may have lost their national form and organization, or their relative standing among the nations of the earth. Thus, the Hebrew race, during many centuries, made supreme contributions to religious thought; and the Greek, during the brief climax of the race, to speculative philosophy, architecture, sculpture, and the drama. The Roman people developed military colonization, aqueducts, roads and bridges, and a great body of public law, large parts of which still survive; and the Italians of the middle ages and the Renaissance developed ecclesiastical organization and the fine arts, as tributary to the splendor of the church and to municipal luxury. England, for several centuries, has contributed to the institutional development of representative government and public justice; the Dutch, in the sixteenth century, made a superb struggle for free thought and free government; France, in the eighteenth century, taught the doctrine of individual freedom and the theory of human rights; and Germany, at two periods within the nineteenth century, fifty years apart, proved the vital force of the sentiment of nationality. I ask you to consider with me what characteristic and durable contributions the American people have been making to the progress of civilization.

The first and principal contribution to which I shall ask your attention is the advance made in the United States, not in theory only, but in practice, toward the abandonment of war as the means of settling disputes between nations, the substitution of discussion and arbitration, and the avoidance of armaments. If the intermittent Indian fighting and the brief contest with the Barbary corsairs be disregarded, the United States have had only four years and a quarter of international war in the one hundred and seven years since the adoption of the Constitution. Within the same period the United States have been a party to forty-seven arbitrations—being more than half of all that have taken place in the modern world. The questions settled by these arbitrations have been just such as have commonly caused wars, namely, questions of boundary, fisheries, damage caused by war or civil disturbances, and injuries to commerce. Some of them were of great magnitude, the four made under the treaty of Washington (May 8, 1871) being the most important that have ever taken place. Confident in their strength, and relying on their ability to adjust international differences, the United States have habitually maintained, by voluntary enlistment for short terms, a standing army and a fleet which, in proportion to the population, are insignificant.

The beneficent effects of this American contribution to civilization are of two sorts: in the first place, the direct evils of war and of preparations for war have been diminished; and secondly, the influence of the war spirit on the perennial conflict between the rights of the single personal unit and the powers of the multitude that constitute organized society—or, in other words, between individual freedom and collective authority—has been reduced to the lowest terms. War has been, and still is, the school of collectivism, the warrant of tyranny. Century after century, tribes, clans, and nations have sacrificed the liberty of the individual to the fundamental necessity of being strong for combined defense or attack in war. Individual freedom is crushed in war, for the nature of war is inevitably despotic. It says to the private person: "Obey without a question, even unto death; die in this ditch, without knowing why; walk into that deadly thicket; mount this embankment, behind which are men who will try to kill you, lest you should kill them; make part of an immense machine for blind destruction, cruelty, rapine, and killing." At this moment every young man in Continental Europe learns the lesson of absolute military obedience, and feels himself subject to this crushing power of militant society, against which no rights of the individual to life, liberty, and the pursuit of happiness avail anything. This pernicious influence, inherent in the social organization of all Continental Europe during many centuries, the American people have for generations escaped, and they show other nations how to escape it. I ask your attention to the favorable conditions under which this contribution of the United States to civilization has been made.

There has been a deal of fighting on the American continent during the past three centuries; but it has not been of the sort which most imperils liberty. The first European colonists who occupied portions of the coast of North America encountered in the Indians men of the Stone Age, who ultimately had to be resisted and quelled by force. The Indian races were at a stage of development thousands of years behind that of the Europeans. They could not be assimilated; for the most part they could not be taught or even reasoned with; with a few exceptions they had to be driven away by prolonged fighting, or subdued by force so that they would live peaceably with the whites. This warfare, however, always had in it for the whites a large element of self-defense — the homes and families of the settlers were to be defended against a stealthy and pitiless foe. Constant exposure to the attacks of savages was only one of the formidable dangers and difficulties which for a hundred years the early settlers had to meet, and which developed in them courage, hardiness, and persistence. The French and English wars on the North American continent, always more or less mixed with Indian warfare, were characterized by race hatred and religious animosity — two of the commonest causes of war in all ages; but they did not tend to fasten upon the English colonists any objectionable public authority, or to contract the limits of individual liberty. They furnished a school of martial qualities at small cost to liberty. In the War of Independence there was a distinct hope and purpose to enlarge individual liberty. It made possible a confederation of the colonies, and, ultimately, the adoption of the Constitution of the United States. It gave to the thirteen colonies a lesson in collectivism, but it was a needed lesson on the necessity of combining their forces to resist an oppressive external authority. The war of 1812 is properly called the Second War of Independence, for it was truly a fight for liberty and for the rights of neutrals, in resistance to the impressment of seamen and other oppressions growing out of European conflicts. The civil war of 1861–65 was waged, on the side of the North, primarily, to prevent the dismemberment of the country, and, secondarily and incidentally, to destroy the institution of slavery. On the Northern side it therefore called forth a generous element of popular ardor in defense of free institutions; and though it temporarily caused centralization of great powers in the government, it did as much to promote individual freedom as it did to strengthen public authority.

In all this series of fightings the main motives were self-defense, resistance to oppression, the enlargement of liberty, and the conservation of national acquisitions. The war with Mexico, it is true, was of a wholly different type. That was a war of conquest, and of conquest chiefly in the interest of African slavery. It was also an unjust attack made by a powerful people on a feeble one; but it lasted less than two years, and the number of men engaged in it was at no time large. Moreover, by the treaty which ended the war, the conquering nation agreed to pay the conquered eighteen million dollars in partial compensation for some of the territory wrested from it, instead of demanding a huge war-indemnity, as the European way is. Its results contradicted the anticipations both of those who advocated and of those who opposed it. It was one of the wrongs which prepared the way for the great rebellion; but its direct evils were of moderate extent, and it had no effect on the perennial conflict between individual liberty and public power.

In the meantime, partly as the results of Indian fighting and the Mexican war, but chiefly through purchases and arbitrations, the American people had acquired a territory so extensive, so defended by oceans, gulfs, and great lakes, and so intersected by those great natural highways, navigable rivers, that it would obviously be impossible for any enemy to overrun or subdue it. The civilized nations of Europe, western Asia, and northern Africa have always been liable to hostile incursions from without. Over and over again barbarous hordes have overthrown established civilizations; and at this moment there is not a nation of Europe which does not feel obliged to maintain monstrous armaments for defense against its neighbors. The American people have long been exempt from such terrors, and are now absolutely free from this necessity of keeping in readiness to meet heavy assaults. The absence of a great standing army and of a large fleet has been a main characteristic of the United States, in contrast with the other civilized nations; this has been a great inducement to immigration, and a prime cause of the country's rapid increase in wealth. The United States have no formidable neighbor, except Great Britain in Canada. In April, 1817, by a convention made between Great Britain and the United States, without much public discussion or observation, these two powerful nations agreed that each should keep on the Great Lakes only a few police vessels of insignificant size and armament. This agreement was made but four years after Perry's naval victory on Lake Erie, and only three years after the burning of Washington by a British force. It was one of the first acts of Monroe's first administration, and it would be difficult to find in all history a more judicious or effectual agreement between two powerful neighbors. For eighty years this beneficent convention has helped to keep the peace. The European way would have been to build competitive fleets, dockyards, and fortresses, all of which would have helped to bring on war during the periods of mutual exasperation which have occurred since 1817. Monroe's second administration was signalized, six years later, by the declaration that the United States would consider any attempt on the part of the Holy Alliance to extend their system to any portion of this hemisphere as dangerous to the peace and safety of the United States. This announcement was designed to prevent the introduction on the American continent of the horrible European system — with its balance of power, its alliances offensive and defensive in opposing groups, and its perpetual armaments on an enormous scale. That a declaration expressly intended to promote peace and prevent armaments should now be perverted into an argument for arming and for a belligerent public policy is an extraordinary perversion of the true American doctrine.

The ordinary causes of war between nation and nation have been lacking in America for the last century and a quarter. How many wars in the world's history have been due to contending dynasties; how many of the most cruel and protracted wars have been due to religious strife; how many to race hatred! No one of these causes of war has been efficacious in America since the French were overcome in Canada by the English in 1759. Looking forward into the future, we find it impossible to imagine circumstances under which any of these common causes of war can take effect on the North American continent. Therefore, the ordinary motives for maintaining armaments in time of peace, and concentrating the powers of government in such a way as to interfere with individual liberty, have not been in play in the United States as among the nations of Europe, and are not likely to be.

Such have been the favorable conditions under which America has made its best contribution to the progress of our race.

There are some people of a perverted sentimentality who occasionally lament the absence in our country of the ordinary inducements to war, on the ground that war develops certain noble qualities in some of the combatants, and gives opportunity for the practice of heroic virtues, such as courage, loyalty, and self-sacrifice. It is further said that prolonged peace makes nations effeminate, luxurious, and materialistic, and substitutes for the high ideals of the patriot soldier the low ideals of the farmer, manufacturer, tradesman, and pleasure-seeker. This view seems to me to err in two opposite ways. In the first place, it forgets that war, in spite of the fact that it develops some splendid virtues, is the most horrible occupation that human beings can possibly engage in. It is cruel, treacherous, and murderous. Defensive warfare, particularly on the part of a weak nation against powerful invaders or oppressors, excites a generous sympathy; but for every heroic defense there must be an attack by a preponderating force, and war, being the conflict of the two, must be judged by its moral effects not on one party, but on both parties. Moreover, the weaker party may have the worse cause. The immediate ill effects of war are bad enough, but its after effects are generally worse, because indefinitely prolonged and indefinitely wasting and damaging. At this moment, thirty-one years after the end of our civil war, there are two great evils afflicting our country which took their rise in that war, namely, (1) the belief of a large proportion of our people in money without intrinsic value, or worth less than its face, and made current solely by act of Congress, and (2) the payment of immense annual sums in pensions. It is the paper-money delusion born of the civil war which generated and supports the silver-money delusion of to-day. As a consequence of the war, the nation has paid $2,000,000,000 in pensions within thirty-three years. So far as pensions are paid to disabled persons, they are a just and inevitable, but unproductive expenditure; so far as they are paid to persons who are not disabled,—men or women,—they are in the main not only unproductive but demoralizing; so far as they promote the marriage of young women to old men, as a pecuniary speculation, they create a grave social evil. It is impossible to compute or even imagine the losses and injuries already inflicted by the fiat-money delusion; and we know that some of the worst evils of the pension system will go on for a hundred years to come, unless the laws about widows' pensions are changed for the better. It is a significant fact that of the existing pensioners of the war of 1812 only twenty-one are surviving soldiers or sailors, while 3826 are widows.[1]

[1] June 30, 1895.

War gratifies, or used to gratify, the combative instinct of mankind, but it gratifies also the love of plunder, destruction, cruel discipline, and arbitrary power. It is doubtful whether fighting with modern appliances will continue to gratify the savage instinct of combat; for it is not likely that in the future two opposing lines of men can ever meet, or any line or column reach an enemy's intrenchments. The machine-gun can only be compared to the scythe, which cuts off every blade of grass within its sweep. It has made cavalry charges impossible, just as the modern ironclad has made impossible the manœuvers of one of Nelson's fleets. On land, the only mode of approach of one line to another must hereafter be by concealment, crawling, or surprise. Naval actions will henceforth be conflicts between opposing machines, guided, to be sure, by men; but it will be the best machine that wins, and not necessarily the most enduring men. War will become a contest between treasuries or war-chests; for now that 10,000 men can fire away a million dollars' worth of ammunition in an hour, no poor nation can long resist a rich one, unless there be some extraordinary difference between the two in mental and moral strength.

The view that war is desirable omits also the consideration that modern social and industrial life affords ample opportunities for the courageous and loyal discharge of duty, apart from the barbarities of warfare. There are many serviceable occupations in civil life which call for all the courage and fidelity of the best soldier, and for more than his independent responsibility, because not pursued in masses or under the immediate command of superiors. Such occupations are those of the locomotive engineer, the electric lineman, the railroad brakeman, the city fireman, and the policeman. The occupation of the locomotive engineer requires constantly a high degree of skill, alertness, fidelity, and resolution, and at any moment may call for heroic self-forgetfulness. The occupation of a lineman requires all the courage and endurance of a soldier, whose lurking foe is mysterious and invisible. In the two years, 1893 and 1894, there were 34,000 trainmen killed and wounded on the railroads of the United States, and 25,000 other railroad employés besides. I need not enlarge on the dangers of the fireman's occupation, or on the disciplined gallantry with which its risks are habitually incurred. The policeman in large cities needs every virtue of the best soldier, for in the discharge of many of his most important duties he is alone. Even the feminine occupation of the trained nurse illustrates every heroic quality which can possibly be exhibited in war; for she, simply in the way of duty, without the stimulus of excitement or companionship, runs risks from which many a soldier in hot blood would shrink. No one need be anxious about the lack of opportunities in civilized life for the display of heroic qualities. New industries demand new forms of fidelity and self-sacrificing devotion. Every generation develops some new kind of hero. Did it ever occur to you that the "scab" is a creditable type of nineteenth century hero? In defense of his rights as an individual, he deliberately incurs the reprobation of many of his fellows, and runs the immediate risk of bodily injury, or even of death. He also risks his livelihood for the future, and thereby the well-being of his family. He steadily asserts in action his right to work on such conditions as he sees fit to make, and, in so doing, he exhibits remarkable courage, and renders a great service to his fellow-men. He is generally a quiet, unpretending, silent person, who values his personal freedom more than the society and approbation of his mates. Often he is impelled to work by family affection, but this fact does not diminish his heroism. There are file-closers behind the line of battle of the bravest regiment. Another modern personage who needs heroic endurance, and often exhibits it, is the public servant who steadily does his duty against the outcry of a party press bent on perverting his every word and act. Through the telegram, cheap postage, and the daily newspaper, the forces of hasty public opinion can now be concentrated and expressed with a rapidity and intensity unknown to preceding generations. In consequence, the independent thinker or actor, or the public servant, when his thoughts or acts run counter to prevailing popular or party opinions, encounters sudden and intense obloquy, which, to many temperaments, is very formidable. That habit of submitting to the opinion of the majority which democracy fosters renders the storm of detraction and calumny all the more difficult to endure—makes it, indeed, so intolerable to many citizens, that they will conceal or modify their opinions rather than endure it. Yet the very breath of life for a democracy is free discussion, and the taking account, of all opinions honestly held and reasonably expressed. The unreality of the vilification of public men in the modern press is often revealed by the sudden change when an eminent public servant retires or dies. A man for whom no words of derision or condemnation were strong enough yesterday is recognized to-morrow as an honorable and serviceable person, and a credit to his country. Nevertheless, this habit of partizan ridicule and denunciation in the daily reading-matter of millions of people calls for a new kind of courage and toughness in public men, and calls for it, not in brief moments of excitement only, but steadily, year in and year out. Clearly, there is no need of bringing on wars in order to breed heroes. Civilized life affords plenty of opportunities for heroes, and for a better kind than war or any other savagery has ever produced. Moreover, none but lunatics would set a city on fire in order to give opportunities for heroism to firemen, or introduce the cholera or yellow fever to give physicians and nurses opportunity for practising disinterested devotion, or condemn thousands of people to extreme poverty in order that some well-to-do persons might practise a beautiful charity. It is equally crazy to advocate war on the ground that it is a school for heroes.

Another misleading argument for war needs brief

notice. It is said that war is a school of national development—that a nation, when conducting a great war, puts forth prodigious exertions to raise money, supply munitions, enlist troops, and keep them in the field, and often gets a clearer conception and a better control of its own material and moral forces while making these unusual exertions. The nation which means to live in peace necessarily foregoes, it is said, these valuable opportunities of abnormal activity. Naturally, such a nation's abnormal activities devoted to destruction would be diminished; but its normal and abnormal activities devoted to construction and improvement ought to increase.

One great reason for the rapid development of the United States since the adoption of the Constitution is the comparative exemption of the whole people from war, dread of war, and preparations for war. The energies of the people have been directed into other channels. The progress of applied science during the present century, and the new ideals concerning the well-being of human multitudes, have opened great fields for the useful application of national energy. This immense territory of ours, stretching from ocean to ocean, and for the most part but imperfectly developed and sparsely settled, affords a broad field for the beneficent application of the richest national forces during an indefinite period. There is no department of national activity in which we could not advantageously put forth much more force than we now expend; and there are great fields which we have never cultivated at all. As examples, I may mention the post-office, national sanitation, public works, and education. Although great improvements have been made during the past fifty years in the collection and delivery of mail matter, much still remains to be done both in city and country, and particularly in the country. In the mail facilities secured to our people, we are far behind several European governments, whereas we ought to be far in advance of every European government except Switzerland, since the rapid interchange of ideas, and the promotion of family, friendly, and commercial intercourse, are of more importance to a democracy than to any other form of political society. Our national government takes very little pains about the sanitation of the country, or its deliverance from injurious insects and parasites; yet these are matters of gravest interest, with which only the general government can deal, because action by separate States or cities is necessarily ineffectual. To fight pestilences needs quite as much energy, skill, and courage as to carry on war; indeed, the foes are more insidious and awful, and the means of resistance less obvious. On the average and the large scale, the professions which heal and prevent disease, and mitigate suffering, call for much more ability, constancy, and devotion than the professions which inflict wounds and death and all sorts of human misery. Our government has never touched the important subject of national roads, by which I mean not railroads, but common highways; yet here is a great subject for beneficent action through government, in which we need only go for our lessons to little republican Switzerland. Inundations and droughts are great enemies of the human race, against which government ought to create defenses, because private enterprise cannot cope with such wide-spreading evils. Popular education is another great field in which public activity should be indefinitely enlarged, not so much through the action of the Federal government,— though even there a much more effective supervision should be provided than now exists,— but through the action of States, cities, and towns. We have hardly begun to apprehend the fundamental necessity and infinite value of public education, or to appreciate the immense advantages to be derived from additional expenditure for it. What prodigious possibilities of improvement are suggested by the single statement that the average annual expenditure for the schooling of a child in the United States is only about eighteen dollars! Here is a cause which requires from hundreds of thousands of men and women keen intelligence, hearty devotion to duty, and a steady uplifting and advancement of all its standards and ideals. The system of public instruction should embody for coming generations all the virtues of the medieval church. It should stand for the brotherhood and unity of all classes and conditions; it should exalt the joys of the intellectual life above all material delights; and it should produce the best constituted and most wisely directed intellectual and moral host that the world has seen.

In view of such unutilized opportunities as these for the beneficent application of great public forces, does it not seem monstrous that war should be advocated on the ground that it gives occasion for rallying and using the national energies?

The second eminent contribution which the United States have made to civilization is their thorough acceptance, in theory and practice, of the widest religious toleration. As a means of suppressing individual liberty, the collective authority of the Church, when elaborately organized in a hierarchy directed by one head and absolutely devoted in every rank to its service, comes next in proved efficiency to that concentration of powers in government which enables it to carry on war effectively. The Western Christian Church, organized under the Bishop of Rome, acquired, during the middle ages, a centralized authority which quite overrode both the temporal ruler and the rising spirit of nationality. For a time Christian Church and Christian State acted together, just as in Egypt, during many earlier centuries, the great powers of civil and religious rule had been united. The Crusades marked the climax of the power of the Church. Thereafter, Church and State were often in conflict; and during this prolonged conflict the seeds of liberty were planted, took root, and made some sturdy growth. We can see now, as we look back on the history of Europe, how fortunate it was that the colonization of North America by Europeans was deferred until after the period of the Reformation, and especially until after the Elizabethan period in England, the Luther period in Germany, and the splendid struggle of the Dutch for liberty in Holland. The founders of New England and New York were men who had imbibed the principles of resistance both to arbitrary civil power and to universal ecclesiastical authority. Hence it came about that within the territory now covered by the United States no single ecclesiastical organization ever obtained a wide and oppressive control, and that in different parts of this great region churches very unlike in doctrine and organization were almost simultaneously established. It has been an inevitable consequence of this condition of things that the Church, as a whole, in the United States has not been an effective opponent of any form of human rights. For generations it has been divided into numerous sects and denominations, no one of which has been able to claim more than a tenth of the population as its adherents; and the practices of these numerous denominations have been profoundly modified by political theories and practices, and by social customs natural to new communities formed under the prevailing conditions of free intercourse and rapid growth. The constitutional prohibition of religious tests as qualifications for office gave the United States the leadership among the nations in dissociating theological opinions and political rights. No one denomination or ecclesiastical organization in the United States has held great properties, or has had the means of conducting its ritual with costly pomp or its charitable works with imposing liberality. No splendid architectural exhibitions of Church power have interested or overawed the population. On the contrary, there has prevailed in general a great simplicity in public worship, until very recent years. Some splendors have been lately developed by religious bodies in the great cities; but these splendors and luxuries have been almost simultaneously exhibited by religious bodies of very different, not to say opposite, kinds. Thus, in New York city, the Jews, the Greek Church, the Catholics, and the Episcopalians have all erected, or undertaken to erect, magnificent edifices. But these recent demonstrations of wealth and zeal are so distributed among differing religious organizations that they cannot be imagined to indicate a coming centralization of ecclesiastical influence adverse to individual liberty.

In the United States, the great principle of religious toleration is better understood and more firmly established than in any other nation of the earth. It is not only embodied in legislation, but also completely recognized in the habits and customs of good society. Elsewhere it may be a long road from legal to social recognition of religious liberty, as the example of England shows. This recognition alone would mean, to any competent student of history, that the United States had made an unexampled contribution to the reconciliation of just governmental power with just freedom for the individual, inasmuch as the partial establishment of religious toleration has been the main work of civilization during the past four centuries. In view of this characteristic and infinitely beneficent contribution to human happiness and progress, how pitiable seem the temporary outbursts of bigotry and fanaticism which have occasionally marred the fair record of our country in regard to religious toleration! If any one imagines that this American contribution to civilization is no longer important,—that the victory for toleration has been already won,—let him recall the fact that the last years of the nineteenth century have witnessed two horrible religious persecutions, one by a Christian nation, the other by a Moslem—one, of the Jews by Russia, and the other, of the Armenians by Turkey.

The third characteristic contribution which the United States have made to civilization has been the safe development of a manhood suffrage nearly universal. The experience of the United States has brought out several principles with regard to the suffrage which have not been clearly apprehended by some eminent political philosophers. In the first place, American experience has demonstrated the advantages of a gradual approach to universal suffrage, over a sudden leap. Universal suffrage is not the first and only means of attaining democratic government; rather, it is the ultimate goal of successful democracy. It is not a specific for the cure of all political ills; on the contrary, it may itself easily be the source of great political evils. The people of the United States feel its dangers to-day. When constituencies are large, it aggravates the well-known difficulties of party government; so that many of the ills which threaten democratic communities at this moment, whether in Europe or America, proceed from the breakdown of party government rather than from failures of universal suffrage. The methods of party government were elaborated where suffrage was limited and constituencies were small. Manhood suffrage has not worked perfectly well in the United States, or in any other nation where it has been adopted, and it is not likely very soon to work perfectly anywhere. It is like freedom of the will for the individual — the only atmosphere in which virtue can grow, but an atmosphere in which sin can also grow. Like freedom of the will, it needs to be surrounded with checks and safeguards, particularly in the childhood of the nation; but, like freedom of the will, it is the supreme good, the goal of perfected democracy. Secondly, like freedom of the will, universal suffrage has an educational effect, which has been mentioned by many writers, but has seldom been clearly apprehended or adequately described. This educational effect is produced in two ways: In the first place, the combination of individual freedom with social mobility, which a wide suffrage tends to produce, permits the capable to rise through all grades of society, even within a single generation; and this freedom to rise is intensely stimulating to personal ambition. Thus every capable American, from youth to age, is bent on bettering himself and his condition. Nothing can be more striking than the contrast between the mental condition of an average American belonging to the laborious classes, but conscious that he can rise to the top of the social scale, and that of a European mechanic, peasant, or tradesman, who knows that he cannot rise out of his class, and is content with his hereditary classification. The state of mind of the American prompts to constant struggle for self-improvement and the acquisition of all sorts of property and power. In the second place, it is a direct effect of a broad suffrage that the voters become periodically interested in the discussion of grave public problems, which carry their minds away from the routine of their daily labor and household experience out into larger fields. The instrumentalities of this prolonged education have been multiplied and improved enormously within the last fifty years. In no field of human endeavor have the fruits of the introduction of steam and electrical power been more striking than in the methods of reaching multitudes of people with instructive narratives, expositions, and arguments. The multiplication of newspapers, magazines, and books is only one of the immense developments in the means of reaching the people. The advocates of any public cause now have it in their power to provide hundreds of newspapers with the same copy, or the same plates, for simultaneous issue. The mails provide the means of circulating millions of leaflets and pamphlets. The interest in the minds of the people which prompts to the reading of these multiplied communications comes from the frequently recurring elections. The more difficult the intellectual problem presented in any given election, the more educative the effect of the discussion. Many modern industrial and financial problems are extremely difficult, even for highly-educated men. As subjects of earnest thought and discussion on the farm, and in the work-shop, factory, rolling-mill, and mine, they supply a mental training for millions of adults, the like of which has never before been seen in the world.

In these discussions, it is not only the receptive masses that are benefited; the classes that supply the appeals to the masses are also benefited in a high degree. There is no better mental exercise for the most highly trained man than the effort to expound a difficult subject in so clear a way that the untrained man can understand it. In a republic in which the final appeal is to manhood suffrage, the educated minority of the people is constantly stimulated to exertion, by the instinct of self-preservation as well as by love of country. They see dangers in proposals made to universal suffrage, and they must exert themselves to ward off those dangers. The position of the educated and well-to-do classes is a thoroughly wholesome one in this respect: they cannot depend for the preservation of their advantages on land-owning, hereditary privilege, or any legislation not equally applicable to the poorest and humblest citizen. They must maintain their superiority by being superior. They cannot live in a too safe corner.

I touch here on a misconception which underlies much of the criticism of universal suffrage. It is commonly said that the rule of the majority must be the rule of the most ignorant and incapable, the multitude being necessarily uninstructed as to taxation, public finance, and foreign relations, and untrained to active thought on such difficult subjects. Now, universal suffrage is merely a convention as to where the last appeal shall lie for the decision of public questions; and it is the rule of the majority only in this sense. The educated classes are undoubtedly a minority; but it is not safe to assume that they monopolize the good sense of the community. On the contrary, it is very clear that native good judgment and good feeling are not proportional to education, and that among a multitude of men who have only an elementary education, a large proportion will possess both good judgment and good feeling. Indeed, persons who can neither read nor write may possess a large share of both, as is constantly seen in regions where the opportunities for education in childhood have been scanty or inaccessible. It is not to be supposed that the cultivated classes, under a régime of universal suffrage, are not going to try to make their cultivation felt in the discussion and disposal of public questions. Any result under universal suffrage is a complex effect of the discussion of the public question in hand by the educated classes in the presence of the comparatively uneducated, when a majority of both classes taken together is ultimately to settle the question. In practice, both classes divide on almost every issue. But, in any case, if the educated classes cannot hold their own with the uneducated, by means of their superior physical, mental, and moral qualities, they are obviously unfit to lead society. With education should come better powers of argument and persuasion, a stricter sense of honor, and a greater general effectiveness. With these advantages, the educated classes must undoubtedly appeal to the less educated, and try to convert them to their way of thinking; but this is a process which is good for both sets of people. Indeed, it is the best possible process for the training of freemen, educated or uneducated, rich or poor.

It is often assumed that the educated classes become impotent in a democracy, because the representatives of those classes are not exclusively chosen to public office. This argument is a very fallacious one. It assumes that the public offices are the places of greatest influence; whereas, in the United States, at least, that is conspicuously not the case. In a democracy, it is important to discriminate influence from authority. Rulers and magistrates may or may not be persons of influence; but many persons of influence never become rulers, magistrates, or representatives in parliaments or legislatures. The complex industries of a modern state, and its innumerable corporation services, offer great fields for administrative talent which were entirely unknown to preceding generations; and these new activities attract many ambitious and capable men more strongly than the public service. These men are not on that account lost to their country or to society. The present generation has wholly escaped from the conditions of earlier centuries, when able men who were not great land-owners had but three outlets for their ambition — the army, the church, or the national civil service. The national service, whether in an empire, a limited monarchy, or a republic, is now only one of many fields which offer to able and patriotic men an honorable and successful career. Indeed, legislation and public administration necessarily have a very second-hand quality; and more and more legislators and administrators become dependent on the researches of scholars, men of science, and historians, and follow in the footsteps of inventors, economists, and political philosophers. Political leaders are very seldom leaders of thought; they are generally trying to induce masses of men to act on principles thought out long before. Their skill is in the selection of practicable approximations to the ideal; their arts are arts of exposition and persuasion; their honor comes from fidelity under trying circumstances to familiar principles of public duty. The real leaders of American thought in this century have been preachers, teachers, jurists, seers, and poets. While it is of the highest importance, under any form of government, that the public servants should be men of intelligence, education, and honor, it is no objection to any given form, that under it large numbers of educated and honorable citizens have no connection with the public service.

Well-to-do Europeans, when reasoning about the working of democracy, often assume that under any government the property-holders are synonymous with the intelligent and educated class. That is not the case in the American democracy. Anyone who has been connected with a large American university can testify that democratic institutions produce plenty of rich people who are not educated and plenty of educated people who are not rich, just as medieval society produced illiterate nobles and cultivated monks.

Persons who object to manhood suffrage as the last resort for the settlement of public questions are bound to show where, in all the world, a juster or more practicable regulation or convention has been arrived at. The objectors ought at least to indicate where the ultimate decision should, in their judgment, rest — as, for example, with the landowners, or the property-holders, or the graduates of secondary schools, or the professional classes. He would be a bold political philosopher who, in these days, should propose that the ultimate tribunal should be constituted in any of these ways. All the experience of the civilized world fails to indicate a safe personage, a safe class, or a safe minority, with which to deposit this power of ultimate decision. On the contrary, the experience of civilization indicates that no select person or class can be trusted with that power, no matter what the principle of selection. The convention that the majority of males shall decide public questions has obviously great recommendations. It is apparently fairer than the rule of any minority, and it is sure to be supported by an adequate physical force. Moreover, its decisions are likely to enforce themselves. Even in matters of doubtful prognostication, the fact that a majority of the males do the prophesying tends to the fulfilment of the prophecy. At any rate, the adoption or partial adoption of universal male suffrage by several civilized nations is coincident with unexampled ameliorations in the condition of the least fortunate and most numerous classes of the population. To this general amelioration many causes have doubtless contributed; but it is reasonable to suppose that the acquisition of the power which comes with votes has had something to do with it.

Timid or conservative people often stand aghast at the possible directions of democratic desire, or at some of the predicted results of democratic rule; but meantime the actual experience of the American democracy proves: 1, that property has never been safer under any form of government; 2, that no people have ever welcomed so ardently new machinery, and new inventions generally; 3, that religious toleration was never carried so far, and never so universally accepted; 4, that nowhere have the power and disposition to read been so general; 5, that nowhere has governmental power been more adequate, or more freely exercised, to levy and collect taxes, to raise armies and to disband them, to maintain public order, and to pay off great public debts — national, State, and town; 6, that nowhere have property and well-being been so widely diffused; and 7, that no form of government ever inspired greater affection and loyalty, or prompted to greater personal sacrifices in supreme moments. In view of these solid facts, speculations as to what universal suffrage would have done in the seventeenth and eighteenth centuries, or may do in the twentieth, seem futile indeed. The most civilized nations of the world have all either adopted this final appeal to manhood suffrage, or they are approaching that adoption by rapid stages. The United States, having no customs or traditions of an opposite sort to overcome, have led the nations in this direction, and have had the honor of devising, as a result of practical experience, the best safeguards for universal suffrage, safeguards which, in the main, are intended to prevent hasty public action, or action based on sudden discontents or temporary spasms of public feeling. These checks are intended to give time for discussion and deliberation, or, in other words, to secure the enlightenment of the voters before the vote. If, under new conditions, existing safeguards prove insufficient, the only wise course is to devise new safeguards.

The United States have made to civilization a fourth contribution of a very hopeful sort, to which public attention needs to be directed, lest temporary evils connected therewith should prevent the continuation of this beneficent action. The United States have furnished a demonstration that people belonging to a great variety of races or nations are, under favorable circumstances, fit for political freedom. It is the fashion to attribute to the enormous immigration of the last fifty years some of the failures of the American political system, and particularly the American failure in municipal government, and the introduction in a few States of the rule of the irresponsible party foremen known as "bosses." Impatient of these evils, and hastily accepting this improbable explanation of them, some people wish to depart from the American policy of welcoming immigrants. In two respects the absorption of large numbers of immigrants from many nations into the American commonwealth has been of great service to mankind. In the first place, it has demonstrated that people who at home have been subject to every sort of aristocratic or despotic or military oppression become within less than a generation serviceable citizens of a republic; and, in the second place, the United States have thus educated to freedom many millions of men. Furthermore, the comparatively high degree of happiness and prosperity enjoyed by the people of the United States has been brought home to multitudes in Europe by friends and relatives who have emigrated to this country, and has commended free institutions to them in the best possible way. This is a legitimate propaganda vastly more effective than any annexation or conquest of unwilling people, or of people unprepared for liberty.

It is a great mistake to suppose that the process of assimilating foreigners began in this century. The eighteenth century provided the colonies with a great mixture of peoples, although the English race predominated then, as now. When the Revolution broke out, there were already English, Irish,

Scotch, Dutch, Germans, French, Portuguese, and Swedes in the colonies. The French were, to be sure, in small proportion, and were almost exclusively Huguenot refugees, but they were a valuable element in the population. The Germans were well diffused, having established themselves in New York, Pennsylvania, Virginia, and Georgia. The Scotch were scattered through all the colonies. Pennsylvania, especially, was inhabited by an extraordinary mixture of nationalities and religions. Since steam-navigation on the Atlantic and railroad transportation on the North American continent became cheap and easy, the tide of immigration has greatly increased; but it is very doubtful if the amount of assimilation going on in the nineteenth century has been any larger, in proportion to the population and wealth of the country, than it was in the eighteenth. The main difference in the assimilation going on in the two centuries is this, that in the eighteenth century the newcomers were almost all Protestants, while in the nineteenth century a considerable proportion have been Catholics. One result, however, of the importation of large numbers of Catholics into the United States has been a profound modification of the Roman Catholic Church in regard to the manners and customs of both the clergy and the laity, the scope of the authority of the priest, and the attitude of the Catholic Church toward public education. This American modification of the Roman Church has reacted strongly on the Church in Europe.

Another great contribution to civilization made

by the United States is the diffusion of material well-being among the population. No country in the world approaches the United States in this respect. It is seen in that diffused elementary education which implants for life a habit of reading, and in the habitual optimism which characterizes the common people. It is seen in the housing of the people and of their domestic animals, in the comparative costliness of their food, clothing, and household furniture, in their implements, vehicles, and means of transportation, and in the substitution, on a prodigious scale, of the work of machinery for the work of men's hands. This last item in American well-being is quite as striking in agriculture, mining, and fishing, as it is in manufactures. The social effects of the manufacture of power, and of the discovery of means of putting that power just where it is wanted, have been more striking in the United States than anywhere else. Manufactured and distributed power needs intelligence to direct it: the bicycle is a blind horse, and must be steered at every instant; somebody must show a steam-drill where to strike and how deep to go. So far as men and women can substitute for the direct expenditure of muscular strength the more intelligent effort of designing, tending, and guiding machines, they win promotion in the scale of being, and make their lives more interesting as well as more productive. It is in the invention of machinery for producing and distributing power, and at once economizing and elevating human labor, that American ingenuity has been most conspicuously manifested. The high price of labor in a sparsely-settled country has had something to do with this striking result; but the genius of the people and of their government has had much more to do with it. As proof of the general proposition, it suffices merely to mention the telegraph and telephone, the sewing-machine, the cotton-gin, the mower, reaper, and threshing-machine, the dish-washing machine, the river steamboat, the sleeping-car, the boot and shoe machinery, and the watch machinery. The ultimate effects of these and kindred inventions are quite as much intellectual as physical, and they are developing and increasing with a portentous rapidity which sometimes suggests a doubt whether the bodily forces of men and women are adequate to resist the new mental strains brought upon them. However this may prove to be in the future, the clear result in the present is an unexampled diffusion of well-being in the United States.

These five contributions to civilization — peace-keeping, religious toleration, the development of manhood suffrage, the welcoming of newcomers, and the diffusion of well-being — I hold to have been eminently characteristic of our country, and so important that, in spite of the qualifications and deductions which every candid citizen would admit with regard to every one of them, they will ever be held in the grateful remembrance of mankind. They are reasonable grounds for a steady, glowing patriotism. They have had much to do, both as causes and as effects, with the material prosperity of the United States; but they are all five essentially moral contributions, being triumphs of reason, enterprise, courage, faith, and justice, over passion, selfishness, inertness, timidity, and distrust. Beneath each one of these developments there lies a strong ethical sentiment, a strenuous moral and social purpose. It is for such work that multitudinous democracies are fit.

In regard to all five of these contributions, the characteristic policy of our country has been from time to time threatened with reversal — is even now so threatened. It is for true patriots to insist on the maintenance of these historic purposes and policies of the people of the United States. Our country's future perils, whether already visible or still unimagined, are to be met with courage and constancy founded firmly on these popular achievements in the past.

SOME REASONS WHY THE AMERICAN REPUBLIC MAY ENDURE

FROM THE "FORUM," OCTOBER, 1894

SOME REASONS WHY THE AMERICAN REPUBLIC MAY ENDURE

THE governments which have been called republics have not, as a rule, exhibited the kind or degree of durability which we desire for our own free government. The American republic has now lasted more than a hundred years; and little Switzerland maintains a precarious existence by favor of powerful neighbors jealous of each other; but the so-called republics of Greece, Rome, and Italy, and two French republics, have perished. Mexico and the republics of Central and South America are insecure and ineffective governments. On the whole, in spite of our instinctive faith in free institutions, we cannot shut our eyes to the fact that the auguries which can be drawn from history are not favorable to the real permanence of any republic.

When we set out to seek reasons for believing that our republic will live longer than other governments which have borne that name, and will altogether escape decline and fall, we cannot but be dismayed to see what great powers and resources the older republics possessed, and what splendid achievements they made, without winning stability and perpetuity from all these powers, resources, and achievements. The republic of Athens, for example, had an art and a literature which have proved themselves immortal. In sculpture and architecture Athens is still supreme; its literature still inspires and guides philosophers, poets, and men of letters in nations unborn when Greece was in her prime. Now art and literature are among the supreme achievements of the human race; yet the example of Athens demonstrates that they cannot of themselves safeguard a republic.

We must not attempt to console ourselves for this painful fact by the thought that an effeminate and peaceful people might excel in art and literature, and that the absence of forceful national qualities might account for the instability of such a people's government. The story of the Roman republic invalidates this theory. For generations the Roman republic was the strongest government on earth; and even now, as we examine the elements of its strength, it seems to us that they might have given durability to that powerful commonwealth. In the first place, it had an admirable body of public law which determined justice between man and man and between man and state; and that body of law was so wise and ample that to-day it is the basis of the public law of the greater part of the populations of Europe. Although this great system of jurisprudence still survives, it did not give undecaying life to the nation which created it. Moreover, the Roman republic possessed the most superb army which has ever existed—an army whose conquests were more extensive and more lasting than the conquests made by the arms of any other state, ancient or modern. The Roman army has never been equaled either as a fighting or as a colonizing force; yet that army did not assure mounting vitality to the Roman commonwealth: on the contrary, it was one of the means of its downfall.

There are some short-sighted people who expect systems of public transportation and intercommunication to secure nations from disintegration; but again the history of Rome teaches the contrary. Rome had a transportation system which, considering the means at the disposal of the engineer at that time, has never been equaled. The Roman roads covered the greater part of Europe and northern Africa, and considerable portions of Asia; and they were so well constructed that parts of them remain to this day. Some of the Roman bridges have stood for twenty centuries unharmed by flood and weather. But this transportation system, vast and perfect as it was, did not prevent the decline and fall of the Roman power.

One might suppose that a nation strong and rich enough to carry out immense public works, such as aqueducts, baths, temples, palaces, and theaters, would necessarily possess also the means of giving durability to their form of government; but the experience of Rome proves that we can rely in our own case on none of these things. The Roman aqueducts, for example, which brought water to all their principal cities, are unequaled to the present day for size, massiveness, and boldness of conception,—partly, to be sure, because the Roman engineers were forced to erect huge structures of masonry, since they had not learned to make large metallic pipes. Rome teaches conclusively that magnitude and splendor of public works have no tendency to guarantee the permanence of a state.

The Italian republics have still another lesson for us. Venice, which possessed an architecture of wonderful beauty, and an art in painting which still remains preëminent, developed these fine arts by means of a wide-spread commerce, which gave its citizens wealth, dignity, and power. It was, moreover, a martial republic. Its very merchants wore swords. Its paintings and palaces are still the admiration of the world; but its commerce has disappeared, and the Venetian republic has long been obliterated. Successful commerce, and fine arts following in its train, provide no security for national perpetuity.

Most of the national resources and achievements which have now been mentioned have a certain material or physical quality. Perhaps we can discern in history some immaterial force, some national sentiment or passion, which can be relied on to give permanence to national institutions. There has been one power in the world on which men have greatly relied for the security of governmental and social institutions—namely, the power of religious enthusiasm; but what does history teach with regard to the efficacy of this sentiment to give security to states? It is easy to find instances of concentrated religious enthusiasm in unified national forms. The Hebrew religion was of this sort. It bound together by a simple faith and a common ritual all the members of a race which possessed extraordinary vitality and persistence; but did it give permanence to Judea? Even as a province or a principality Judea has disappeared. The race persists, but without a country or a capital. The Arabic civilization was carried from Asia, through Africa, into Spain by Moslem religious enthusiasm. It was a civilization which had fine arts, chronicles, and for the higher classes a delicate and luxurious mode of life. Its soldiers have never been surpassed for fervent devotion. But this concentrated religious zeal, effective as it was for conquest, did not preserve the Arabic civilization, which has disappeared from the face of the earth. Christian experience points to the same conclusion. Spain, for example, drove out the Moors and the Jews, exterminated the Protestants, and made itself Roman Catholic unitedly and fervently; but that single Roman Catholic belief and ritual did not preserve for Spain its once preëminent position in Europe. On the contrary, Spain, become single in religious opinion and practice, languished, retrograded, and lost place among the leaders of civilization. In the present century it is a striking fact that the three nations which have given the greatest proofs of constitutional vigor — namely, Germany, England, and the United States—are those which in religious opinions and practices are very heterogeneous, so that no concentrated religious fervor can possibly melt and unite all their people. We cannot believe, then, that religious enthusiasm, however unified and concentrated, can guarantee the permanent existence of a state.

Great public powers, splendid arts, noble literature, wide-spread commerce, and exalted religious sentiment have, then, all failed to secure the continuance of states. Perhaps a humbler achievement of recent times may prove more effectual —namely, the achievement of general, diffused physical well-being. There seem to be a good many social philosophers in these days who believe that the general diffusion of physical comforts, and the accessibility of easy modes of life for large numbers of people, will have some tendency to give permanence to the institutions under which these material goods are secured; that the power which man has won over nature through the study of chemistry, physics, and natural history, means stability for the institutions under which these conquests have been achieved. May not these theorizers be right? Will not growing wealth, ease, and comfort guarantee the state, provided that these advantages be within reach of the many? The answer to this question must depend on the spiritual use made of added physical comfort. A nation is after all but the agglomeration of an immense number of individuals; and the moral condition of a nation can be nothing but the result of the morality prevailing among the individuals who compose it. Comfort, ease, and wealth must have on a nation almost the same effects that they have on an individual. Now, softness and ease of life do not always make for manliness and virtue. It is not generally supposed that riches increase the probability of enduring vitality for a family or a social class. The common opinion is that wealth and luxury make it, not easier, but harder to bring up children to serviceable citizenship. All persons who have been concerned with education during the past forty years—which is the period of most rapid increase in diffused physical comfort for all classes, and in wealth and luxury for considerable numbers—recognize that great efforts are necessary in order to bring up successfully the children of the luxurious classes; because they lack the natural training to service which children get in families where every member has habitually to contribute to the common maintenance. It is harder, not easier, for the rich man than for the poor man to bring up his children well. Families of moderate means have a great advantage over the rich in this respect. In this matter of material well-being there is surely some question concerning the profitable degree of comfort and ease. By common consent there is a degree of ease which debilitates rather than invigorates. The general fact seems to be that the effect of material prosperity on the development of an individual or the duration of a family depends on the use made of added wealth and comfort. When added material resources produce in the individual, or in the family, additional mental and moral resources, all the additions work together for good; otherwise added wealth is a hindrance and not a help. When a mechanic, a clerk, a farmer, or a laborer doubles his income and his expenditures, it does not necessarily follow that the mode of life of himself and his family will be purer, more refined, and more intellectual. It may be improved, or it may not be. In the same way, it would be the intellectual and moral effects of a higher degree of physical ease and comfort enjoyed by a whole people, which would determine whether the material gain were a good thing or an evil. If diffused prosperity made a people lazy, selfish, and sensual, as it easily might, it would not contribute to the permanence of their nationality or their government. It is not the climates which are always soft, warm, and caressing which produce the most vigorous races of men. While we see plainly that extreme poverty is an evil and a danger alike for the individual, the family, and the state, we can place no reliance on diffused physical well-being as a source of public security, until we can be assured of its effects on the motives, affections, and passions of the people. There is no sure hope in either increase or redistribution of wealth.

If, then, we would find reasons for believing that the American republic will live, when other republics have not lived, we must seek for intellectual and moral causes of permanence which are comparatively new in the world, or at least which have much fuller play in recent than in earlier times.

The first moral cause of permanence of which the American republic has the advantage is the principle of toleration in religion — a principle which, though not recently enunciated (nobody has ever stated it better than William the Silent), has been very recently put in practice, not, by any means, in all parts of the civilized world, but in a few favored regions, and notably in the United States. On one of the tablets of the Water-gate at Chicago was written this sentence: "Toleration in religion the best fruit of the last four centuries." This statement is no exaggeration but the literal truth. Toleration in religion is absolutely the best fruit of all the struggles, labors, and sorrows of the civilized nations during the last four centuries. The real acceptance of this principle cannot be carried back more than fifty years. Even now it is not accepted everywhere — far from it; but it is accepted in the United States more widely and completely than in any other country, and here lies one of the chief hopes for the permanence of our institutions. We are delivered from one of the worst terrors and horrors of the past. What suffering the human race has endured from religious wars, persecutions, and exterminations! From these woes, and from all apprehension of them, the people of the American republic are delivered. We owe to this principle, however, much more than deliverance from evils; for it is a positive promoter of good-will and mutual respect among men, and of friendly intercourse unembarrassed by religious distinctions. That this beneficent principle has freer play here than it has ever had elsewhere, gives one firm ground for believing that our republic may attain a permanence never before attained.

Another mental and moral force which makes for the permanence of our institutions is universal education. This is a new force in the world, not in action in any land before this century. It has not existed more than twenty years in such a civilized country as France; it dates only from 1870 in England. It is not yet true that education is universal even in our own country; but the principle of universal education finds general acceptance, and the practical results approximate more and more, as time goes on, to the requirements of the theoretical principle. In all civilized countries continuous effort is made to bring the practice up to the level of the theory. Within three generations immense progress has been made; and it now seems as if a perfectly feasible development of this principle in practice must work a profound change in human society within a comparatively small number of future generations. Must we not hope everything from this new factor in civilized life,—from the steady cultivation in all classes of correct observation, just reasoning, and the taste for good reading? Must we not hope to be delivered from a thousand evils which are results of ignorance and unreason? It is reasonable to expect that even the evils of inherited vicious tendencies and habits will be mitigated by universal education. It is always through the children that the best work is to be done for the uplifting of any community. When we consider for how few years in the history of mankind this practice of general education has prevailed, and to how few generations it has ever been applied, we cannot but find in this new practice great hope for the development of the intelligence and the morality needed to secure the permanence of free institutions. It is a commonplace that republican institutions are built on education; but we hardly realize how new that commonplace is. Plato taught that the industrial and producing classes needed no education whatever. None of the republics which have died had anything more than a small educated class. The masses of their people grew up and lived in crassest ignorance. The great change in regard to the education of the people which the present century has witnessed is not confined to mere primary instruction. That primary instruction is of course the most widely diffused, and imparts to the masses the art of reading, which is the principal vehicle for the subsequent cultivation of the intelligence. Beyond this primary instruction, about five per cent. of all the children in the United States receive the more elaborate training of secondary schools and normal schools. Of this five per cent. a fair proportion attend colleges and universities. This attainment of secondary, or higher, instruction by one child in twenty in the United States is quite as novel a social fact as the attainment of primary instruction by the other nineteen. Universal suffrage prolongs in the United States the effect of universal education; for it stimulates all citizens throughout their lives to reflect on problems outside the narrow circle of their private interests and occupations, to read about public questions, to discuss public characters, and to hold themselves ready in some degree to give a rational account of their political faith. The duties of republican citizenship, rightly discharged, constitute in themselves a prolonged education, which effectively supplements the work of schools and colleges.

A third reason for believing that our institutions will endure is to be found in the fact that a better family life prevails among our people than was known to any of the republics which have perished, or, indeed, to any earlier century. The family, not the individual, is the tap-root of the state, and whatever tends to secure the family tends to secure the state. Now family life — under which term may properly be included all the complex relations between husband and wife, and parents and children — is gentler in this century, and particularly in the United States, than it has ever been. Family discipline has become, even within thirty years, much gentler than it ever was before. The relations of husband and wife have also become juster. In the savage state the superior physical strength of the man, his greater freedom from occasional or periodical bodily limitations, and his greater enterprise and boldness, made the relation of husband and wife very like that of master and slave. Civilization has steadily contended against that savage inheritance; and has aimed through public law at the emancipation of the weaker sex and the establishment of equality in the relation of the sexes. A single illustration—the laws affecting the transmission of property—must suffice. American legislation on this subject is the most just the world has seen. Under the feudal system it was almost necessary to the life of that social organization that, when the father died, the real estate—which was generally the whole estate—should go to the eldest son, over the head of the mother; for the son inherited his father's responsibilities in war, in productive industries, and in society. The son, not the wife, was the husband's heir. In France to-day, if a man dies leaving a wife and children, a large share of his property must go to his children. He is not free, under any circumstances, to give it all to his wife. A prescribed portion must by law go to the children over the head of their mother. The children are his children, and the wife is not recognized as an equal owner. It is the man who is the head of that group of human beings, and a large share of his property must go to his children. Again we see in public law an assertion of the lower place of the woman. But how is it in our own country? In the first place, we have happily adopted a valuable English measure, the right of dower; but this measure, though good so far as it goes, gives not equality but a certain protection. Happily, American law goes farther, and the wife may inherit from the husband the whole of his property. She must receive a part of it; but he, under certain restrictions intended to prevent frauds on creditors, may give her the whole. On the other hand, the wife, if she has property, may give the whole of it to the husband. Here is established in the law of inheritance a relation of equality between husband and wife — a relation which is the happiest, most just, and most beneficent for the man, the woman, their children, and the state. It is an indirect advantage of our laws and customs concerning the inheritance of property that they promote the redistribution of wealth accumulated in single hands. The custom of treating all children alike in testamentary dispositions obviously tends in this direction; and the practice of leaving property to women promotes the redistribution of wealth, because women are, as a rule, less competent than men either to keep money or to make it productive. There is a real safeguard in these customs against the undue increase of wealth and luxury. That gentleness and justice in family life should have been greatly promoted under the American republic, not among a small minority of the people, but among the masses, may well give us a lively hope for the permanence of the institutions under which these benefits have been attained. Whatever regulates wisely the relations of the sexes, and increases domestic happiness, increases also social and governmental stability.

Pursuing the idea that the promotion of diffused happiness promotes governmental stability, we observe next that certain means of public happiness have recently been liberally provided in many American communities, at public expense, with great intelligence and by deliberate design. During the last twenty-five years, strenuous efforts have been made in many municipalities to promote public happiness by giving opportunities to the multitude for the enjoyment of fresh air and natural beauty. One of the most striking social phenomena in the United States of recent years has been the sudden creation of public parks and playgrounds, constructed and maintained at public expense. At bottom, the meaning of this sudden development is that the people seek to procure for themselves, and are procuring, increased means of health and happiness. They have still much to learn in regard to utilizing the means provided, for our native population does not take naturally to fresh air, family holidays, and out-of-door meals. They have been too long unwonted to these wholesome delights. This public park and garden movement has only just begun; but the improvement made within twenty years gives the strongest possible hope for the rapid spread of this wise public policy. European municipalities have often been enabled to provide themselves with parks and gardens by appropriating royal domains, estates of nobles, or disused forts and fortifications. The democratic American communities have enjoyed no such facilities, but have been obliged to buy the reservations — often at great cost — and create or restore the needed beauties of park or garden. That the democracy should manifest both the will and the capacity to accomplish such beneficent and far-seeing undertakings, is a good omen of durability for that form of government. The provision of free libraries and museums of natural history and fine arts, at public expense, or by the combination of private endowments with public appropriations, is another evidence of the disposition of the democracy to provide the means of public cultivation and enjoyment. Much of this good work has been done within the past forty years, and very little such work was ever done before by a popular government. The American cities have also grappled intelligently with the serious problems of water-supply, sewerage, and preventive medicine, although the suddenness and volume of the movement of the population into large towns and cities have greatly increased the normal difficulty of these problems.

Another new and effective bulwark of state is to be found in the extreme publicity with which all American activities are carried on. Many people are in the habit of complaining bitterly of the intrusion of the newspaper reporter into every nook and corner of the state, and even into the privacy of home; but in this extreme publicity is really to be found a new means of social, industrial, and governmental reform and progress. As Emerson said, "Light is the best policeman." There are many exaggerations, perversions, and inaccuracies in this publicity; but on the whole it is a beneficent and a new agency for the promotion of the public welfare. Such publicity has become possible partly through man's new power over nature, as seen in the innumerable applications of heat and electricity, and partly through the universal capacity to read. For almost all social, industrial, and political evils publicity gives the best hope of reasonable remedy. Publicity exposes not only wickedness, but also folly and bad judgment. It makes crime and political corruption more difficult and far less attractive. The forger, burglar, and corruptionist need secrecy, for two reasons: first, that they may succeed in their crimes; and secondly, that they may enjoy the fruits of their wickedness. The most callous sinner finds it hard to enjoy the product of his sin if he knows that everybody is aware how he came by it. No good cause ever suffered from publicity; no bad cause but instinctively avoids it. So new is this force in the world, that many people do not yet trust it, or perceive its immense utility. In cases of real industrial grievances or oppressions, publicity would be by far the quickest and surest means of cure — vastly more effective for all just ends than secret combinations of either capitalists or laborers. The newspapers, which are the ordinary instruments of this publicity, are as yet very imperfect instruments, much of their work being done so hastily and so cheaply as to preclude accuracy; but as a means of publicity they visibly improve from decade to decade, and, taken together with the magazines and the controversial pamphlet, they shed more light on the social, industrial, and political life of the people of the United States than was ever shed before on the doings and ways of any people. This force is distinctly new within this century, and it affords a new and strong guarantee for the American republic.

Within the past fifty years there has been developed, for the conduct of business, education, and charity, an agency which may fairly be called new —namely, the corporation. Although a few charitable, trading, and manufacturing corporations were of earlier origin,—some of which became famous,—the great development of corporate powers and functions has all taken place within fifty years, since the application of the principle of limited liability. Thousands upon thousands of corporations are now organized in the United States, and are actively carrying on a great variety of industrial and social operations. Millions of Americans get their livings and pass their lives in the service of these corporations. As a rule, the employees of corporations receive wages or salaries, and have no further interest in the business. We are so familiar with this state of things that we do not realize its absolute novelty. It has practically been created within the lifetime of persons who are not yet old. In the service of corporations, there is seldom any element of personal devotion, such as existed in other times between subject and sovereign, or between retainer and feudal chief; but there is a large element of fidelity and loyalty, which is becoming of greater and greater importance in the formation of the national character. A considerable portion of all the business, charity, and education carried on in the United States is well conducted by the faithful and loyal servants of corporations, as every one will plainly see so soon as he takes account of his own contacts in daily life with the work of corporations, and compares them with his contacts with the work of individuals or of partnerships. This corporation service affords a new discipline for masses of people; and it is a discipline of the highest value toward inducing stability and durability in governmental institutions. The service of a town or city, of a state, or the national government is really a kind of corporation service, carried on at present, to be sure, under unfavorable conditions, the public service being subject to evils and temptations from which private corporation service is for the most part exempt, and yielding to those who pay its cost less for their money than they get from any other kind of corporation. In all probability these unfavorable conditions will prove to be temporary. From the frequent occurrence of strikes on railroads and in mines we get an impression that there is little fidelity in the service of corporations; but it must be remembered that the organization of American railroads and mining companies is, with some notable exceptions, very inferior to the organization of other corporations, and that the laborers in the lower grades of these two employments are distinctly of an inferior sort. Most of these railroad and mining corporations have never adopted any of the means which European experience has shown to be efficacious for attaching their employees permanently to their service. For the most part, they claim the right to act on the brutal principle of instant dismissal without notice or cause assigned. If we direct our attention to the banks, trust companies, insurance companies, manufacturing corporations, colleges, universities, endowed schools, hospitals and asylums of the country, we shall realize that the quality of corporation service is really good, and that the great majority of corporation servants exhibit, in high degree, the admirable virtues of fidelity and loyalty. The successful career of the new companies which insure fidelity is an interesting corroboration of this observation. Even the railroads and the mines exhibit from time to time fine examples of fidelity on the part of large bodies of their employees, in spite of extremely adverse conditions, such as the presence of serious bodily danger, and the seductions of some ill-managed unions which claim to represent the permanent interests of workingmen. There can be no better preparation for faithful and loyal service to the government than faithful and loyal service to a corporation which conducts a business of magnitude and recognized utility. In these days of comprehensive trusts and far-reaching monopolies we see clearly that such agencies directly prepare the way for governmental assumption of their powers and functions. The wider and more comprehensive the monopoly, the stronger becomes the argument for the assumption of that business by the government. Indeed, the government is the only agency which should be trusted with a complete monopoly. At any rate, the presumption is in favor of government conduct of any business which has complete possession of the market. The corporation, then, is not simply a means of aggregating small capitals and utilizing them in large blocks; it is also an agency for training masses of people to the high virtues of fidelity and loyalty—virtues which cannot but secure the state. At the present stage of progress, with all corporations so new in the world, society suffers through them various evils, such as oppressive monopoly, destructive competition, political corruption, and occasionally inefficiency and obstructiveness; but on the whole this new agency is of incalculable value to modern society, and, in time to come, will prove a firm buttress of free institutions.

The recent attempts to carry out general strikes in industries which produce or distribute necessaries of life have demonstrated that society will not endure a suspension of labor in such industries for more than a few days. The reason is that men are much more dependent on each other than they used to be. The extreme division of labor, which has more and more characterized the normal industrial methods in civilized states since the beginning of the present century, has brought about a mutual dependence of man on man and community on community, which is a strong guarantee of the permanence of free institutions. Adam Smith dealt with this great subject of the division of labor in 1776; but the present century has seen the principle wrought out in detail, and carried through every branch of industry — indeed, the last fifty years have witnessed extensive new applications of the principle. In the savage state each family is tolerably independent of every other, as regards food, clothing, and shelter. Fifty years ago a New England farmer raised on his own farm most of the materials which supplied him and his family with food, clothing, fire, and shelter; but now, when three fifths of the population of New England live in large towns or cities, when the New England farm no longer produces either wheat or wool, and when every urban household imports the whole of its food and clothing, and all its materials for light and heat, the dependence of every little group of New Englanders on numerous other persons, near and remote, has become well-nigh absolute. All civilized mankind lives under similar conditions of interdependence. The sense of dependence is of course mutual, and with it goes some recognition of common aims and hopes among the different sorts and conditions of men. This sense of common interests is something very different from the sentiment of human equality. It is a feeling of unity, not of equality. It has a firm foundation in facts; whereas the notion that men are equal is plainly false, unless it be strictly limited to the political significance of equality, namely, to equality before the law and in regard to the right of suffrage. It is a feeling which leads naturally to a sense of human brotherhood. In a family the feeling of mutual dependence and mutual support is one of the roots of family affection. In the same way, in the larger human brotherhood the mutual dependence which division of labor has brought about strengthens the feeling of unity. The doctrine of human brotherhood has been taught for thousands of years. It is all contained in two words — "Our Father"; but, though accepted by seers and philosophers, it has been little realized in practice by the multitude. There are many signs of the wide and steady spread of the realized acceptance of this doctrine in practice. The theory, long current in the world, gets more and more applied in institutions, in business, and in society. The fact of intimate mutual dependence extends to different states and nations. A federation of States like the American Union affords a favorable field for the practical realization by masses of people of the truth of the affirmation St. Paul frequently repeated, "We are members one of another." It gives excellent opportunities for observing that the misfortune of one State is invariably the misfortune of all; that no State can suffer in its crops, or its industries, or its moral standards, without involving the others in loss and damage. Under a federated government like our own, the conditions under which such deductions as these may be made are simpler than they can possibly be when the experiences of different nations living under different forms of government and under different legislation, must be compared. In spite, therefore, of local and sectional jealousies and oppositions, the American people have come to accept as literal truth St. Paul's statement, "And whether one member suffer, all the members suffer with it." The doctrine is old; but the realization of the doctrine is new. This realization of an ancient truth marks again the progress of society toward practical acceptance of the conception that there is a genuine unity of aims and hopes among all men, an acceptance which of itself will prove a stout bulwark of free institutions.

We now come to certain abstract considerations which probably supply the firmest grounds for hopeful anticipations concerning the future of free institutions, though to some minds they will doubtless seem intangible and unsubstantial. In recent times, serious changes have taken place in regard to the highest hopes, aspirations, and ideals of mankind. These ideal conceptions have been slowly wrought out in the minds of students, philosophers, and poets, and have been cherished by the few; but suddenly, within the past two generations, they have found acceptance with multitudes of men. This sudden acceptance is the combined result of the rapid progress of scientific knowledge during the last fifty years, and of the general ability of the people to read. These changes of expectation, aspiration, and faith are of course only moral forces; but they are forces which greatly affect the sum of human happiness. As has already been repeatedly intimated, the stability of governments depends largely on the just answer to the question — Do they provide the necessary conditions of happy human life? The first change of expectation which claims attention is the changed sentiment of the people toward what is new, and therefore untried. The American people, as a rule, approach a new object, a new theory, or a new practice, with a degree of hope and confidence which no other people exhibit. The unknown is to the savage terrible; the dark has been dreadful, and evil has always been imagined of it; many highly civilized people have an aversion to things novel; but for us Americans so many new things have proved to be good things, that we no longer look on what is novel with suspicion and distrust. Our continent is new, and has proved to be rich; our machinery is new, and has proved to be useful; our laws are many of them new, but they have proved helpful. The people have traversed many wilds and wastes, but have passed them with safety, and found good in the unexplored and unknown. The untried is therefore for us no longer terrible, or, at least, to be suspected. Hope and expectation of good spring in our hearts, as never before in the hearts of former generations.

Furthermore, the changes which have taken place in the realized doctrines of Christianity concerning the origin and nature of man are very reassuring for those who believe in the possibility of developing a nation of freemen capable of orderly self-government. The old conceptions of the fall of man and of the total depravity of the race were good foundations for the *régime* of a beneficent despot, but not for the *régime* of self-governing freemen. The modern doctrine of the steady ascent of man through all his history is necessarily welcome to republicans, because it justifies their political beliefs. Again, enlarged knowledge of the nature of the universe, and a more accurate view of man's humble place in it, have also contributed to the prevalence of a humane philosophy which is a security for good governments. It was, on the whole, an unwholesome conception that the universe was made for man, and that he was the rightful master of it all. Out of that prodigious piece of ignorant assumption came many practical wrongs toward animals and inferior races of men. To a more cheerful outlook the gradual triumph of science over many terrors and superstitions has contributed, as has also the growing power of men to resist or moderate the effects of catastrophes like storms, droughts, famines, and pestilences. The earth and the universe are brighter and less terrible than they were. There is even a greater brightening in man's spiritual landscape. No cherished ideal of our race has undergone a more beneficent change during the present century than the ideal of God; and this change makes strongly for the happiness of mankind. The Christian Gospel has just begun to be realized. We have just begun to understand that God is love. He has been an awful ideal of justice and wrath — an angry deity whose chief functions were punishment and vengeance. The world He made was full of evil; the men He made were all depraved, and most of them hopelessly so. This ideal of divinity, however influential, did not increase human cheerfulness and joy. Although it lingers still in creeds, consecrated formulæ, and ancient hymns, it has practically ceased to be believed by considerable numbers of men, both churched and unchurched. The ideal which replaces it is one of supreme power and love, filling the universe, working through all human institutions, and through all men. This ideal promotes happiness and joy. It is not new; but it is newly realized by multitudes. Now, these beneficent changes in the spiritual conceptions of large numbers of men have taken place since our country took on its present governmental structure; and they have lent and will lend to that structure a firm support, because they contribute generously to the happiness and true spirituality of the people.

Finally, the object of religion and the aim of its ministers have become wonderfully different, since the American republic was established, from what they were in ancient or mediæval times, or even down to the opening of this century. The religions of the ancient world had very little to do with morality. They were propitiatory and protective. The Christian religion and its ministers for the last fifteen hundred years were chiefly concerned with the conciliation of an offended God, the provision of securities for individual happiness in a future life,— these securities being attainable by persons whose mode of life in this world had been of questionable or even vicious quality,—and the offering of joys in another world as consolation or compensation for sufferings or evils in this. Since the beginning of this century a revolution has occurred, which has been felt more or less in every branch of the Christian Church and in almost every Christian nation, but has had a broad sweep in the United States. The primary objects of religion and its ministers in our day and country are more and more to soften and elevate the characters and lives of men in this world, and to ameliorate the common lot. The improvement of character and conduct in the individual, in society, and in the state during this present life is now becoming the principal aim of many churches and their ministers. The progressive churches are all of this mind; and even the most conservative—like the Roman Catholic and the Presbyterian—plainly exhibit this tendency. By the multitude of the unchurched, also, it is generally understood that there is no angry God to propitiate, and that the only way to take security for the morrow, whether in life or in death, is to do well the duties of to-day. Religion, by devoting itself to the elevation of human character, becomes a prop and stay of free institutions, because these rest ultimately on the character of the citizen.

These, then, are some of the new principles and forces which make for the permanence of the republic: toleration in religion; general education; better domestic relations; attention to the means of public health and pleasure; publicity; corporation service; increased mutual dependence of man on man, and therewith a growing sense of brotherhood and unity; the greater hopefulness and cheerfulness of men's outlook on man, the earth, the universe, and God; and finally, the changing objects and methods of religion and its institutions. It is the working of these principles and forces, often unrecognized, which has carried the republic safely through many moral difficulties and dangers during the past thirty years. These things, and not its size and wealth, make us love our country. These things, we believe, will give the American republic long life. These bulwarks of the commonwealth will prove all the stronger and more lasting, because women as well as men can work on them, and help to transmit them, ever broader and firmer, from generation to generation.

THE WORKING OF THE AMERICAN DEMOCRACY

ADDRESS

Delivered Before The Fraternity Phi Beta Kappa, of Harvard University, June 28, 1888

THE WORKING OF THE AMERICAN DEMOCRACY

I PURPOSE to examine some parts of the experience of the American democracy, with the intention of suggesting the answers to certain theoretical objections which have been urged against democracy in general, and of showing in part what makes the strength of the democratic form of government.

For more than a hundred years there has been among civilized nations a decided set of opinion toward democratic institutions; but in Europe this set has been determined rather by unfavorable experience of despotic and oligarchic forms of government than by any favorable experience of the democratic form. Government by one and government by a few have been tried through many centuries, by different races of men, and under all sorts of conditions; but neither has ever succeeded — not even in England — in producing a reasonably peaceful, secure, and also happy society. No lesson upon this subject could be more forcible than that which modern Europe teaches. Empires and monarchies, like patriarchies and chieftainships, have doubtless served their turn; but they have signally failed to realize the social ideals — some ancient and some modern in origin — which have taken firm hold of men's minds since the American Revolution. This failure extends through all society, from top to bottom. It is as conspicuous in the moral condition of the upper classes as in the material condition of the lower. Oligarchies call themselves aristocracies; but government by the few has never really been government by the best. Therefore mankind tends to seek the realization of its ideals in broad-based forms of government.

It can hardly be said that Europe has any experience of democracy which is applicable to a modern state. Gallant little Switzerland lives in a mountain fastness, and exists by the sufferance of powerful neighbors, each jealous of the other. No lessons for modern use can be drawn from the transient city democracies of ancient or medieval times. The city as a unit of government organization has gone forever, with the glories of Athens, Rome, and Florence. Throughout this century a beneficent tendency has been manifested toward the formation of great national units. Witness the expansion of Russia and the United States, the creation of the German empire, the union of Austria, Hungary, and Bohemia, and the unification of Italy. At least, within these great units prevail a common peace and an unrestricted trade. The blessings which result from holding vast territories and multitudes under one national government are so great that none but large governments have any future before them. To succeed, democracy must show itself able to control both territory and population on a continental scale; therefore its methods must be representative — which means that they are necessarily deliberative, and are likely to be conservative and slow. Of such government by the many, Europe has no trustworthy experience, either in ancient or in modern times. The so-called democracies of Greece and Rome were really governments by a small caste of free citizens ruling a multitude of aliens and slaves: hasty and tyrannical themselves, they naturally prepared the way for tyrants. Yet when all the world were slaves, that caste of free citizens was a wonderful invention. France, since the Revolution, has exhibited some fugitive specimens of democratic rule, but has had no stable government of any sort, whether tyranny, oligarchy, or democracy. In short, such experience as Europe has had of so-called democracies—with the exception of admirable Switzerland — is worse than useless; for it is thoroughly misleading, and has misled many acute observers of political phenomena.

In this absence of available European experience, where can mankind look for trustworthy evidence concerning the practical working of democratic institutions? Solely to the United States. The Australasian colonies will before long contribute valuable evidence; but at present their population is small, and their experience is too recent to be of great value to students of comparative politics. Yet it is upon experience, and experience alone, that safe conclusions can be based concerning the merits and the faults of democracy. On politics, speculative writing—even by able men like Sir George Cornewall Lewis and Sir Henry Maine—is as perilous as it is on biology; and prophecy is still more dangerous. To the modern mind, ideal states like Plato's Republic, Sir Thomas More's Utopia, and Saint Augustine's Civitas Dei, are utterly uninteresting—particularly when they rest upon such visionary postulates as community of goods and community of wives and children. The stable state must have its roots in use and wont, in familiar customs and laws, and in the inherited habits of successive generations. But it is only in the United States that a well-rooted democracy upon a great scale has ever existed; and hence the importance of accurate observation and just judgment of the working of American democratic institutions, both political and social. Upon the success of those institutions rest the best hopes of the world.

In discussing some parts of our national experience, I intend to confine myself to moral and intellectual phenomena, and shall have little to say about the material prosperity of the country. The rapid growth of the United States in population, wealth, and everything which constitutes material strength is, indeed, marvelous; but this concomitant of the existence of democratic institutions in a fertile land, rich also in minerals, ores, oil, and gas, has often been dilated upon, and may be dismissed with only two remarks: first, that a great deal of moral vigor has been put into the material development of the United States; and secondly, that wide-spread comfort ought to promote rather than to hinder the civilizing of a people. Sensible and righteous government ought ultimately to make a nation rich; and although this proposition cannot be directly reversed, yet diffused well-being, comfort, and material prosperity establish a fair presumption in favor of the government and the prevailing social conditions under which these blessings have been secured.

The first question I wish to deal with is a fundamental one: How wisely, and by what process, has the American people made up its mind upon public questions of supreme difficulty and importance? Not how will it, or how might it, make up its mind; but how has it made up its mind? It is commonly said that the multitude, being ignorant and untrained, cannot reach so wise a conclusion upon questions of state as the cultivated few; that the wisdom of a mass of men can only be an average wisdom at the best; and that democracy, which in things material levels up, in things intellectual and moral levels down. Even De Tocqueville says that there is a middling standard of knowledge in a democracy, to which some rise and others descend. Let us put these speculative opinions, which have so plausible a sound, in contrast with American facts, and see what conclusions are to be drawn.

The people of this country have had three supreme questions to settle within the last hundred and thirty years: first, the question of independence of Great Britain; secondly, the question of forming a firm federal union; and thirdly, the question of maintaining that union at whatever cost of blood and treasure. In the decision of these questions, four generations of men took active part. The first two questions were settled by a population mainly English; but when the third was decided, the foreign admixture was already considerable. That graver or more far-reaching political problems could be presented to any people, it is impossible to imagine. Everybody can now see that in each case the only wise decision was arrived at by the multitude, in spite of difficulties and dangers which many contemporary statesmen and publicists of our own and other lands thought insuperable. It is quite the fashion to laud to the skies the second of these three great achievements of the American democracy; but the creation of the Federal Union, regarded as a wise determination of a multitude of voters, was certainly not more remarkable than the other two. No government—tyranny or oligarchy, despotic or constitutional—could possibly have made wiser decisions or executed them more resolutely, as the event has proved in each of the three cases mentioned.

So much for the wisdom of these great resolves. Now, by what process were they arrived at?

In each case the process was slow, covering many years during which discussion and debate went on in pulpits, legislatures, public meetings, newspapers, and books. The best minds of the country took part in these prolonged debates. Party passions were aroused; advocates on each side disputed before the people; the authority of recognized political leaders was invoked; public spirit and selfish interest were appealed to; and that vague but powerful sentiment called love of country, felt equally by high and low, stirred men's hearts and lit the intellectual combat with lofty emotion. In presence of such a protracted discussion, a multitude of interested men make up their minds just as one interested man does. They listen, compare what they hear with their own experience, consider the bearings of the question on their own interests, and consult their self-respect, their hopes, and their fears. Not one in a thousand of them could originate, or even state with precision, the arguments he hears; not one in a thousand could give a clear account of his own observations, processes of thought, and motives of action upon the subject, —but the collective judgment is informed and guided by the keener wits and stronger wills, and the collective wisdom is higher and surer in guiding public conduct than that of one mind or of several superior minds uninstructed by million-eyed observation and million-tongued debate.

In all three of the great popular decisions under consideration, most remarkable discernment, patience, and resolution were, as a fact, displayed. If these were the average qualities of the many, then the average mental and moral powers of the multitude suffice for greatest deeds; if they were the qualities of the superior few infused into the many by speech and press, by exhortation, example, and leadership, even then the assertion that the operative opinions of the unlearned mass on questions of state must necessarily be foolish, their honesty only an ordinary honesty, and their sentiments vulgar, falls to the ground. The multitude, it would seem, either can distil essential wisdom from a seething mass of heterogeneous evidence and opinion, or can be inspired, like a single individual, from without and above itself. If the practical wisdom of the multitude in action be attributed to the management or to the influence of a sagacious few, the wise result proves that these leaders were well chosen by some process of natural selection, instead of being designated, as in an oligarchy, by the inheritance of artificial privileges.

It is fair to say that one reason why democratic decisions of great public questions are apt to turn out well, and therefore to seem to posterity to have been wise, is, that the state of the public mind and will is an all-important factor in determining the issue of such questions. Democracy vigorously executing its own purpose demonstrates by the issue its wisdom before the event. Indeed, this is one of the most legitimate and important advantages of the democratic form of government.

There is a limited sense in which it is true that in the United States the average man predominates; but the political ideas which have predominated in the United States, and therefore in the mind and will of the average man,—equality before the law, national independence, federation, and indissoluble union,—are ideas not of average but of superlative merit. It is also true that the common school and the newspaper echo received opinion, and harp on moral commonplaces. But unfortunately there are many accepted humane opinions and ethical commonplaces which have never yet been embodied in national legislation,—much less in international law,—and which may therefore still be repeated to some advantage. If that comprehensive commonplace, "Ye are all members one of another," could be realized in international relations, there would be an end of war and industrial isolation.

Experience has shown that democracy must not be expected to decide wisely about things in which it feels no immediate concern. Unless its interests are affected or its sentiments touched, it will not take the pains necessary to arrive at just conclusions. To engage public attention sufficiently to procure legislation is the reformer's chief difficulty in a democracy. Questions of war, peace, or human rights, and questions which concern the national unity, dignity, or honor, win the attention of the many. Indeed, the greatest political questions are precisely those in which the many have concern; for they suffer the penalties of discord, war, and public wrong-doing. But it is curiously difficult to secure from multitudes of voters effective dealing with questions which relate merely to taxation, expenditure, administration, trade, or manufactures. On these lesser matters the multitude will not declare itself until evils multiply intolerably. We need not be surprised, however, that the intelligence and judgment of the multitude can be brought into play only when they think their own interests are to be touched. All experience, both ancient and modern, shows that when the few rule, they do not attend to the interests of the many.

I shall next consider certain forms of mental and moral activity which the American democracy demands of hundreds of thousands of the best citizens, but which are without parallel in despotic and oligarchic states. I refer to the widely diffused and ceaseless activity which maintains, first, the immense Federal Union, with all its various subdivisions into States, counties, and towns; secondly, the voluntary system in religion; and thirdly, the voluntary system in the higher instruction.

To have carried into successful practice on a great scale the federative principle, which binds many semi-independent States into one nation, is a good work done for all peoples. Federation promises to counteract the ferocious quarrelsomeness of mankind, and to abolish the jealousy of trade; but its price in mental labor and moral initiative is high. It is a system which demands not only vital force at the heart of the state, but a diffused vitality in every part. In a despotic government the intellectual and moral force of the whole organism radiates from the central seat of power; in a federal union political vitality must be diffused throughout the whole organism, as animal heat is developed and maintained in every molecule of the entire body. The success of the United States as a federal union has been and is effected by the watchfulness, industry, and public spirit of millions of men who spend in that noble cause the greater part of their leisure, and of the mental force which can be spared from bread-winning occupations. The costly expenditure goes on without ceasing, all over the country, wherever citizens come together to attend to the affairs of the village, town, county, or State. This is the price of liberty and union. The well-known promptness and skill of Americans in organizing a new community result from the fact that hundreds of thousands of Americans — and their fathers before them — have had practice in managing public affairs. To get this practice costs time, labor, and vitality, which in a despotic or oligarchic state are seldom spent in this direction.

The successful establishment and support of religious institutions, — churches, seminaries, and religious charities, — upon a purely voluntary system, is another unprecedented achievement of the American democracy. In only three generations American democratic society has effected the complete separation of church and state, a reform which no other people has ever attempted. Yet religious institutions are not stinted in the United

States; on the contrary, they abound and thrive, and all alike are protected and encouraged, but not supported, by the state. Who has taken up the work which the state has relinquished? Somebody has had to do it, for the work is done. Who provides the money to build churches, pay salaries, conduct missions, and educate ministers? Who supplies the brains for organizing and maintaining these various activities? This is the work, not of a few officials, but of millions of intelligent and devoted men and women scattered through all the villages and cities of the broad land. The maintenance of churches, seminaries, and charities by voluntary contributions and by the administrative labors of volunteers, implies an enormous and incessant expenditure of mental and moral force. It is a force which must ever be renewed from generation to generation; for it is a personal force, constantly expiring, and as constantly to be replaced. Into the maintenance of the voluntary system in religion has gone a good part of the moral energy which three generations have been able to spare from the work of getting a living; but it is worth the sacrifice, and will be accounted in history one of the most remarkable feats of American public spirit and faith in freedom.

A similar exhibition of diffused mental and moral energy has accompanied the establishment and the development of a system of higher instruction in the United States, with no inheritance of monastic endowments, and no gifts from royal or ecclesiastical personages disposing of great resources derived from the state, and with but scanty help from the public purse. Whoever is familiar with the colleges and universities of the United States knows that the creation of these democratic institutions has cost the life-work of thousands of devoted men. At the sacrifice of other aspirations, and under heavy discouragements and disappointments, but with faith and hope, these teachers and trustees have built up institutions, which, however imperfect, have cherished scientific enthusiasm, fostered piety, literature, art, and maintained the standards of honor and public duty, and steadily kept in view the ethical ideas which democracy cherishes. It has been a popular work, to which large numbers of people in successive generations have contributed of their substance or of their labor. The endowment of institutions of education, including libraries and museums, by private persons in the United States, is a phenomenon without precedent or parallel, and is a legitimate effect of democratic institutions. Under a tyranny — were it that of a Marcus Aurelius — or an oligarchy — were it as enlightened as that which now rules Germany — such a phenomenon would be simply impossible. The University of Strasburg was lately established by an imperial decree, and is chiefly maintained out of the revenue of the state. Harvard University has been 250 years in growing to its present stature, and is even now inferior at many points to the new University of Strasburg; but Harvard is the creation of thousands of persons, living and dead, rich and poor, learned and simple, who have voluntarily given it their time, thought, or money, and lavished upon it their affection; Strasburg exists by the mandate of the ruling few directing upon it a part of the product of ordinary taxation. Like the voluntary system in religion, the voluntary system in the higher education fortifies democracy; each demands from the community a large outlay of intellectual activity and moral vigor.

There is another direction in which the people of the United States have spent and are now spending a vast amount of intellectual and moral energy—a direction not, as in the three cases just considered, absolutely peculiar to the American republic, but still highly characteristic of democracy. I mean the service of corporations. Within the last hundred years the American people have invented a new and large application of the ancient principle of incorporation. We are so accustomed to corporations as indispensable agents in carrying on great public works and services, and great industrial or financial operations, that we forget the very recent development of the corporation with limited liability as a common business agent. Prior to 1789 there were only two corporations for business purposes in Massachusetts. The English general statute which provides for incorporation with limited liability dates only from 1855. No other nation has made such general or such successful use of corporate powers as the American—and for the reason that the method is essentially a democratic method, suitable for a country in which great individual or family properties are rare, and small properties are numerous. Freedom of incorporation makes possible great combinations of small capitals, and, while winning the advantages of concentrated management, permits diffused ownership. These merits have been quickly understood and turned to account by the American democracy. The service of many corporations has become even more important than the service of the several States of the Union. The managers of great companies have trusts reposed in them which are matched only in the highest executive offices of the nation; and they are relatively free from the numerous checks and restrictions under which the highest national officials must always act. The activity of corporations, great and small, penetrates every part of the industrial and social body, and their daily maintenance brings into play more mental and moral force than the maintenance of all the governments on the Continent combined.

These propositions can easily be illustrated by actual examples. I find established at Boston, for instance, the headquarters of a railroad corporation which employs 18,000 persons, has gross receipts of about $40,000,000 a year, and on occasion pays its best-paid officer a salary of $35,000. I find there also the central office of a manufacturing establishment which employs more than 6000 persons, has a gross annual income of more than $7,000,000, and pays its best-paid officer $20,000 a year. The gross receipts of the Pennsylvania Railroad system are

$115,000,000 a year, the highest-paid official of the company receives a salary of $30,000, and the whole system employs 100,000 men. A comparison of such figures with the corresponding figures for the prosperous and respectable Commonwealth of Massachusetts is not uninstructive. The gross receipts of the Commonwealth are about $7,000,000 a year, the highest salary it pays is $6,500, and there are not more than 6,000 persons in its employ for any considerable part of the year.

In the light of such facts, it is easy to see some of the reasons why American corporations command the services of men of high capacity and character, who in other countries or in earlier times would have been in the service of the state. In American democratic society corporations supplement the agencies of the state, and their functions have such importance in determining conditions of labor, diffusing comfort and general well-being among millions of people, and utilizing innumerable large streams and little rills of capital, that the upper grades of their service are reached by merit, are filled, as a rule, upon a tenure during good behavior and efficiency, are well paid, and have great dignity and consideration. Of the enormous material benefits which have resulted from the American extension of the principle of incorporation, I need say nothing. I wish only to point out that freedom of incorporation, though no longer exclusively a democratic agency, has given strong support to democratic institutions; and that a great wealth of intellect, energy, and fidelity is devoted to the service of corporations by their officers and directors.

The four forms of mental and moral activity which I have been considering — that which maintains political vitality throughout the Federal Union; that which supports unsubsidized religious institutions; that which develops the higher instruction in the arts and sciences, and trains men for all the professions; and that which is applied to the service of corporations — all illustrate the educating influence of democratic institutions — an influence which foreign observers are apt to overlook or underestimate. The ballot is not the only political institution which has educated the American democracy. Democracy is a training-school in which multitudes learn in many ways to take thought for others, to exercise public functions, and to bear public responsibilities.

So many critics of the theory of democracy have maintained that a democratic government would be careless of public obligations, and unjust toward private property, that it will be interesting to inquire what a century of American experience indicates upon this important point. Has there been any disposition on the part of the American democracy to create exaggerated public debts, to throw the burden of public debts on posterity rather than on the present generation, or to favor in legislation the poorer sort as against the richer, the debtor as against the creditor?

The answer to the question is not doubtful. With the exception of the sudden creation of the great national debt occasioned by the Civil War, the American communities have been very moderate in borrowing, the State debts being for the most part insignificant, and the city debts far below the English standard. Moreover, these democratic communities, with a few local and temporary exceptions, pay their public debts more promptly than any state under the rule of a despot or a class has ever done. The government of the United States has once paid the whole of its public debt, and is in a fair way to perform that feat again. So much for democratic treatment of public obligations.

It is conceivable, however, that the popular masses should think it for their own interest to keep down and pay off public indebtedness, and yet should discriminate in legislation in favor of the majority who are not well off, and against the minority who are. There are two points, and only two points, so far as I know, at which permanent American legislation has, as a fact, intentionally discriminated in favor of the poor. The several States, as a rule, exempt from taxation household effects and personal property to a moderate amount, and the tools of farmers and mechanics. The same articles and a few others like them are also commonly exempted from attachment for debt, together often with a homestead not exceeding in value one thousand dollars. The exemptions from attachment, and even those from taxation, will cover all the property of many poor persons and families; yet this legislation is humane and worthy of respect, being analogous to the common provision which exempts from all taxation persons who, by reason of age or infirmity, may, in the judgment of the assessors, be unable to contribute to the public charges. It is intended to prevent cases of hardship in the collection either of taxes or of debts; and doubtless the exemptions from attachment are designed also to leave to the debtor a fair chance of recovery.

After observing the facts of a full century, one may therefore say of the American democracy that it has contracted public debt with moderation, paid it with unexampled promptness, acquired as good a public credit as the world has ever known, made private property secure, and shown no tendency to attack riches or to subsidize poverty, or in either direction to violate the fundamental principle of democracy, that all men are equal before the law. The significance of these facts is prodigious. They mean that, as regards private property and its security, a government by the many, for the many, is more to be trusted than any other form of government; and that as regards public indebtedness, an experienced democracy is more likely to exhibit just sentiments and practical good judgment than an oligarchy or a tyranny.

An argument against democracy, which evidently had great weight with Sir Henry Maine, because he supposed it to rest upon the experience of mankind, is stated as follows: Progress and reformation have always been the work of the few, and have been opposed by the many; therefore democracies will be obstructive. This argument is completely refuted by the first century of the American democracy, alike in the field of morals and jurisprudence, and the field of manufactures and trade. Nowhere, for instance, has the great principle of religious toleration been so thoroughly put in practice as in the United States; nowhere have such well-meant and persistent efforts been made to improve the legal status of women; nowhere has the conduct of hospitals, asylums, reformatories, and prisons been more carefully studied; nowhere have legislative remedies for acknowledged abuses and evils been more promptly and perseveringly sought. There was a certain plausibility in the idea that the multitude, who live by labor in established modes, would be opposed to inventions which would inevitably cause industrial revolutions; but American experience completely upsets this notion. For promptness in making physical forces and machinery do the work of men, the people of the United States surpass incontestably all other peoples. The people that invented and introduced with perfect commercial success the river steamboat, the cotton-gin, the parlor-car and the sleeping-car, the grain-elevator, the street railway—both surface and elevated—the telegraph, the telephone, the rapid printing-press, the cheap book and newspaper, the sewing-machine, the steam fire-engine, agricultural machinery, the pipe-lines for natural oil and gas, and machine-made clothing, boots, furniture, tools, screws, wagons, fire-arms, and watches—this is not a people to vote down or hinder labor-saving invention or beneficent industrial revolution. The fact is that in a democracy the interests of the greater number will ultimately prevail, as they should. It was the stage-drivers and inn-keepers, not the multitude, who wished to suppress the locomotive; it is some publishers and typographical unions, not the mass of the people, who wrongly imagine that they have an interest in making books dearer than they need be. Furthermore, a just liberty of combination and perfect equality before the law, such as prevail in a democracy, enable men or companies to engage freely in new undertakings at their own risk, and bring them to triumphant success, if success be in them, whether the multitude approve them or not. The consent of the multitude is not necessary to the success of a printing-press which prints twenty thousand copies of a newspaper in an hour, or of a machine cutter which cuts out twenty overcoats at one chop. In short, the notion that democracy will hinder religious, political, and social reformation and progress, or restrain commercial and industrial improvement, is a chimera.

There is another criticism of the working of democratic institutions, more formidable than the last, which the American democracy is in a fair way to dispose of. It is said that democracy is fighting against the best-determined and most peremptory of biological laws, namely, the law of heredity, with which law the social structure of monarchical and oligarchical states is in strict conformity. This criticism fails to recognize the distinction between artificial privileges transmissible without regard to inherited virtues or powers, and inheritable virtues or powers transmissible without regard to hereditary privileges. Artificial privileges will be abolished by a democracy; natural, inheritable virtues or powers are as surely transmissible under a democracy as under any other form of government. Families can be made just as enduring in a democratic as in an oligarchic State, if family permanence be desired and aimed at. The desire for the continuity of vigorous families, and for the reproduction of beauty, genius, and nobility of character is universal. "From fairest creatures we desire increase" is the commonest of sentiments. The American multitude will not take the children of distinguished persons on trust; but it is delighted when an able man has an abler son, or a lovely mother a lovelier daughter. That a democracy does not prescribe the close intermarriage which characterizes a strict aristocracy, so-called, is physically not a disadvantage, but a great advantage for the freer society. The French nobility and the English House of Lords furnish good evidence that aristocracies do not succeed in perpetuating select types of intellect or of character.

In the future there will undoubtedly be seen a great increase in the number of permanent families in the United States—families in which honor, education, and property will be transmitted with reasonable certainty; and a fair beginning has already been made. On the quinquennial catalogue of Harvard University there are about five hundred and sixty family stocks, which have been represented by graduates at intervals for at least one hundred years. On the Yale catalogue there are about four hundred and twenty such family stocks; and it is probable that all other American colleges which have existed one hundred years or more show similar facts in proportion to their age and to the number of their graduates. There is nothing in American institutions to prevent this natural process from extending and continuing. The college graduate who does not send his son to college is a curious exception. American colleges are, indeed, chiefly recruited from the sons of men who were not college-bred themselves; for democratic society is mobile, and permits young men of ability to rise easily from the lower to the higher levels. But on the other hand nothing in the constitution of society forces men down who have once risen, or prevents their children or grandchildren from staying on the higher level if they have the virtue in them.

The interest in family genealogies has much increased of late years, and hundreds of thousands of persons are already recorded in printed volumes which have been compiled and published by voluntary contributions or by the zeal of individuals. In the Harvard University Library are four hundred and fifteen American family genealogies, three quarters of which have been printed since 1860. Many of these families might better be called clans or tribes, so numerous is their membership. Thus of the Northampton Lyman family there were living, when the family genealogy was published in 1872, more than four thousand persons. When some American Galton desires in the next century to study hereditary genius or character under a democracy, he will find ready to his hand an enormous mass of material. There are in the United States one hundred and forty-eight historical societies, most of them recently established, which give a large share of their attention to biography, genealogy, necrology, and kindred topics. Persons and families of local note, the settlement and development of new towns, and the rise of new industries are commemorated by these societies, which are accumulating and preserving materials for the philosophical historian who shall hereafter describe the social condition of a democracy which in a hundred years overran the habitable parts of a continent.

Two things are necessary to a family permanence—education and bodily vigor, in every generation. To secure these two things, the holding and the transmission of moderate properties in families must be so well provided for by law and custom as to be possible for large numbers of families. For the objects in view, great properties are not so desirable as moderate or even small properties, since the transmission of health and education with great properties is not so sure as with small properties. It is worth while to inquire, therefore, what has been accomplished under the reign of the American democracy in the way of making the holding and the transmission of small properties possible. In the first place, safe investments for moderate sums have been greatly multiplied and made accessible, as every trustee knows. Great trust-investment companies have been created expressly to hold money safely, and make it yield a sure though small income. The savings-bank and the insurance company have been brought to every man's door, the latter insuring against almost every kind of disaster to which property and earning capacity are liable. Life insurance has been regulated and fostered, with the result of increasing materially the stability of households and the chances of transmitting education in families. Through these and other agencies it has been made more probable that widows and orphans will inherit property, as well as easier for them to hold that property securely—a very important point in connection with the permanence of families, as may be strikingly illustrated by the single statement that eighteen per cent. of the students in Harvard College have no fathers living. Many new employments have been opened to women, who have thus been enabled more easily to hold families together and educate their children. Finally, society has been saved in great measure from war and revolution, and from the fear of these calamities; and thus family property, as well as happiness, has been rendered more secure.

The holding and the transmission of property in families are, however, only means to two ends—

namely, education and health in successive generations. From the first, the American democracy recognized the fact that education was of supreme importance to it — the elementary education for all, the higher for all the naturally selected; but it awakened much later to the necessity of attending to the health of the people. European aristocracies have always secured themselves in a measure against physical degeneration by keeping a large proportion of their men in training as soldiers and sportsmen, and most of their women at ease in country seats. In our democratic society, which at first thought only of work and production, it is now to be seen that public attention is directed more and more to the means of preserving and increasing health and vigor. Some of these means are country schools for city children, country or seaside houses for families, public parks and gardens, out-of-door sports, systematic physical training in schools and colleges, vacations for business and professional men, and improvements in the dwellings and the diet of all classes. Democracy leaves marriages and social groups to be determined by natural affiliation or congeniality of tastes and pursuits, which is the effective principle in the association of cultivated persons under all forms of government. So far from having any quarrel with the law of hereditary transmission, it leaves the principle of heredity perfectly free to act; but it does not add to the natural sanctions of that principle an unnecessary bounty of privileges conferred by law.

From this consideration of the supposed conflict between democracy and the law of heredity the transition is easy to my last topic; namely, the effect of democratic institutions on the production of ladies and gentlemen. There can be no question that a general amelioration of manners is brought about in a democracy by public schools, democratic churches, public conveyances without distinction of class, universal suffrage, town-meetings, and all the multifarious associations in which democratic society delights; but this general amelioration might exist, and yet the highest types of manners might fail. Do these fail? On this important point American experience is already interesting, and I think conclusive. Forty years ago Emerson said it was a chief felicity of our country that it excelled in women. It excels more and more. Who has not seen in public and in private life American women unsurpassable in grace and graciousness, in serenity and dignity, in effluent gladness and abounding courtesy? Now, the lady is the consummate fruit of human society at its best. In all the higher walks of American life there are men whose bearing and aspect at once distinguish them as gentlemen. They have personal force, magnanimity, moderation, and refinement; they are quick to see and to sympathize; they are pure, brave, and firm. These are also the qualities that command success; and herein lies the only natural connection between the possession of property and nobility of character. In a mobile or free society the excellent or noble man is likely to win ease and independence; but it does not follow that under any form of government the man of many possessions is necessarily excellent. On the evidence of my reading and of my personal observation at home and abroad, I fully believe that there is a larger proportion of ladies and gentlemen in the United States than in any other country. This proposition is, I think, true with the highest definition of the term "lady" or "gentleman;" but it is also true, if ladies and gentlemen are only persons who are clean and well-dressed, who speak gently and eat with their forks. It is unnecessary, however, to claim any superiority for democracy in this respect; enough that the highest types of manners in men and women are produced abundantly on democratic soil.

It would appear then from American experience that neither generations of privileged ancestors, nor large inherited possessions, are necessary to the making of a lady or a gentleman. What is necessary? In the first place, natural gifts. The gentleman is born in a democracy, no less than in a monarchy. In other words, he is a person of fine bodily and spiritual qualities, mostly innate. Secondly, he must have, through elementary education, early access to books, and therefore to great thoughts and high examples. Thirdly, he must be early brought into contact with some refined and noble person — father, mother, teacher, pastor, employer, or friend. These are the only necessary conditions in peaceful times and in law-abiding communities like ours. Accordingly, such facts as the following are common in the United States: One of the numerous children of a small farmer manages to fit himself for college, works his way through college, becomes a lawyer, at forty is a much-trusted man in one of the chief cities of the Union, and is distinguished for the courtesy and dignity of his bearing and speech. The son of a country blacksmith is taught and helped to a small college by his minister; he himself becomes a minister, has a long fight with poverty and ill-health, but at forty-five holds as high a place as his profession affords, and every line in his face and every tone in his voice betoken the gentleman. The sons and daughters of a successful shopkeeper take the highest places in the most cultivated society of their native place, and well deserve the preëminence accorded to them. The daughter of a man of very imperfect education, who began life with nothing and became a rich merchant, is singularly beautiful from youth to age, and possesses to the highest degree the charm of dignified and gracious manners. A young girl, not long out of school, the child of respectable but obscure parents, marries a public man, and in conspicuous station bears herself with a grace, discretion, and nobleness which she could not have exceeded had her blood been royal for seven generations. Striking cases of this kind will occur to every person in this assembly. They are every-day phenomena in American society. What conclusion do they establish? They prove that the social mobility of a democracy, which permits the excellent and well-endowed of either sex to rise and to seek out each other, and which gives every advantageous variation or sport in a family stock free opportunity to develop, is immeasurably more beneficial to a nation than any selective in-breeding, founded on class distinctions, which has ever been devised. Since democracy has every advantage for producing in due season and proportion the best human types, it is reasonable to expect that science and literature, music and art, and all the finer graces of society will develop and thrive in America, as soon as the more urgent tasks of subduing a wilderness and organizing society upon an untried plan are fairly accomplished.

Such are some of the reasons drawn from experience for believing that our ship of state is stout and sound; but she sails —

> . . . the sea
> Of storm-engendering liberty —

the happiness of the greatest number her destined haven. Her safety requires incessant watchfulness and readiness. Without trusty eyes on the lookout, and a prompt hand at the wheel, the stoutest ship may be dismantled by a passing squall. It is only intelligence and discipline which carry the ship to its port.

THE FORGOTTEN MILLIONS

A STUDY OF THE COMMON AMERICAN MODE OF LIFE

PUBLISHED IN THE "CENTURY MAGAZINE," AUGUST, 1890

7*

THE FORGOTTEN MILLIONS

IT is the fashion to discuss social questions, and to bring to the discussion many prepossessions and not a little warmth of imagination. The anarchist, socialist, and nationalist, each for his own reasons, have all an interest in magnifying and proclaiming every wrong, evil, and danger which can possibly be attributed to industrial conditions. In every important strike the strikers endeavor to enlist public sympathy by giving vivid descriptions of the injuries against which they protest by quitting work. Newspapers and magazines find it profitable to print minute accounts of the cruelest industrial practices, the most revolting human habitations, and the most depraved modes of life which can anywhere be discovered — in miners' camps, factory villages, or city slums. The evils described are real, though perhaps exaggerated; and the average reader, whose sympathy is moved day after day by some new tale of injustice and distress, gradually loses all sense of the proportion of good to evil in the social organism.

He does not observe that, whereas almost all the evils portrayed are developed in unnatural agglomerations of population, three quarters of the American people do not live in dense settlements, but are scattered over great areas, only one quarter of the population living within groups so large as four thousand persons. It has not been brought home to him that even in such a hideous mass of misery as East London sixty-two per cent. of the population live in comfort and with an upward tendency. He tends to forget the great comfortable, contented mass of the people in his eager sympathy with some small fraction which is miserable and embittered; and little by little he comes to accept the extreme view that the existing social order is all wrong, although he knows perfectly well that the great majority of people, even in the worst American towns and cities, live comfortably and hopefully, and with as much contentment and gladness as can be expected in people of their rather joyless lineage.

In this fortunate land of ours the antidote for this empoisoned state of mind is the careful study of communities which illustrate the commonest social conditions and the commonest modes of life. By observing with accuracy the commonest social conditions of to-day, we also qualify ourselves as well as possible for imagining the probable social conditions of to-morrow; for it is the common, not the exceptional, conditions of the present which predict and prepare the conditions of the future. At the risk of dwelling upon elementary principles in popular government, and of describing as unknown things familiar to many country-bred Americans, I therefore purpose to delineate with some minuteness the mode of government, mode of life, and general social condition of the people who make up the sparsely settled town of Mount Desert, situated on the island of that name which lies on the east side of the wide Penobscot Bay. I select this remote and poor town simply because I am well acquainted with the habits and conditions of its people; there are doubtless thousands of towns which would answer my general purpose just as well.

The island of Mount Desert is divided into three townships. The northeastern portion is the town of Eden; the southwestern is Tremont; and the intermediate third is the town of Mount Desert, incorporated in 1789. The town lies upon the sea at both ends and is irregular in shape; but its major axis, which runs about N. W. by W. and S. E. by E., is 12 miles long, and its width perpendicular to this axis varies from 3½ to 5 miles. Its area is therefore about fifty square miles, the greater part of this area being occupied by salt-water inlets, fresh-water ponds, and rocky hills. The population, which in 1880 numbered 1017, probably numbered about 1400 in 1889, the polls having increased in that interval from 243 to 337. There is but one village proper in the town, namely, Somesville, at the head of Somes Sound; though there are several other small groups of houses, as at Northeast Harbor, Seal Harbor, and

Pretty Marsh. In general the population is scattered along the shores of the sea and the inlets. The number of houses in the town in the summer of 1889 was about 280, of which about one tenth were for summer use only. The average number of persons to a house is therefore between five and six. The surnames which are common in the town are chiefly English (Wall, Davis, Grover, Clement, Dodge, Lynam, Bracy, Savage, Kimball, Smallidge, Jordan, Gilpatrick, Roberts, Manchester, Atherton, Richardson, Somes, Wasgatt, Smith, Freeman, Bartlett, and Carter); but a few, such as Murphy, Callahan, and Fenelly, indicate an Irish descent, near or remote. The government is by town-meeting,— an unqualified democracy,— and the officers annually elected are three selectmen, who also serve as assessors and overseers of the poor, a treasurer, a town clerk, a commissioner of roads (not chosen in 1890), and a superintendent of schools. Most of these officials are paid by the day, and their total cost to the town is decidedly modest ($400 to $500 a year). More than half the polls usually attend town-meetings, and take part in State and National elections. A fair number at the March town-meeting is 175; but at the Presidential election in 1888, 225 men voted, 140 for Harrison and 85 for Cleveland. The motive of many of the voters who give a day to the annual town-meeting is to keep down the tax-levy, and to resist appropriations which benefit part of the town rather than the whole. Since each voter has the keenest appreciation of the fact that he is to pay his share of every appropriation, the tendency of the town-meeting is rather to niggardliness than to extravagance; yet new appropriations, or increases of appropriations, which can be shown to be for the common interest, have a fair chance of success.

In striking contrast to the common relation in cities and large towns between the number of taxpayers and the number of voters is the relation between these two numbers in Mount Desert. The taxpayers in Mount Desert are much more numerous than the polls, because many women, children, and non-residents are taxed. Thus in 1889 the taxpayers numbered 578, of whom 176 were non-residents; but these non-resident taxpayers are mostly people of the same county (Hancock), who formerly lived in the town, or have bought land there on speculation. The number of persons from without the State who had built houses in the town for summer occupation was only sixteen down to the summer of 1889.

The largest tax paid in the town for that year was $152; and the rate being $33 on $1000, this largest tax implied a valuation of $4606.06 for the estate which was assessed highest. The incidence of the whole tax-levy, as shown in the following table, is interesting because it exhibits approximately the distribution of property among the townspeople. There are no rich persons in the town; very few who have not acquired some property; and fewer still who are not in condition to bear their share of the public burdens.

263	persons, or estates,	paid each	a tax	between	$0	and	$5
105	"	"	"	"	5	"	10
102	"	"	"	"	10	"	20
47	"	"	"	"	20	"	30
29	"	"	"	"	30	"	40
9	"	"	"	"	40	"	50
6	"	"	"	"	50	"	60
5	"	"	"	"	60	"	70
3	"	"	"	"	70	"	80
3	"	"	"	"	80	"	90
2	"	"	"	"	100	"	110

1 person, or estate, paid between $90 and $100; one paid $127; one $150; and one $152.

The principles on which the taxes are levied are highly instructive—this obscure, poor, and sparsely settled town having long practised a method of taxation far more conservative than the methods which prevail in the rich and populous New England communities. In the first place, the valuation is low and the rate high, the valuation remaining very constant and the rate being determined each year by the amount which the town votes to raise. A low valuation tends to keep the State and county taxes low, although the returns of town valuations are subject to correction by a State Valuation Commission. Secondly, the assessors pay no attention to speculative or fancy values. Thus, although a village lot may have been actually bought at the rate of $500 an acre, it continues to be valued for purposes of taxation at, say, $30 an acre, as if it were tillage land. If a cottage which cost $2000 is let for the summer for $300, it nevertheless continues to be valued at, say, $700. Thirdly, no attempt is made to tax things invisible and undiscoverable, although the laws of Maine prescribe the taxation of bonds, money at interest, and other forms of personal property which are easily concealed. The items on the assessors' books consist exclusively of things which are under the public eye.

The low valuation for purposes of taxation is, on the whole, more acceptable to each taxpayer than an accurate or supposed market-price valuation would be; and it is a more stable basis for the annual assessment of the necessary taxes. The annual valuations, whether of real estate or of personal property, are never appealed to as indicating market-price or actual value. The items on the assessors' books (which are open to inspection by any citizen) are divisible into real estate, personal property, and polls—land and buildings constituting the real estate; cattle, horses, mules, sheep, swine, pleasure carriages, musical instruments, household furniture above $200 in value, logs, timber, boards, vessels, and stock in trade or employed in arts, constituting the personal property. All these things are visible to every neighbor. No inquisitorial methods are necessary, and no returns of property under oath are asked for. Stock in trade is roughly estimated at low figures, the contents of a well-filled country variety store, for example, being valued at $500 year after year. For purposes of taxation the land is divided into mowing or tillage, pasture and unimproved land. From

$10 to $30 per acre is the common valuation for tillage land; $4 per acre is the commonest valuation of pasture land; and for unimproved land the range of valuation is from $4 to $20 per acre, according to its capacities. These valuations are still persisted in, although the access of summer visitors since 1880 has given a high speculative value to some shore and village lots.

This method of taxation is perfectly natural under the conditions which have existed in the town since its first settlement in 1760. The things taxed have made up the entire property of the people for generations, and for practical purposes they are still the only forms of property and capital in the town. The interests of the permanent residents explain the wise neglect of the assessors to take account of the altered values of shore and village house-sites. The greater part of the land which has acquired, since 1880, a relatively high value, because of the summer immigration, belongs to permanent residents, who hold it tenaciously, and mean to live on a part of it. If this land were assessed for taxation at the prices its owners ask for it, the present owners could not long continue to hold it.

The total valuation has of course risen considerably since the town began to be a summer resort, but is still very moderate. Indeed, it would no more than make a decent little property for a respectable merchant in New York or Chicago. The increase is mainly due to new buildings, $40,000 of this increase being assessed to permanent residents, and $50,000 to summer residents. The following table shows the steps of the increase:

VALUATION OF THE TOWN OF MOUNT DESERT.

	1880	1881	1882	1883	1884
Real estate of residents	$62,531	$60,999	$85,393 (real and personal estate of residents)	$64,470	$68,203
Personal estate of residents	24,228	20,755		24,189	24,610
Real and personal estate of non-residents[1]	8,553	11,413	17,698	19,111	20,911
Total	$95,312	$93,167	$103,091	$107,770	$113,724

	1885	1886	1887	1888	1889
Real estate of residents	$72,326	$73,884	$89,157	$98,090	$104,453
Personal estate of residents	24,479	24,399	24,809	28,976	30,793
Real and personal estate of non-residents[1]	23,178	24,526	39,575	50,270	58,273
Total	$119,983	$122,809	$153,541	$177,336	$193,519

It is noticeable that the personal property assessed to permanent residents did not increase at all between 1880 and 1887. The amount of vessel property diminished in this interval, and until 1887 the increase in other forms of personal property did not more than make good that loss.

A rate of $33 on every $1000 of the total valuation yields in most years, when added to the poll taxes ($3 a poll), the money needed to meet the annual appropriations. What are those appropria-

[1] The personal property assessed to non-residents is insignificant in amount.

tions?—or, in other words, for what do the voters spend the money which they have themselves contributed? The following table answers this question for the years 1880, 1885, 1889, and 1890, the year 1880 being before the invasion of the town by summer visitors, and the year 1889 being the year of largest appropriations:

APPROPRIATIONS MADE AT THE MARCH TOWN-MEETING.

For	1880		1885
State and county taxes	$1,055.60		$833.48
Common schools	733.60		813.60
Roads and bridges	575.00		1,400.00
Town charges	600.00		400.00
Poor	1,200.00		1,100.00
Bridge at Little Harbor Brook	150.00	Repairing Beach Hill Road	100.00
		Bridge at Somesville	100.00
		Land damage on road at Pretty Marsh	30.00
Total	$4,314.20	Total	$4,777.08

For	1889		1890
State and county taxes	$789.98		$800.00
Common schools	813.60		813.60
Roads and bridges	2,500.00		2,000.00
Town charges	1,000.00		800.00
Poor	1,200.00		1,000.00
Road at Northeast Harbor	750.00	Bridge at Northeast Harbor	60.00
Damage on a horse	25.00	Repairing two hills on Southwest Harbor road	300.00
Memorial day expenses	15.00	Free high school	150.00
Free high school[1]	200.00	To buy school books	800.00
Total	$7,293.58	Total	$6,723.60

[1] The first appropriation for a high school was made in 1886.

State and county taxes used to absorb nearly a quarter of the whole tax levy, but of late years have required less than one eighth.

For common schools the town appropriates just what the Maine statute requires, namely, eighty cents for each inhabitant according to the last census; but this small appropriation is supplemented by a grant from the State of nearly as much more, which is derived from the school fund, the bank tax, and a tax of one mill on every dollar of valuation throughout the State. In addition to the town tax for schools, a separate district tax is occasionally levied for school buildings. For the year ending April 1, 1889, the number of scholars was 406, and the State grant of $712.11 added to the town appropriation of $813.60 made the whole sum available for common schools $1525.71, or $3.76 for each scholar for the year. Since 1886 the town has also appropriated annually from $100 to $200 a year for a high school, the State giving as much as the town raises, but not exceeding $250.

Roads and bridges have been the largest item on the list of appropriations since 1884, and have of late absorbed from one third to three sevenths of the entire tax-levy. This expenditure has undoubtedly been judicious; for driving is one of the principal pastimes of the summer visitors, and gives profitable employment at that season to the horses and vehicles of the permanent residents. Moreover, the roads and bridges, having necessarily been constructed originally in the cheapest possible manner as regards both laying out and surface, were costly in wear and tear of animals and vehicles, and costly also in annual repairs. Indeed, within the memory of men of middle age, communication between the different settlements of the town was mainly by water, and the "stores" were situated near sheltered landings, rather than at cross-roads or corners. Of late years a fair proportion of the annual outlay on the roads has been devoted to permanent improvements, like the construction of adequate culverts and gutters and the reduction of the steepest grades.

The appropriation for the care of the town poor has been the next largest appropriation since 1884; but before that year it was usually the largest of the appropriations, as, for instance, in 1880, when it was more than one fourth of the whole tax-levy. The theory on which the voters act in making this appropriation is that the town is to take care of the incapable, crippled, and aged who are without means of support. No one in the town is to be hungry or cold. If some unusual misfortune overtakes a family ordinarily self-supporting,— like diphtheria among the children, or the prolonged sickness of the breadwinner,— that family is to be helped temporarily by the town. In short, everybody who has a domicile in the town is assured of a bare livelihood at all times, and of aid under special misfortunes. The idea that it is the duty of the town to take care of its poor is firmly planted in the mind of every inhabitant. The town officers will try to prevent an hereditary or constitutional pauper from acquiring a domicile in the town; they will try to establish elsewhere shiftless families that are apt to need aid; but they will relieve every case of destitution which fairly belongs in the town. There is no poor-house; so that persons who cannot support themselves are boarded and lodged in private houses at the expense of the town. Besides this idea of the town's duty toward the unfortunate and incapable there is planted in the breast of the rural New Englander another invaluable sentiment, namely, that "to come on the town" is the greatest of misfortunes and humiliations. Few aged people "come on the town." When a man and wife who have brought up a family get past work, they not infrequently, with the consent of the whole family, give a deed of their land and buildings to one of the married sons or daughters in consideration of an assured maintenance during their lives. This arrangement is generally regarded as one creditable to all parties, being in fact a natural substitute for an annuity.

The appropriation for town charges covers the town officers' bills by the day, the discount on taxes, abatements, stationery, and incidentals. On the whole, the town is well served at small charge. In the appropriations for 1890 a new item appears, namely, "to buy school-books." The city practice of providing free text-books as well as free tuition for all children had just penetrated to this island town.[1]

[1] It is interesting to compare the public expenditures of a poor Maine town like Mount Desert with those of a comparatively rich Massachusetts town like Concord. For 1888–89 the expenditures of

An interesting element in the well-being of this rural population is their school system. It has already appeared that the town appropriations for schools are very small, and that even after the addition of the liberal aid given by the State the total sum available per child is not more than one-fifth of the sum ordinarily available in New England cities and towns in which the population is large and dense. The average annual expenditure per child in Massachusetts since 1883 has been about $20. What do the people of Mount Desert, who by annual vote make the minimum provision for schools, get for their money? The number of schoolhouses in the town was ten in 1889, and, on the average, school is kept in every schoolhouse for two terms of about nine weeks each in a year. The summer schools are usually kept by women, who

Concord, excluding payments on a new high-school building and payments of principal and interest on the town debt, amounted to $54,135.48. Only 77 per cent. of these expenditures were for the same objects as the expenditures at Mount Desert. The other 23 per cent. were for street-lamps, police, sewers, sidewalks, the fire department, the public library, the cemetery, and public grounds, none of which luxuries are provided at Mount Desert. The expenditures in the two towns in 1888–89 for the same objects compare as follows:

	Concord expenditures.	Per cent. of total expenditures.	Mt. Desert appropriations.	Per cent. of total appropriations.
State and county tax........	$6,603.59	12.2	$789.98	10.8
Schools, excluding new buildings..................	14,751.59	27.2	1,013.60	13.9
Roads and bridges...........	10,881.29	20.0	3,275.00	44.9
General expenses............	5,023.06	9.8	1,000.00	13.7
Poor.........................	4,209.14	7.8	1,200.00	16.4
	$41,468.67	77.	$7,278.58	99.7

are paid from $4.50 to $5 a week besides their board and lodging; the winter schools, by men, who are paid about $40 a month, besides their board and lodging. In addition, the so-called high school is kept three terms of ten weeks each, but in three different districts. Eighteen weeks in the year are all the schooling a Mount Desert boy can get until he is far enough advanced to go to the high school for ten weeks more. Moreover, the two terms in each year are far apart, so that the pupil forgets a good deal between terms. The teachers are in many cases untrained for their work, or very imperfectly trained. In spite of their limited opportunities, however, all the children of the town learn to read, write, and cipher well enough for practical purposes, and better than some children in cities and large towns who have twice the amount of

The striking differences are on schools, roads and bridges, and poor. The percentage expenditures on poor and on roads and bridges at Mount Desert are more than double the percentage expenditures for the corresponding objects at Concord. On the other hand, the percentage expenditure on schools is very little larger in Concord than in Mount Desert; for the State aid given to Mount Desert, which is not included in the foregoing table, nearly doubles the appropriation made at town-meeting; whereas the aid which Concord receives from Massachusetts is insignificant, but is included in the table. The percentage of the total valuation of the town appropriated to schools in Concord in 1888–89 was .45 of one per cent.; the percentage of the Mount Desert valuation appropriated to schools in the same year was .52 of one per cent. Concord has only two and a half times the population of Mount Desert, but nearly twenty times the valuation. It is possible, however, that the Concord valuation represents more accurately than that of Mount Desert the actual property of the inhabitants. Concord has not twice as many school-children as Mount Desert, but spends on schools seven times the money.

schooling,—and that under skilful teachers,—but pass the rest of their time under unfavorable conditions in crowded tenements and streets. The favorable result depends, first, on the keenness of the children's desire to learn; and, secondly, on the general home training. In an ordinary Mount Desert household, men, women, and children all work with their hands for the common support and satisfaction. The children help the elders in the common family interest as soon as they can rock a cradle, drive a cow, sweep a floor, or bring from the post-office the precious weekly newspaper. Yet the children's labor, unlike factory work, is wholesome for body and mind. They thus acquire at home, in the best way, habits of application and industry which stand them in good stead during the short weeks of their scanty school terms.

It must be confessed that the town was but ill supplied with churches before the advent of the summer visitor. Before 1881 there was but one church in the town, and that one did not always have a minister, and was practically inaccessible from large portions of the town. The native population, as a rule, felt no need of rites or sacraments; they were seldom christened or baptized, and were generally married by a justice, and buried by some minister imported for the occasion. A careful justice requires the town clerk's certificate of five days' intention of marriage. It has long been the custom to bury the dead near the houses where they had lived; so that on almost every farm one or more small burial lots are to be seen, inclosed with a wooden fence, and containing a few marble headstones, some wild roses, and perhaps a mountain-ash or some maples. There were but few church members in the town, such as there were being Baptists, Methodists, or Congregationalists. By the zeal of summer residents and visitors who were devoted to the Episcopal Church, two chapels have been built in the town, in which the worship of that church is maintained all the year round; and last summer (1889) a small Union church was also finished by the combined efforts of permanent and summer residents. It was, and still is, the practice of the natives of the town to secure a little preaching by inviting a minister or a theological student who lives in some neighboring town to preach once every other Sunday, or once every month, in one of the schoolhouses, and to accept as payment the proceeds of the collection taken up at the meeting, a guarantee being sometimes given that the collection should amount to a specified sum. The same minister could serve in this way four of the scattered settlements, provided he were strong enough to endure the inevitable exposure and fatigue. One who remembers the Mount Desert preaching procured in this fashion forty years ago describes the regular discourses of his youth as "them worm sermons"; but allusions to the worms which destroy this body, and to the undying worm in hell, are now heard but rarely. Singing by the local choir adds to the interest of these religious meetings, which indeed answer pretty well the common church purpose of bringing people together in search of edification, uplifting, and friendly communion. At Northeast Harbor the Union church, instead of the bare schoolhouse, is now used in precisely this way, it being quite impossible for the few residents to provide a salary for a settled minister. Sunday-schools are from time to time carried on in some of the schoolhouses by the efforts of a few public-spirited persons, men and women, who make use of the printed lessons and guides which the various Protestant denominations provide in great abundance. Adults as well as children attend these Sunday-schools.

In 1889 there were eleven general, or variety, "stores" in the town, and nine trades were practised, namely, the trades of the carpenter, painter, paperhanger, milliner, blacksmith, harness-maker, plumber, mason, and undertaker. These are, of course, the trades first needed in small communities. A little lumber is still sawed; in winters when ice fails on the Hudson some ice is cut for shipping, and cord-wood is cut for home use and for shipping; but the only considerable industry in the town is quarrying and cutting granite. The commonest product of the quarries is paving-stones; but stones of large size, for building purposes, are also produced. The splitting out of paving-stones is piece-work, at which a strong and skilful man can earn good wages ($3 to $5 a day); but it is hard work, and it cannot be pursued more than six or seven months out of the year. Almost every young man follows the sea for a time in either fishing- or coasting-vessels; and almost every householder does a little farming—that is, he makes some hay, raises pease, beans, beets, carrots, and potatoes for his family, and keeps a few hens, a pig, and one or two cows. The proceeds of a lucky season in a mackerel-catcher or "banker" are sometimes sufficient to build a house for the young fisherman, particularly if only two or three of the rooms are plastered at first. A young man who has laid up money enough to build a small house, and furnish two rooms in it, is in a position to marry and settle down; and a young woman who, with the assistance of her parents, has saved one or two hundred dollars by working in summer hotels or teaching, is distinctly a desirable match—first, because she has proved her capacity; and secondly, because she has capital. There is probably not an able-bodied man in the town, leaving out the summer residents, who does not work a great deal with his hands. The doctor is also a farmer; and the minister at Somesville, when there is one, probably raises his own vegetables, takes care of his horse, and saws, splits, and carries in his wood. Almost all the men are rough carpenters and painters, and they are equally at home on a boat, a jigger, or a buckboard. The most substantial citizens work on the roads; tend their live-stock; milk the cows; drive buckboards; cut ice and wood; haul stone, firewood, and lumber; bring sand, gravel, and brick in scows; go a-fishing or tend lobster-pots. Ten years ago many of the women spun the wool of their own sheep into yarn, besides making all the family clothes, taking care of the poultry, making butter, and doing all the household work. The girls work very hard in the summer boarding-houses of the island for eight or ten weeks, but do not, like the Nova Scotia girls, seek domestic service far away from home. From the necessity of the case, division of labor is not carried far in the town, and most of the people learn to do many things passably rather than any one thing perfectly.

The diet of the population is sufficiently varied, and is agreeable to them; but it is perhaps somewhat defective in the elements needed to form bone and muscle. This chemical defect may possibly account for the premature decay of the young people's teeth, which is noticeable in many cases. The staples of their food are white flour, corn-meal, sugar, butter, lard, stewed fruit (apples, crab-apples, damsons, bog and mountain cranberries, blueberries, raspberries, and prunes), beans, salt pork, salt and fresh fish (cod, haddock, mackerel, alewives, smelts, and frost-fish), clams, lobsters, fresh vegetables and berries in summer, tea and coffee, salt and spices. Fresh meat is too costly for common use, except in midwinter, when large pieces can be bought at wholesale prices and kept frozen. Moreover, the women, as a rule, do not use beef and mutton to advantage, because they do not know how to make the savory stews, broths, and soups which French and Canadian women prepare from the cheapest pieces of meat.

Instead of boiling or stewing a piece of the round of beef, for example, the Mount Desert cooks broil or fry it in thin slices, the product being, of course, dry, tough, and indigestible. Eggs are too useful for barter at the "store" to be eaten freely, and chickens must be sold to extravagant summer residents, or to collectors of poultry for city markets. The diet of the inhabitants of Mount Desert might be greatly improved at very small cost if they would only adopt oatmeal from the Scotch, pea-soup from the Canadians, sausage from the Germans, and the *pot-au-feu* from the French. It should be observed, however, that their present diet is satisfactory to them. They like hot bread made in fifteen minutes by the aid of chemical baking-powders; they are used to cakes, doughnuts, pies, and sweet sauces, and they probably would not like the more nutritious and more nitrogenous diet which their summer visitors affect.

The cost of bringing up a family of five or six children comfortably in the town of Mount Desert does not exceed $250 a year, if the house, a garden-patch, and a cow-pasture be already provided from savings of the husband and wife before marriage, and if the family, as a whole, have normal health and strength. Very few heads of families earn more than that sum in a year; for, although a day's wages in summer are commonly $1.75, work is scarce, the winter is long, and few men can get more than five months' employment at these wages in a year. The man and boys of a family can, however, do much for the common support, even when there is no work at wages to be had. They can catch and cure fish, dig clams, trap lobsters, pick the abundant blueberries on the rocky hills in August, and shoot ducks at the seasons of migration. Wild nature still yields to the skilful seeker a considerable quantity of food without price. Dwellers in a city may wonder how it is possible for a family to live so cheaply, but there is no mystery about it. There is no rent to pay; the schools are free; water costs nothing; the garden-patch yields potatoes and other vegetables, and the pasture milk and butter; two kerosene lamps and a lantern supply all the artificial light needed, at a cost not exceeding $2 a year; the family do all their own work without waste; there is but one fire, except on rare occasions, and that single fire is in a stove which delivers all its heat into the house; the wife and daughters knit the family stockings, mittens, and mufflers, mend all the clothes, and for the most part make all their own. The ready-made clothing which the men buy at the stores is very cheap ($10 to $15 a suit), being made of cotton with but a small admixture of wool. The cloth is strong and warm, and looks fairly well when new, but soon fades and wears shabby. For children the old clothes of their elders are cut down, the wear being thus brought on new places. The Hessian country girl wears proudly her grandmother's woolen petticoats, and well she may, for they are just as good and handsome as they were sixty years ago. A Scotch shepherd's all-wool plaid withstands the wind and the rain for a lifetime. The old Swiss porter, who is carrying the mounted traveler's valise over the Gemmi, puts on when the shower begins a thick woolen jacket of a rich brown color, with the remark, "The rain won't wet me, sir; this coat has kept me dry for twenty-five years." The American farmer and laborer use no such good materials as these, and therefore they and their children look shabby most of the time; but their clothes are very cheap in first cost, and, like the cotton clothes of the Chinese, they answer the main purposes of all clothing. In a city the best clothes of the family must be often put on; in the country but seldom. Shoes and boots must be bought for the whole household, but these articles are also very cheap in New England, and the coarser sorts are durable in proportion to their price. For protection from rain the Mount Desert man who is obliged to be out-of-doors in bad weather uses, in sailor-fashion, not rubber clothing, but suits of oiled cotton cloth, which keep out not only water but wind, last long, and cost little ($2 to $3 a suit). However hard it may be for city people to understand it, the fact remains that $250 a year is a sum adequate to the comfortable and wholesome support of a family of seven or eight persons in the town of Mount Desert, provided that a house, a garden, and a pasture are secured to them.

The people are, as a rule, well satisfied with their surroundings and their mode of life. Why should they not be? They are individually self-supporting and independent; they manage their town affairs, as free citizens should, with frugality and conservatism, feel no external restraints, and, being quite ignorant of the practical working of the national tariff, are conscious of no burdens which are not self-imposed. They are not anxious about the morrow, for their well-being does not depend on any single industry, or on the good feeling or good judgment of any one man or set of men. They all feel sure of a modest livelihood while health and strength last, and the poorest know that in emergencies they can rely on help from the common purse or from sympathetic neighbors. If the father of a family break his leg just when the winter supply of wood should be sawed and split, the men and boys of the neighborhood hold a "chopping-bee" at the house, and in a day the winter's supply of fuel is prepared and piled ready for use. If the cow of a poor family dies, the friends club together to provide another. Such poverty as exists in the town is the result of disease, bad habits, or shiftlessness. The persons supported by the town in 1888–89 were two orphan children, two insane adults, one boy in the reform school, and one infirm woman. If the wife is lazy, careless, or wasteful, the family cannot thrive. "That woman will throw more good stuff out of the window with a spoon than her husband can roll in at the door in a wheelbarrow," said a town official in describing the causes of the straitened condition of a family which sometimes needed the help of the town. A good proportion of the families of the town are thrifty, kindly, and intelligent, and there are helpfulness and self-respect throughout their households, and therefore comfort and contentment. Of course there are some blackish sheep; and, as in all small communities, there are some quarrels between neighbors who ought to be friends, and some chronic misunderstandings and antagonisms between kindred families which ought to be united. One must not imagine that people who live in the country are *ipso facto* more virtuous and high-minded than people of the same stock who live in the city. It is really no easier for people of small means than for those of large means to avoid becoming penurious and worldly minded. Bunyan's man with a muck-rake, who could look no way but downward, raked to himself, not coins and rubies, but the straws, the small sticks, and the dust of the floor. In making a bargain with a Mount Desert man one must not expect to find him less skilful and wary than a city Yankee. On the contrary, he may appear more suspicious, because he is less self-confident. The men do not always take their hats off in the house, even in the presence of women, and men, women, and children are habitually reticent and undemonstrative in manner. One who engages a Mount Desert laborer or mechanic to do a piece of work will probably receive the impression that it is the employed who consents to do a favor to the employer. On the other hand, the employer is pretty sure to get a fair day's work done. The butcher, the fish-dealer, and the grocer dispense their goods for a consideration, to be sure, but chiefly, it would appear, to accommodate their neighbors. "Can you let me have some eggs to-day?" or, "can you spare me some halibut" is a natural mode of opening a negotiation for these commodities. In short, the manners of the people express the independence they feel; and if they have not so much responsiveness and alertness as city people, it is because they have not so much practice in meeting strangers.

But perhaps to people who live crowded together in closely-built cities the life of a Mount Desert family seems solitary and dreary. They cannot hear the newsboys' and hucksters' cries, the rattle of vehicles and clatter of hoofs on stone pavements, the buzz and rumble of electric cars, and the screaming of factory whistles. They cannot see the thronged street and the gay shop windows, the electric lights, the grand houses, and the public monuments. They cannot ride on street-cars, parade on Main Street or Fifth Avenue, and visit at pleasure the dime museum, the dog, cat, horse, or baby show, or the negro minstrels. These indeed are some of the sights, sounds, and social privileges which are denied to a rural and seaboard population. Still they have compensations. They hear the loud monotone of the surf on the outer islands, the splash of the waves on the inner beaches, the rushing of the brook, the cawing of crows, the songs of robins and thrushes, and the rustling of the leaves in the breeze. They see the sky, the sea, the woods, the ponds, and the hills in all the varying lights and shadows of summer and winter, morning and evening, sunshine and storm. Then, too, they have many social enjoyments. Town-meeting gives the men a whole day of pleasure: first, the long drive or walk in company to the meeting-place; then the morning session; then the dinner provided by public-spirited women for twenty or twenty-five cents a head, the proceeds to go for some public object, like a plank sidewalk or a fence for the cemetery; then the afternoon session, big with important issues; and then the cheerful return home. Sewing-circles are maintained in the most populous neighborhoods—sometimes two in the same neighborhood, one for the mature matrons and another for the girls. A circle sews, not for the poor,—for there are none,—but for some public object, like an organ for the Sunday meeting, or a library for the Sunday-school; and when it holds its sale of the articles it has made, it gives a supper-party—admission ten, fifteen, or twenty cents, according to the costliness of the supper. There are hulled-corn suppers, ice-cream suppers, strawberry suppers, and turkey suppers. Then there are dancing-schools and singing-schools, and latterly there have been choir rehearsals in addition. Now and then a traveling showman summons the population to his ten-cent show. Occasionally a combination of native talent gives a recital or a little play. The "lodge" draws the men together, and the women too, for simple entertainments. The necessity of giving and receiving help in household emergencies adds variety to the lives of the women. If the mother of a family is disabled somebody must go and help her, for few families can afford to hire assistance. The neighbors do the work until an aunt, a sister, or a niece can arrive from the mainland or from some other part of the island. There is no little visiting for pleasure among relations, the visits lasting, not twenty minutes or through a single meal, as among hurrying city people, but for several days. Thus a Mount Desert man and wife will go to Bangor in the fall, when the steamboat fares are reduced one half, and pay a week's visit to some cousins who live in that metropolis; in the next June the Bangor cousins will return the visit. The cost of the exchange of visits is only the steamboat fares; for the two families have just about the same food and mode of life, and what the hosts expend the guests save. The system may be extended even to remote places like Massachusetts. A married aunt in Boston entertains her nephew and his wife for a week in the early spring; the next summer the aunt comes alone to Mount Desert, and spends a fortnight with her nephew. Of course the men get more variety than the women, because they often work in "crews," as on vessels, on the roads, on new buildings, and in the quarries; and also because they travel more by land and by sea, vote, serve on juries, and act as town and county officers.

The people of Mount Desert are free and at ease, very conservative for the familiar reason "we 're well 'nough 's we air," and very indifferent to the social speculations of nervous residents in cities. The single tax on land strikes them as absurd. The socialists' proposition that the community owes everybody at least a livelihood seems to them an old story. "It has always been so in this town," they truly say. Whether or no cities should make their own gas, as the Nationalists propose, is a matter of profound indifference to them. Kerosene is their reliance. On the question whether Government should manage the telegraphs — the other practical proposal of the Nationalists — they might possibly have an opinion in the negative, because they suffer from the wretched management of their post-offices by the National Government. The postmasters are frequently changed, the routes are badly arranged, and the mails are carried by horses which can hardly drag one foot after another. "The meanest and worst-used horses on our roads are hitched to the United States stage," said an indignant villager last summer. They hear of strikes, lock-outs, and boycotts in remote regions like New York, Pittsburg, and Chicago with much the same sort of pitying interest that the tenement-house horrors, the midsummer slaughter of infants, the great conflagrations, and the multitude of accidents, crimes, and disasters which happen amid a dense population excite in them. "Why will people stay in such places?" "How thankful we ought to be that we don't live in cities," are common expressions among them. It is difficult to transplant Mount Desert people. They prefer their sterile but beautiful island to any other place in the world, and if they leave it for a time they are always desiring and expecting to return to it. Factory operatives, unsatisfied mechanics, and city folks generally—they would say—may find as much fault as they please with the constitution of their own society, and may upset their social pyramid as often as they choose, provided it be clearly understood that the institutions and society of Mount Desert are to be left untouched, since they are already perfectly satisfactory to all concerned.

The manners and customs of the people of the town have thus far been very little affected by the inroad of summer visitors. About a dozen families have learned to take boarders, and have enlarged their houses considerably for this purpose; a few more families have sold portions of their farms, and with the proceeds have built for themselves better houses; and there is more work both for men and women in summer than there used to be. Still the habits of the people are essentially unchanged, and the town is managed precisely as it was before 1881.

Now this sequestered, wholesome, and contented community affords a fair type of the organization of basal American society. Due allowance made for differences of climate, soil, diet, and local usage, this is very much the way in which from thirty to forty millions of the American people live.

FAMILY STOCKS IN A DEMOCRACY

Published in the "Forum," 1890

FAMILY STOCKS IN A DEMOCRACY

IN an address before the Phi Beta Kappa Society of Harvard University two years ago, I endeavored to show, among other things, that democratic government, as distinguished from aristocratic or autocratic government, has no quarrel, as has been alleged, with the biological law of hereditary transmission; that families can be made just as enduring in a democratic as in an oligarchic state; and that the highest types of manners in men and women are produced abundantly on democratic soil. I maintained that the social mobility of a democracy, which permits the excellent and well-endowed of either sex to rise unimpeded from lower to higher levels, and to seek each other out, and which gives every advantageous variation in a family stock free opportunity to develop, is immeasurably more beneficial to a nation than any selective in-breeding, founded on class distinctions, that has ever been devised. I pointed out that democracy promotes the transmission and development of inheritable virtues and powers, although it does not add to the natural sanctions of the law of heredity an unnecessary bounty of privileges conferred by law, and, indeed, abolishes the legal transmission of artificial privileges. On that occasion I had no time to do more than to mention some of the means of perpetuating good family stocks in a democracy. It seems to me, however, that the principal means of preserving useful families in democratic society ought to be fully discussed; because the family, rather than the individual, is the important social unit; because the perpetuation of sound families is of the highest social interest; and because the democratic form of government is that form which in a few years, or a few generations, will prevail all over the civilized world. To that discussion I venture to contribute the following considerations.

It must be observed, in the first place, that the social freedom and mobility which permit every superior person to rise to his appropriate level in democratic society would be doubtful advantages, if for every person or family which should rise another should sink. If society as a whole is to gain by mobility and openness of structure, those who rise must stay up in successive generations, that the higher levels of society may be constantly enlarged, and that the proportion of pure, gentle, magnanimous, and refined persons may be steadily increased. New-risen talent should reinforce the upper ranks. New families rising to eminent station should be additions to those which already hold high place in the regard of their neighbors, and should not be merely substitutes for decaying families. In feudal society, when a man had once risen to high rank, there were systematic arrangements, like primogeniture and entailed estates, for keeping his posterity in the same social order. A democratic society sanctions no such arrangements, and does not need them; yet for the interests of the state, the assured permanence of superior families is quite as important as the free starting of such families.

Before going further, I ought to explain what I mean by good, or superior, family stocks. I certainly do not mean merely rich families. Some rich families are physically and morally superior; others are not. Obviously, in our country sudden and inordinate wealth makes it not easier, but harder, to bring up a family well. Neither do I have sole reference to professional or other soft-handed people who live in cities. On the contrary, such persons often lack the physical vigor which is essential to a good family stock. I have in mind sturdy, hard-working, capable, and trustworthy people, who are generally in comfortable circumstances simply because their qualities are those which command reasonable material, as well as moral, success. I have in mind, for instance, a family whose members have multiplied and thriven in one New England village for 130 years, always industrious, well-to-do, and respected, but never rich or highly educated, working with their hands, holding town and county offices, leading in village enterprises, independent, upright, and robust. I have in mind the thousand family stocks which are represented by graduates, at intervals, for one hundred years or more, on the catalogues of Harvard and Yale colleges — families in which comfort, education, and good character have been transmitted, if riches or high place have not. The men of a good family stock may be farmers, mechanics, professional men, merchants, or that sort of men of leisure who work hard for the public. But while I give this broad meaning to the term "good family stocks," I hold that one kind of family ought especially to be multiplied and perpetuated, namely, the family in which gentle manners, cultivated tastes, and honorable sentiments are hereditary. Democracy must show that it can not only ameliorate the average lot, but also produce, as the generations pass, a larger proportion of highly cultivated people than any other form of government.

What, then, are the means of perpetuating good family stocks in a democracy? The first is country life. In this regard, democracies have much to learn from those European aristocracies which have proved to be durable. All the vigorous aristocracies of past centuries lived in the country a large part of the year. The men were soldiers and sportsmen, for the most part, and lived on detached estates sparsely peopled by an agricultural and martial tenantry. They were oftener in camp than in the town or city. Their women lived in castles, halls, or châteaux in the open country almost the whole year, and their children were born and brought up there. The aristocratic and noble families of modern Europe still have their principal seats in the country, and go to town only for a few months of the year. These customs maintain vigor of body and equability of mind. It is not necessary, however, to go to Europe to find illustrations of modes of life favorable to the healthy development and preservation of superior families. In the last century, and in the early part of this century, the country minister and the country lawyer in New England were often founders, or members by descent, of large and vigorous family stocks, in which well-being and well-doing were securely transmitted. Their lives were tranquil, simple, not too laborious, and sufficiently intellectual; and their occupations took them much out of doors. They had a recognized leadership in the village communities where they made their homes, and also in the commonwealth at large. They took thought for education in general, and for the recruiting of their own professions; and they had a steadying and uplifting sense of responsibility for social order and progress, and for state righteousness. In many cases they transmitted their professions in their own families. So excellent were these combined conditions for bringing up robust and capable families, that to-day a large proportion of New England families of conspicuous merit are descended on one side or the other from a minister or a lawyer.

In American society of to-day the conditions of professional and business life are ordinarily unfavorable to the establishment of families in the country. The great industries are carried on at centers of dense population; trade is concentrated in large towns and cities; lawyers, journalists, and artists of every degree, medical specialists, architects, and consulting engineers, must all spend their days in cities. The well-educated country minister and country lawyer have almost disappeared. Population tends more and more to concentrate in dense masses. In a few of our older States, from 50 to 75 per cent. of the whole population live in groups or assemblages numbering 8000 persons or more. City life is changeful, noisy, exciting, and hurrying; country life is monotonous, leisurely, and calm. For young children particularly, the necessary conditions of dense populations are unfavorable. How great the difference is between an urban and a rural population in the average age of all who die, may be conveniently illustrated from the registration reports of Massachusetts, which have now been published for 47 years, and are believed to be reasonably accurate. In the thirty years from 1850 to 1880, the average age of all the persons who died in Suffolk County, an urban county on the seaboard, was 23⅓ years; the corresponding age in Barnstable, a rural county on the same seaboard, was 37; in Franklin, an inland rural county, it was 38½; while in the island county of Nantucket it was very nearly double the average age at death in Suffolk, namely, 46.15. The same reports show that the annual death-rate is uniformly higher in the densely populated counties than in the sparsely populated ones. Other causes besides density of population contribute to produce these striking results; but the main fact remains that a family which lives in the country has a better chance of continuance than one which lives in the city. Moreover, if we study the family histories of the actual leaders, for the time being, in business and the professions in any American city, we shall usually find that a very large proportion of them were country-bred. The country breeding gives a vigor and an endurance which in the long run outweigh all city advantages, and enable the well-endowed country boys to outstrip their city-bred competitors.

A very practical question, then, is how to resist, in the interest of the family, the tendency to live in cities and in large towns. For families in easy circumstances there is no better way than that which European experience has proved to be good, namely, the possession of two houses, one in the country and the other in the city, the first to be occupied for the larger part of the year; but this method is costly, and involves a good many things not noticed at first sight. Thus, for example, it involves the employment of governesses and tutors for children under fifteen years of age, and the use of country boarding-schools to some extent for older children. It involves, also, the exercise of hospitality on a large scale, in order to secure social variety in the country house. It needs, too, good postal facilities, circulating libraries, fair roads, and some smooth, sheltered footpaths. During the past thirty years there has been in the eastern States a great increase in the number of families using two houses, and the tendency in such families has been to spend a longer and longer time in the country or by the seaside. Colleges, academies, and private schools have arranged their terms and vacations to meet this growing practice; that is, they have a summer vacation of from three to four months. Teachers of music and the fine arts in the cities have no lessons to give from the first of June to the first of October. A large number of students in Harvard College get engagements to teach for the summer in families, or groups of families, which are living in the mountains, in the open country, or by the sea. College undergraduates used to teach country district schools for twelve weeks in the winter; they now teach in families, or at summer resorts, for twelve weeks in the summer. These facts, and many others which might be cited, indicate a wholesome change in the habits of well-to-do families, in favor of country life.

The next change for the better to be noticed is the adoption of suburban life by great numbers of families, both poor and well-to-do, the heads of which must do their daily work in cities. Recent improvements in steam and electric railway transportation make it easy for a family man, whose work is in the city from eight or nine o'clock to five or six o'clock, to live fifteen or even twenty miles from his office or shop. The chances are strong that the death-rate in an open-built suburb, provided with good water and good sewers, will be decidedly lower than in the city; indeed, that it will not be more than from one half to three quarters of the city death-rate. In the suburb are better air, more sun, and a more tranquil life. This method obtains more and more in the Atlantic States north of the Potomac, in England, and in Australia. The advantages of suburban residence may, however, be almost neutralized for the men, if the daily travel to and fro is made wearisome, annoying, or unwholesome. It is always to be wished that the ride home from shop or office should be a refreshment instead of an added labor. In many American cities the means of communication between the business quarters and the suburban residence quarters are so thoroughly bad that for the men it is a positive hardship to live in the suburbs. It is said that in some of the new cities of Australia, parks have been laid out between the business and the residence quarters, so that the daily rides between the two districts may always be agreeable.

A third mode of combating the ill effects of density of population, and of giving city families some of the advantages of country life, is by increasing in cities the provision of public squares, gardens, boulevards, and public parks. The city open square or garden is one thing, and the city park quite another; the former being properly an open-air sitting-room or nursery for the neighboring people, the second being a large piece of open country brought into the city. Both are needful in much larger number and area than it has been the custom to provide in American cities. It is important also to cultivate among our people the habit of using all the squares and parks they have, for Americans are very far behind Europeans in the intelligent use of such reservations. To this end the foreign custom of half-holidays in the various trades is an excellent one, particularly if the half-holidays are taken on Wednesdays or Saturdays, when there are half-holidays in the public schools. To promote healthy family enjoyments among laboring people, ten hours' labor a day, with a half-holiday once a week, is a much better industrial arrangement than nine hours' labor every day in the week.

An important advantage which country life has over city life is that it requires, permits, or encourages out-of-door occupations for men, women, and children. The farmer and his boys habitually work in the open air; the mill-hand, clerk, machinist, teacher, lawyer, and minister work in-doors, often in positively bad air. To offset the evil effects of in-door occupations, every city family which aspires to vigor and permanence should assiduously seek fresh air and out-of-door pleasures or occupations. All children in well-to-do families should be taught to walk long distances, to swim and to row, and to ride on horseback. Girls need these accomplishments as much as boys. In this matter, also, democratic society must learn from aristocratic. Rich people used always to be great landowners; now, unfortunately, people may be rich and yet own nothing but stocks and bonds—not even one house. European nobilities were always an agricultural class, loving good land and good crops, rejoicing in horses, dogs, and cattle, and delighting in hunting, fishing, shooting, racing, and all other forms of open-air sport. Men, women, and children rode on horseback habitually, and took long journeys in that wholesome way. Their castles and halls were so open to the air and so little warmed, that even their in-door life was not so enervating as ours. If modern democratic families are to be perpetuated like ancient aristocratic families, they must live as robust and healthy lives. If the family occupations are not manual, the boys should learn to use some tools—the gardener's, carpenter's, turner's, blacksmith's, machinist's, founder's, or plumber's—and the girls should learn to cut out, sew, knit, and cook; and whether the family occupations are manual or not, out-of-door life should be cultivated to the utmost. Americans have not the skill of Europeans in availing themselves of every chance to eat or work in the open air, under the shelter of a tree or of a vine-clad arbor. Neither the poorer sort nor the richer possesses this skill, or feels an irrepressible desire for such opportunities. One often sees, in the suburbs of our cities, large and costly houses placed in lots so small that the owners and their families have hardly more room for out-of-door pleasures than they would have in a city block. Many a rich American, who occupies without any scruple a house worth $100,000, will hesitate to keep open, for the use of his family and for the indirect advantage of his neighbors, an acre of suburban land worth only $50,000. The Germans, in their native country, excel in the out-of-door habit. Every restaurant and beer-garden must have some space out of doors, however small, for the use of its patrons in the warmer half of the year. Every school takes care of the natural-history rambles of its pupils. In the long vacation, walking-journeys for the boys are arranged and conducted by the teachers. Families devote a part of every Sunday in good weather to some open-air excursion. In some of the smaller manufacturing towns of Germany, on a pleasant half-holiday, it seems as if the whole population had deserted the houses, and had taken to the open air in the streets, squares, and gardens. It is extraordinary how little provision has been made in most American towns and cities for the out-of-door enjoyments of the population. Even when public squares and gardens have been reserved or purchased, they are often left in an unkempt condition and without proper police protection, and are not provided with seats, shelters from sun and wind, sand-heaps for little children, gymnastic apparatus for older boys and girls, and open-air restaurants at which simple refreshments may be obtained. As compared with European governments, American democratic government seems to take no thought whatever for the healthful enjoyments of an urban population.

I venture to state next the proposition, that a permanent family should have a permanent dwelling-place, domicile, or home town. In older societies this has always been the case. Indeed, a place often lent its name to a family. In American society the identification of a family with a place is comparatively rare. In American cities and large towns there are as yet no such things as permanent family houses. Even in the oldest cities of the East, hardly any family lives in a single house through the whole of one generation, and two successive generations are rarely born in the same house. Rapid changes of residence are the rule for almost everybody, so that a city directory which is more than one year old is untrustworthy for home addresses. The quick growth of the chief American cities, and the conversion of residence quarters into business quarters, partly account for the nomadic habits of their inhabitants; but the inevitable loss of social dignity and repose, and the diminution of local pride and public spirit, are just as grievous as if there were no such physical causes for the restlessness of the population. The human mind can scarcely attribute dignity and social consideration to a family which lives in a hotel, or which moves into a new flat every first of May.

In the country, however, things are much better. In the older States there are many families which have inhabited the same town for several generations, a few which have inhabited the same house for three generations, and many farms that have been in the same family for several generations;

and in more and more cases prosperous men, who have made money in business or by their professions, return to the places where their ancestors lived, and repossess themselves of ancestral farms which had passed into other hands. In the country it is quite possible, under a democratic form of government, that a permanent family should have a permanent dwelling; and in any village or rural town such a family dwelling is always an object of interest and satisfaction. To procure, keep, and transmit such a homestead is a laudable family ambition. It can be accomplished wherever testamentary dispositions are free, and the object in view is considered a reasonable and desirable one. It must be confessed, however, that very few country houses in the United States have thus far been built to last. We build cheap, fragile, and combustible dwellings, which, as a rule, are hardly more durable than the paper houses of the Japanese. Nevertheless, our families might at least do as well as the Japanese families, which are said to live a thousand or fifteen hundred years on the same spot, although in a series of slight houses.

The next means of promoting family permanence is the transmission of a family business or occupation from father to sons. In all old countries this inheritance of a trade, shop, or profession is a matter of course; but in our new society, planted on a fresh continent, it has not been necessary thus far for every family to avail itself, in the struggle for a good living, of the advantage which inherited aptitude gives. But as population grows denser and competition for advantageous occupations grows more strenuous, and as industries become more refined and more subdivided, the same forces which have produced the transmission of occupations in families in Europe and Asia will produce it here. The children of the ribbon-weaver can learn to weave ribbons quicker and better than any other children; the son of a physician has a better chance than the son of a tanner to learn the art of medicine, and besides, he may possess an inherited faculty for medical observation; the son of a lawyer can be quietly inducted into his father's business with great advantage to both father and son. In all such cases, success depends on the hearty coöperation of the children, who may be impelled to work either by ambition and by an inherited disposition, or by the healthy stimulus of impending want. Under right conditions, a transmitted business tends to make a sound family more secure and permanent, and a permanent family tends to hold and perfect a valuable business. This principle, which is securely founded on biological law, applies best in the trades and professions, in ordinary commerce, and in the industries which do not require immense capitals; but in Europe many vast industries and many great financial and mercantile concerns are family properties, and there is in our own country already a distinct tendency to this family management of large businesses, as being more economical and vigilant than corporate management, and more discerning and prompt in selecting and advancing capable men of all grades. The principle seems frequently to fail in this country in regard to the sons of uneducated men who have become very rich through some peculiar skill or capacity of their own which is not transmissible, or at least is not transmitted. The difficulty seems to be that the sons feel no sense of responsibility for their privileges and no inducement to work. Brought up to do nothing, they sink into the life of mere idlers, and are dispossessed by hard-working and ambitious men of the very business which the fathers created, and would gladly have had their sons inherit.

The most important of all aids in perpetuating sound family stocks is education. Whatever level of education a family has reached in one generation, that level at least should be attained by the succeeding generation. It is a bad sign of family continuance if a farmer, who was himself sent away from home to a country academy for two or three terms, does not give his son the same or a corresponding opportunity. It is a bad sign if a clerk in the city, who himself went through the high school, is content that his son should stop at the grammar school. It is a bad sign if a professional man, whose father sent him to college, cannot do as much for his son. Diminution of educational privileges in a family generally means either decline in material prosperity or loss of perception of mental and spiritual values. The latter loss is a deal worse than loss of property in its effect on family permanence; for low intellectual and moral standards are fatal to family worth, whereas countless excellent families meet with reverses in business, suffer losses by flood or fire, or confide in untrustworthy persons, and yet survive with all their inherent mental and spiritual excellences. In a righteous democracy the qualities which make a family permanent are purity, integrity, common sense, and well-directed ambition. Neither plain living nor rich living is essential, but high thinking is. Now, the ultimate object of education, whether elementary, secondary, or higher, is to develop high thinking. What, for example, is the prime object of teaching a child to read? Is it that he may be able to read a way bill, a promissory note, or an invoice? Is it that he may be better able to earn his living? No! These are merely incidental and comparatively insignificant advantages. The prime object is to expand his intelligence, to enrich his imagination, to introduce him to all the best human types both of the past and of the present, to give him the key to all knowledge, to fill him with wonder and awe, and to inspire him with hope and love. Nothing less than this is the object of learning to read; nothing better or more vital than this is the object of the most prolonged and elaborate education. The improvement of the human being in all his higher attributes and powers is the true end; other advantages are reaped on the way, but the essential gain is a purified, elevated, and expanded mind. We often hear it said that high-school graduates have learned too much, or have been trained out of their sphere,— whatever that may mean,— and that colleges do not produce the captains of industry. Such criticisms fly very wide of their mark. They do not conform to the facts, and they betray in those who make them a fundamental misconception of the ultimate object of all education. The object of education and of family life is not to promote industry and trade; rather the supreme object of all industry and trade is to promote education and the normal domestic joys. We should not live to work, but work to live—live in the home affections, in the knowledge and love of nature, in the delights of reading and contemplation, in the search for truth, and in the worship of the beautiful and good. In urging this view of the object of education, I have presented the only argument needed to convince a fair-minded man that the family which would last must look to the education of its children.

A few words ought to be said on wise marriage, for that wisdom is of as much consequence to family permanence in a democracy as in any other state of society. In the first place, reasonably early marriages are desirable, from the point of view of family permanence, because they give better promise of children, and because the children of an early marriage will be sooner ready to aid the parents or the surviving parent. A farmer who marries at twenty-two may have helpful children by the time he is thirty-five. A professional man, or a mechanic, who marries at twenty-four, may have a son ready to take up his business by the time the father is fifty; whereas, if he delays marriage until he if thirty-four, he cannot have his son for a partner until he is himself approaching sixty. It is a bad sign that among rich and well-to-do Americans marriage begins to be unduly postponed; but this evil is a limited one, because it affects only a very small proportion of the population, and often works its own cure by extinguishing the families which persistently practise it. Secondly, free selection of mates, under the guidance of mutual affinities and repulsions, is the democratic method in marriage; and biological science indicates that this is probably the best possible way of producing and maintaining a vigorous race. Selective in-breeding, such as has been attempted in noble families in Europe, has not succeeded; selection superintended by elders, as in France, certainly works no better than free selection; and marriage by commercial arrangement, or by purchase more or less disguised, whether of the woman by the man or of the man by the woman, is certainly not conducive either to family happiness or to family permanence in our day, whatever it may have been in patriarchal or matriarchal times. Every principle of political and social freedom tends to confirm and to establish the practice of unrestricted freedom of selection in marriage; so that we may well believe that American practices in this regard will ultimately become universal. With a view to family permanence and to continuous improvement, there are two directions in which the common American marriage practices might be improved. In the first place, among attractions for either sex, physical strength and constitutional vigor and promise should count for more than they generally do; and among repulsions, constitutional weakness or delicacy and bad bodily inheritances should also count for more. Secondly, engagements to marry should not be made until the education of both parties has been completed, and their tastes and capacities have become tolerably well defined. Many ill-assorted marriages result from engagements made before one of the parties has attained his or her mental growth, or become acquainted with his or her powers and inclinations.

Suggestions are frequently made nowadays that the human race could be improved by utterly abolishing the institution of the family, and applying to men and women the methods of breeding which are successfully applied to domestic animals. All these suggestions fly in the face of every doctrine of human rights which mankind has been painfully trying for centuries to establish, and which at last it sees recognized by a considerable portion of the race. Moreover, in the domestic animals men have sought to reproduce and to develop certain bodily powers; they have not had to deal with mental and spiritual gifts. They have sought the best trotters among horses, the best milkers among cows, and the best layers among hens. The problem of improving the human race is infinitely more complex; for the main improvements to be sought, although undoubtedly having a physical basis, are improvements in mental and spiritual powers, the relations of which to the body are by no means understood. To the solution of this more complex and more recondite problem the results obtained in the breeding of valuable varieties of domestic animals contribute hardly anything of value. Meantime, the family remains the most sacred, durable, and potent of human institutions, and through it must be sought the replenishment and improvement of society.

If adequate laws and institutions provide for the safe holding and transmission of property, whatever promotes thrift and accumulation of property in families promotes family permanence. Democracy distrusts exaggerated accumulations of property in single hands; but it firmly believes in private property to that extent which affords reasonable privacy for the family, promotes family continuance, and gives full play to the family motive for making soil, sea, and all other natural resources productive for human uses. Thus democratic legislation incorporates and protects savings banks, trust companies, insurance companies of all kinds, benefit societies, and coöperative loan and building associations, which are all useful institutions for promoting thrift, if they are vigilantly watched and wisely controlled by the state. But the most direct legislative contribution to family permanence, apart from marriage and divorce laws, is to be found in the laws regulating the transmission of land, buildings, implements, wagons, vessels, household goods, and domestic animals, both by will or contract and in the absence of will or contract. The great majority of families hold no other kinds of property than these, the ancient and universal kinds. Stocks and bonds, forms of property which have practically been created within forty years, are held only by an insignificant proportion of families; so that legislation affecting unfavorably the transmission of these new forms of property from one generation to another could not be very injurious to the family as an institution. For example, succession taxes on stocks and bonds might be imposed without serious harm. On the other hand, any legislation which should destroy or greatly impair the inheritable value of land, or of improvements on land, would be a heavy blow at family permanence, particularly in a state where land is for the most part owned by the occupiers. The farm, the village lot, and the town or city house with its appurtenances and contents, constitute transmissible family property in the vast majority of cases. In the interests of the family, democratic legislation on inheritances should chiefly regard, not the few estates which are counted in hundreds of thousands of dollars, but the millions which are counted in hundreds of dollars. Inheritances of a few hundreds of dollars have a great importance from the point of view of family permanence; for most inheritances are on that scale, and five hundred dollars means a favorable start in life for any young working man or woman. The proposal to destroy by taxation the transmissible value of land seems to be aimed at the few unreasonably rich, but it would strike hardest the frugal and hard-working millions.

Lastly, family permanence is promoted by the careful training of successive generations in truth, gentleness, purity, and honor. It is a delightful fact that these noble qualities are in the highest degree hereditary, and just as much so in a democratic as in an aristocratic society. They are to be acquired also by imitation and association; so that a good family stock almost invariably possesses and transmits some of them. Truth is the sturdiest and commonest of these virtues; gentleness is a rarer endowment; purity and honor are the finest and rarest of them all. In a gentleman or a lady they are all combined. Democratic society has already proved that ladies and gentlemen can be made much more quickly than people used to suppose; but since it has been in existence hardly one hundred years, it has not yet had time to demonstrate its full effect in producing and multiplying the best family stocks. It has already done enough, however, to justify us in believing that in this important respect, as in many others, it will prove itself the best of all forms of social organization.

Does any one ask, Why take so much thought for the permanence of superior families? I reply that the family is the main object of all the striving and struggling of most men, and that the welfare of the family is the ultimate end of all industry, trade, education, and government. If the family under a democratic form of government is prosperous and permanent, the state, and civilization itself, will be safer and safer through all generations.

EQUALITY IN A REPUBLIC

From the "Cambridge Magazine," May, 1896

EQUALITY IN A REPUBLIC

MANY people are much disappointed because it has turned out that our free institutions do not produce equality of condition among the citizens. The motto of the French Revolution was, "Liberty, Equality, Fraternity"; and it was expected of the American republic that it would prevent the existence of great distinctions in regard to wealth between its citizens, and tend decidedly toward equal conditions for all. An experience of a little over one hundred years has demonstrated that republican institutions do not prevent the existence, on the one hand of a very rich class, and on the other of a very poor class; and that between these two extremes every possible variety of condition may exist. In some respects free institutions do certainly tend to equality. Thus, they make all citizens equal as regards the suffrage, the security of life and property, and the duty of obedience to the laws; they abolish hereditary privileges, such as titles, transmissible offices, monopolies, or sinecures; but they do not interfere with the accumulation of property, or with the transmission from generation to generation of property and of all that property can procure for its owner.

Looking back on this experience, it seems as if any one might have known from the beginning that a legal state of secure individual liberty could not but produce in the long run great inequalities of condition. The state of society at large under freedom is perfectly illustrated by the condition of things in a university, where the choice of studies is free, and every student is protected and encouraged in developing to the utmost his own gifts and powers. In Harvard University, for example, thousands of students enjoy an almost complete liberty in the selection of their studies, each man being encouraged to select those subjects in which he most easily excels, and consequently finds most enjoyment and most profit. The result is that no two students in the University are pursuing the same subjects with the same success — that is, attaining the same intellectual results in the same time. If a student at the beginning of his course has some advantage over his fellows in the study of Latin or chemistry, at the end of four years his advantage will have been greatly increased by the elaborate training in Latin or chemistry which he has procured. The difference between him and his associates in his acquired knowledge of Latin or chemistry will have become greater and greater, and his superior capacity for acquiring a still further knowledge of the subject will be much more marked at the end of the course than it was at the beginning. As one thousand students that entered together advance through the college, they become more and more unlike in their capacities and attainments, the difference in capacity being much more important than the difference in attainment. This is the inevitable result of the policy of freedom of studies. Under any policy—the most repressive conceivable—it would be impossible to keep the students alike in attainments and capacities during four years, even if they were alike at the start. The only means of turning them out at the end of a four years' course in a tolerably even condition would be to prescribe rigidly the same group of subjects for every student, and to repress in every way possible the unusual gifts of the superior students, while stimulating to the utmost the slow wits of the dullards and sluggards—that is, a despotic government would be required to produce by artificial restrictions some approach to equality of mental condition at graduation.

In American public schools,—in which far too many pupils are placed before one teacher, and a strict grading system is employed as a means of helping her to perform her impossible task,—we have an illustration of the attempt to produce from many hundreds, or even thousands, of children an approximately uniform product representing an average of the bright and the dull. This method does not succeed in producing mental uniformity; and, though it fails to average the children, the attempt is the greatest evil in American public schools. The manual-training schools, which have come into existence in many communities within the last fifteen years, afford a valuable illustration of the inevitable diversity of mental product even under a discipline intended to be uniform. In such training of the eye and hand as lessons in carpentry, forging, drawing, molding, and turning afford, it proves impossible to keep the different members of a class together in simultaneous exercises. The members of a class started on the same day in forging, for example, soon get separated, simply because one boy can do a great deal more work and better work than another. Some boys are slow to attain any excellence at all in work of eye and hand, while others take naturally to fine handiwork. In every trade the same irrepressible differences between workmen constantly appear. They are differences in physical organization, and also in disposition and will-power; and they last through life, and indeed go on increasing from youth to age. No restrictions have yet been devised which abolish these differences. It may be agreed by workmen in the same trade that a uniform number of hours shall constitute a day's work, and uniform pay be given for that uniform day's work. It may be agreed that no mason shall lay more than a specified number of bricks in a day, or that no compositor shall set more than a specified number of ems in a day; and yet, in spite of these sacrifices of individual liberty, the differences between workmen will remain; and it will be found that employers exhibit decided preferences in selecting hands, so that this man will always have work and that man will seldom have it. In short, the only way to bring about uniform earning-power is to establish some kind of despotism, or some system of voluntarily assumed restrictions on individual liberty. Under an absolute despotism, such as that of the Sultan of Morocco or the Khalifa of the Sudan, under which all property is held only at the will of the ruler, and every distinction or public station proceeds solely from him, and may be at any moment withdrawn by him, a kind of equality may exist among all the subjects of the despot. There is no freedom to rise, and the man who has been lifted up may at any moment be cast down to the lowest social stage. In dependence on the will of the despot great inequalities of condition may temporarily exist; but they have no security or permanence. Before the one tyrant all subjects are in some sense equal, even military rank being held only at the will of the despot. The subjects of such a government are not free to exercise their different individual capacities, and there results a low, though level, social state.

These familiar illustrations prepare us to accept the proposition that public freedom must result in inequalities of condition among the citizens; and indeed that is just what has happened in our republic. If all the property in the United States should be evenly distributed among all the citizens to-morrow, on the day after to-morrow inequality of condition would again be established, because all men would be legally free to put into play, in security, their very different gifts and powers for the acquisition and accumulation of property.

But some one may say: Granted that in any one generation the powers of acquisition of the different citizens must be very unequal, and that hence great differences of property must arise, might not these differences, which really depend on the liberty and security which free institutions provide, be made non-transmissible, so that each new generation should be obliged to begin over again the differentiating process? There are two answers to this question. In the first place, the distribution by the state of possessions accumulated by one citizen, among other citizens who had no obvious part in earning them, could not be effected without pauperizing the recipients of the unearned bounty; and secondly, all social experience teaches that the family motive gives the strongest impulsion toward industry, frugality, and disinterestedness. It is ultimately for the family that most men and women struggle and labor all their lives. It is on the family, and not on the individual that states are built. It is the family virtues which make commonwealths possible. The transmission of property, therefore, from father or mother to children has always been safeguarded in every civilized community. It is a right quite as precious to the man of small property as to the man of large property — indeed, more precious. It is a right which everybody is interested in who has any property at all, and any family at all; and though some modern states have ventured to prescribe in some respects how an owner shall distribute his estate among his heirs, no state has ever ventured to deny or abolish this right of distribution. It is one of the elements of our republican freedom in the United States that wills are subjected to much fewer restraints and limitations than they are in most European countries, and this freedom tends strongly to the distribution of properties at death.

We have seen during the last forty years in the United States the development of a disposition among rich people to tie up their estates in trust, in order to hold the properties together for the common benefit of descendants, and to prevent their being wasted by youthful or unintelligent heirs.

Whether this process be socially mischievous, or not, has not yet been determined by experience. If it prove to be injurious, it can easily be checked by legislation. In the meantime, there are two methods in use for securing public benefits from great private properties. The first is the voluntary method of public benefaction which many rich Americans adopt; the second is the succession tax, which appropriates for the public benefit a percentage of all estates which rise above a very moderate limit—a percentage which is small on lineal inheritances and larger on collateral inheritances. Succession taxes are on the whole far the most desirable form of taxation on personal property; for they have the advantage of being levied within a moderate number of years on all the personal property in the community.

It being thus clear that individual liberty in a free state must lead to inequality of possessions, it remains to ask: Is this condition of things to be regretted? Is it desirable that conditions as regards property should be equal? All the analogies of nature and all human experience seem to me to indicate that a society in which there were no varieties of condition would be unnatural, monotonous, stupid, and unprogressive. Civilization means infinite differentiation under liberty. An interesting human society must include individuals of very various gifts and powers. If all women were equally beautiful, the race would hardly know what beauty was. If no man could be more judicious, inventive, or far-seeing than another, progress would be impossible. Society would be as dull as a prairie or an ocean would be, if it were left without the atmospheric changes which give variety to such monotonous plains.

Let us then distinctly abandon equality of possessions as one of the objects which republican institutions aim at, and let us substitute for this foreign conception the object expressed in the word unity. Social unity is consistent with great social diversities. "There are diversities of gifts; but the same spirit." Let us substitute for the French motto, "Liberty, Equality, Fraternity," an Anglo-Saxon motto—"Freedom, Unity, Brotherhood." Those three ideas go well together, and express a lofty and practicable social aim. The fate of free institutions is not to be settled on any issue of poverty or wealth. It is their effect on public health — physical and moral — which is to determine their destiny. Republicans may be either rich or poor, with safety to the State; but they cannot be corrupt in body or soul without bringing the republic to its fall.

ONE REMEDY FOR MUNICIPAL MISGOVERNMENT

PUBLISHED IN THE "FORUM," OCTOBER, 1891

ONE REMEDY FOR MUNICIPAL MISGOVERNMENT

IN these days, when so many sanguine philanthropists are advocating large extensions of governmental activity, and indeed are hoping for a beneficent reorganization of society, in which popular governments shall plan, order, make, store, and distribute everything,—all without unduly abridging individual liberty,—it may be wholesome to discuss sometimes the practical shortcomings of democratic government within its present rather limited field. Before we take courage to believe that governmental management would be successful in many new fields and on a much larger scale, we ought to be satisfied with the results of that management within its actual province. It is more instructive to discuss shortcomings close at hand than those remote, and evils right under the eyes of the people than those they can hardly discern. To discuss the evils which attend municipal government is, therefore, more edifying than to consider the evils of the national and state administrations.

In peaceful times the national government is remote from the daily life of the average citizen. Its wastefulness does not come home to him. Its corrupting patronage and jobbery are unperceived by him. Errors in the financial policy of the government become plain to him only when he experiences their ill effects. The post-office is the only function of the national government which concerns him intimately, and that function is really a simple business, and has always been a government monopoly; so that the average citizen who gets his mail with tolerable regularity, and has no experience of any other method of sending letters and newspapers, generally thinks that the post-office business is as well done by government as it could be by any agency. Municipal functions, on the other hand, touch the average citizen very nearly. It makes a great difference to him whether the city keeps good schools or bad, and clean streets or dirty, supplies him with pure or impure water, and taxes him fairly or unfairly. Moreover, all critics of the working of the institutions of the United States during the last fifty years—whether friendly or hostile, whether foreign or native—agree that municipal government has been the field in which the least efficiency for good has been exhibited and the greatest positive evils have been developed. To what causes the existing evils of municipal government in the United States are to be ascribed, and in what direction the remedies are to be sought, are, therefore, questions of the profoundest interest for the average citizen, as well as for the social philosopher. It is easy to attribute these evils to the inherent viciousness and recklessness of the urban population — wickedness and folly which are more and more effective for evil as the proportion of urban to rural population rises. It is easy for people whose forefathers came to this western world one or more generations ago to believe that the people who have just come are the source of all municipal woes. But neither of these explanations can be accepted as probable or reasonable. When we examine the working of the American democracy on the greatest state questions,— such as independence of Great Britain, the federation of the States, and the indissoluble union of the States, — we find that the democracy has dealt wisely with these great questions, and just as wisely in the generation of 1860–90 as in the generations of Revolutionary times. We observe that, in the management of a great national debt, our democracy has exhibited better judgment, and, on the whole, juster sentiments, than any oligarchy or tyranny has ever exhibited. We see that private property is more secure under the democratic form of government than under any other form. We find that there has been an unequaled amount of diffused intellectual and moral energy among the mass of the people during the last forty years; and we are sure that the democratic form of government, working in combination with democratic social mobility, is eminently favorable to religious, social, and industrial progress. Into the immense material development of the period since the civil war there has gone a deal of sound moral force as well as of mental and physical activity. The census teaches us that the proportion of the urban to the rural population has rapidly increased during the last thirty years; but these new city people have all come in from the country. During this same period, rural town governments have fully maintained their excellence, and have in many States exhibited a new efficiency and enterprise; as, for example, in the development of primary and secondary education, the maintenance of free libraries, the restriction of the liquor traffic, and the improvement of bridges and highways. I submit, therefore, that there is no good reason to believe in any wide-spread and progressive demoralization of the mass of the population, whether urban or rural. I would not be understood, however, to maintain that there have not been particular spots or particular occasions, some of them conspicuous, where failure and disgrace have resulted from moral causes; such as indifference on the part of voters to the bad character of the men they voted for; the corrupt procuring of votes in return for appointments, licenses, or tariffs; or the importation into municipal affairs of passions aroused in national party strife. My contention is, that, in spite of these manifestations, there is no good reason to believe that American constituencies, whether large or small, have frequently been dishonest or corrupt at heart, although they have sometimes chosen dishonest or corrupt agents.

The theory that the immigration of a few millions of foreigners within thirty years is the true cause of municipal evils in the United States must also be rejected, although the too quick admission to the suffrage of men who have had no acquaintance with free institutions has doubtless increased the evils of city government in a few localities. The great majority of the immigrants have been serviceable people; and of late years many of them — particularly the Germans, English, Scotch, Scandinavians, and Swiss — have had a better education than the average rural American can obtain. The experienced voters of the country cannot shelter themselves behind the comparatively small contingent of the inexperienced, particularly when the former are wholly responsible for admitting the latter to the suffrage.

I venture to suggest in this paper another explanation (a partial one, to be sure) of the comparative failure of municipal government in the United States — an explanation which points to a remedy.

It is observable that the failures of the democratic form of government have occurred chiefly in those matters of municipal administration which present many novelties, and belong to the domain of applied science: such as the levying of taxes; the management of water-supplies and drainage systems; the paving, lighting, and cleaning of highways; the control of companies which sell in city streets light, heat, power, transportation for persons, and communication by electricity; the care of the public health; and the provision of proper means of public enjoyment, such as open squares, gardens, and parks. All these matters require for their comprehension and proper management a high degree of scientific training, and all of them require the continuous execution, through many years, of far-reaching plans. I proceed to consider each of the topics I have mentioned, with the intention of showing that antiquated methods of municipal administration, and particularly short and insecure tenures for the heads of departments, are responsible for the greater part of the municipal evils which are bringing discredit on free institutions, and that the altered nature and conditions of municipal business require that these old methods, which answered very well in earlier times, be fundamentally reformed.

In the course of this rapid sketch it will appear at various points that the monarchical and aristocratic governments of Europe have grappled with modern municipal problems much more successfully than our democratic government. The discussion will, I think, suggest that explanations of this result, so unsatisfactory to lovers of liberty, are to be found in the slowness of a democracy to change governmental methods, and in the comparatively small and temporary influence of political and administrative leaders under a form of government which makes frequent appeal to universal suffrage.

I begin with the levying of municipal taxes. One of the greatest mischiefs in American municipal government is the system of local taxation;

for this system is, in many places, an effective school in evasion and perjury, and, as a rule, an agency of stinging injustice. The trouble is two-fold.

In the first place, the incidence of taxes is one of the most difficult subjects in political economy, and very few American legislators know anything about it. More than that, very few Americans in any profession or walk of life know anything about it. The colleges and universities of the country are greatly to blame for this condition of things. They never began to teach political science in any serious way till about twenty years ago. The generation of men now in their prime either never studied any political economy at all, or studied it in one small text-book for a few hours a week for perhaps half a year, at school or college; or they picked up a few notions about it in the intervals of professional or business occupation after they had entered upon their life-work. The number of living Americans who have any thorough and systematic knowledge of the principles of political economy, including the incidence of taxes, is absolutely insignificant; and these few are mostly either professors, or business-men who have been also life-long students. The average business-man and the average professional man have never given any attention to the science, except perhaps to some little scrap of it, like the doctrine of protection, which has temporarily had some political interest.

Secondly, the forms of property have changed so

prodigiously within forty years, that a theory of assessment which worked reasonably well before 1850 has become thoroughly mischievous in 1890. The old theory of taxation was, that every man should be assessed at his home on all his property. It was all there, or it returned thither periodically, like his ox-cart or his vessel. If, by rare chance, a man had property out of the town where he lived, it was a piece of real estate, which was to be assessed for taxes in the town where it lay, and there only. Nowadays in cities this is all changed. In the country and in remote communities by the sea, the lakes, and the rivers, the old forms of property —namely, lands, buildings, implements, live-stock, carriages, and vessels—remain the same that they were fifty years ago, and in such communities there is no difficulty about the assessment and incidence of taxes; but in all the urban populations there are innumerable forms of property which are of very recent creation. The various bonds of railroad, telegraph, telephone, land and bridge companies—which are a kind of preferred stock, without any liability or any voting-power—have been almost entirely created within thirty years. The English statute which provides for incorporation with limited liability dates only from the year 1855. The innumerable stocks of transportation, financial, and manufacturing companies have almost all been created since the present type of American municipality was established. The history of Harvard University, like that of any old institution, illustrates the newness of these forms of property which have become so common. In 1860 only two per cent. of the quick capital of Harvard University was in railroad stocks and bonds; now fifty per cent. is so invested. If we go back in the history of the university thirty years more, to the year 1830, we find that the university owned neither stock nor bond, except fifty-two shares in a Boston bank, one share in a local canal, and certain interests in three wooden bridges leading out of Boston. Legislators, assessors, and voters have been quite unable to grasp the new situation so suddenly created. They have been unable to master quickly enough the new conditions. The conservatism of a democracy is intense, partly because the average voter is afraid of administrative novelties, and partly because inexperienced officials necessarily follow precedent. The more rapid the change of officials, the more surely will this unreasoning following of precedent prevail. A new official is afraid to depart from custom, lest he fall into some dangerous or absurd difficulty. Yet to follow precedent when conditions have changed is the surest way to fall into both absurdity and danger. Clinging to the old theory that a man was to be taxed at the place of his residence on all of his property,—a perfectly good theory under former conditions, and, indeed, under present conditions among a rural population,—American legislators and assessors have endeavored to tax at the place of residence property which did not lie there, never returned thither, and was wholly invisible there. Hence all the inquisitorial methods of assessment which disgrace the American cities.

At present, in many States of the Union the attempt is made to tax the house and the mortgage on it, the merchant's stock and the note he gave for the money with which he bought it, a railroad and the bonds which built it. So far as this method is successful, it falsifies the total valuation of the country, and produces inequality and injustice in the distribution of the public burdens. So far as it is unsuccessful, it causes another kind of injustice, excites suspicions and enmities among neighbors, and dulls the public conscience. These grave evils take effect, for the most part, in urban communities, and there work their most serious mischiefs. Yet they result from popular persistence in a theory which was perfectly good no long time ago, and from the inability of ill-trained and often-changed officials to adapt public policy quickly to new conditions of finance and trade very suddenly created. To deal wisely with public taxation in the face of rapid and progressive changes in business and social conditions requires on the part of the tax officials exact knowledge, sound judgment, wide experience, and continuous service: in short, it requires highly trained experts, serving the public on independent tenures, for long terms.

The management of water-supplies and drainage systems is another municipal function which is of recent growth and of a highly scientific character. As a regular part of city business it has all been created within fifty years. I was brought up in one of the best built houses in Boston, situated near the top of Beacon Hill. The house-drainage was discharged into a cesspool in the rear of the lot, and the whole family drank the water from a deep well which was not more than fifty feet from the cesspool. Moreover, five private stables stood near the rear of the lot, all of them but a short distance from the well; and the natural slope of the land was from the stables and the cesspool toward the well. There was at that time no sewerage system in the city of Boston and no public water-supply.

The mayor of Boston is elected to-day in the same way and for the same term as in those not remote times; but his functions and the whole municipal business which he superintends have utterly changed. I need not say that the provision of adequate supplies of wholesome water in a large city is a work of great and increasing difficulty, which can be successfully managed only by men who have received an elaborate training, and have labored for years continuously in that one field. The difficult subjects of average annual precipitation, natural watersheds, prevention of pollution, and effective distribution, will always task the full powers of gifted men who have received the best possible training. Continuity of policy is of great importance in regard to the water-supply of any large population. The same may be said of the related problem of sewerage. The disposition of the fluid and semi-fluid refuse of cities is an engineering problem which presents great variety in different localities, and almost always great difficulty. In our expanding cities the moment one difficulty or danger is overcome, another presents itself. The planning of sewerage works preëminently requires foresight; and durability is always a primary merit in their construction. That the water-works and sewerage system of a great municipality should be under the charge of constantly shifting officials is irrational to the last degree. The forms and methods of our city governments were determined when no such problems were to be solved by city agents.

I turn next to the care of highways, including paving, lighting, and cleaning. It is unnecessary to dilate upon the intelligence and skill which are needed in modern cities for the right conduct of this department of the public work. The services of engineers of the highest intelligence and skill, and of the highest professional honor and business capacity, are constantly required. In the great European capitals, these departments of municipal service are admirably managed by men trained, in schools long famous, expressly for the planning and direction of such public works, and kept in service, like officers of the army and navy, during good behavior and efficiency. There is not a great capital in Europe—I had almost said there is not even a small city—which does not immeasurably excel in the care of its highways the best governed of American cities. The monarchical and bureaucratic governments of Europe see to it that city streets and country highways are smooth, hard, and clean. The streets of European capitals, and their public squares, are incessantly swept and washed, and all rubbish, manure, and offal are promptly removed; but in most American cities the manure of animals, the sputa of human beings, and much other vegetable and animal refuse are suffered to dry up, and blow about as dust. The footways in American cities are as inferior to those of foreign cities as the carriage-ways, in respect to convenience and cleanliness, except, indeed, that there are some portions of the oldest European cities in which originally no footways were provided. Spain is not considered a particularly clean country; but I remember sitting down in a small public square in Seville to eat an orange, and so absolutely tidy was the inclosure that I could see no place where it was possible to leave the skin of the orange, and I had to carry it away with me. The inferiority of American cities in this respect is not due to lack of sufficient expenditure on the highways: it is due primarily to the fact that competent experts are not steadily employed to direct this important branch of municipal business, and, secondarily, to a flood of abuses which become possible in the absence of competent and honest supervision. There is no point at which municipal government in the United States has been so complete a failure as here. It has disastrously failed to provide for the convenience and comfort of the people in a matter which seriously affects the daily well-being of every inhabitant.

I speak next of an important municipal function which is of very recent origin, which, indeed, has hardly as yet been developed at all; namely, the control in the public interest of the companies which sell light, heat, power, transportation, and telegraphic or telephonic communication. The value of these franchises has only recently been demonstrated; and the many ways in which these companies may affect the business interests, and the comfort, health, and pleasure of a compact community, are not yet fully developed. The introduction of electricity for all these purposes, except heating, has very recently greatly modified the methods of the purveying corporations. Not a single American city has succeeded in dealing with these serviceable monopolies justly and at the same time to the public advantage; and, so long as the present modes of electing and organizing a municipal government continue in this country, we may well despair of seeing any effective control over these corporations exercised in the public interest. They are controlled in Europe by skilful engineers whose duty is to the public, and whose authority is exercised steadily and independently. This grave municipal problem is, however, very new. It is only about forty years since the first street-railways were built in the United States; the telephone seems to many of us a thing of yesterday; and the introduction of electric lights and electric cars is quite within the memory of children still in school. Within five years a wholly new class of municipal difficulties has arisen from the multiplication of overhead wires, for all sorts of purposes, along and across the public highways. How absurd it is to expect an effective discharge of supervisory functions over these novel and enterprising corporations, which are eagerly pursuing their private interests, from city officials who are elected by universal suffrage once a year or once in two years, or who depend for their positions on the single will of an official so elected!

One would imagine, *a priori*, that a "government by the people, for the people," would always have been careful of the people's health; but here we come upon one of the most conspicuous failures of free institutions in urban populations. Democratic government is at present at a serious disadvantage, in comparison with aristocratic and monarchical governments, as regards the care of the public health. The evidence of that disadvantage is of two sorts. In the first place, there are several cities in the United States which already, in spite of their comparative newness, have a death-rate absolutely higher than that of the best conducted cities of Europe. London, with its six millions of people, has habitually a lower death-rate than Boston, New York, Brooklyn, or Chicago. A few facts must suffice to illustrate this point. In the third quarter of 1889, the summer quarter, Chicago, Boston, and New York had a higher death-rate than Rome, Milan, and Turin, in hot Italy. In the fourth quarter, Chicago had a higher death-rate than Copenhagen, Christiania, Prague, Hamburg, Bremen, Cologne, Dresden, Leipsic, Berlin, Lyons,

Amsterdam, Edinburgh, Sheffield, Birmingham, Liverpool, or London. In the first quarter of 1890, the death-rate in New York was a little higher than the mean rate in the twenty-eight great English towns, including London, some of those great towns being confessedly in habitually bad sanitary condition. The population of New York is about equal to that of Berlin. In the first quarter of 1890, the deaths in New York were at the annual rate of 28.8 persons in every 1000, against 23.3 in Berlin—a fact which means that in those three months 2600 persons more died in New York than in Berlin, although New York has great advantages over Berlin as regards both climate and situation. In the fourth quarter of 1890, the death-rate in New York and Brooklyn was higher than in Berlin by more than 3 in 1000. In the second place, in those American cities which have made some effort to preserve the public health and to lower the death-rate, no such success has rewarded the effort as in many European cities, although the newness of most American cities should give them a great advantage over the European. London, which is supposed to contain in East London the largest mass of human misery in the civilized world, is the best example in the world of sanitary success. Berlin is another striking example of sanitary success under extremely unfavorable conditions. Before 1871 the annual death-rate in Berlin had for thirty years been from 37 to 39 per 1000. Of late years, 21 to 23 per 1000 have been common rates—an immense annual saving of life, which is chiefly due to the construction of a good water-supply and a good sewerage system. The worst district of Glasgow — No. 14, a physical and moral plague-spot — had in 1871 a population of 14,000 and a death-rate of 42.3 per 1000; in 1881 a population of about 8000 and a death-rate of 38.3; in 1888 a population of about 7000 and a death-rate of 32.45. No American city has obtained sanitary successes like these. Boston among cities, and Massachusetts among States, have taken as much pains in sanitary matters as any American communities, yet the death-rate has not been reduced during the past twenty-five years, either in the city or in the State at large. How much saving of life is possible under favorable conditions may be inferred from two comparisons. In the year 1888, the death-rate in Boston was 24.57 per 1000: in the adjoining, or rather interjected, town of Brookline, it was 11.43. In urban England, the death-rate during the last quarter of 1890 was 21.2 per 1000: among the remaining population, it was 17.5 per 1000.

What are the reasons of the comparative inefficiency of democratic government in the care of the public health? I maintain that they are not vice and criminal negligence, but ignorance and unwisdom. Is it not obvious that the care of the public health requires a high degree of intelligence and of scientific training in the officers who have charge of it, and that our system of municipal administration almost precludes the employment of such competent officers? Preventive medicine is a comparatively new science, and it has been more effectively cultivated in Europe than in this country, partly because the methods of municipal administration which there prevail give a chance for putting its principles into practice which American methods have not given. In its respect for personal liberty and the rights of the individual, democracy lets ignorance and selfishness poison water-supplies with fecal matter, distribute milk infected with diphtheria, scarlet-fever, or tuberculosis, and spread contagious diseases by omitting the precautions of isolation and disinfection. Clearly, this feebleness of democracy is largely due to ignorance. Aristocratic and autocratic governments have learned quicker than democracies the economic and humane value of sanitary science, and have applied that science more promptly and efficiently. If the sufferings inflicted on the poorer and less intelligent portions of the community, and the economic losses inflicted on the whole community, by incompetent practitioners of medicine and surgery, could be brought home to American legislators, the quacks and charlatans would have short shrift, in spite of the inevitable interference with so-called private rights. Registration acts for practitioners of medicine would then be promptly passed, and vigorously enforced. In like manner, if a democracy were only persuaded that contagious diseases — like yellow fever, small-pox, and diphtheria — might be closely restricted by isolation, the present careless methods of dealing with these scourges would soon be as obsolete as surgery and midwifery without antiseptics. The multitude does not know how typhoid fever lurks in contaminated water; it does not comprehend either the suffering or the economic loss which inevitably falls on any population breathing polluted air, or drinking polluted water; it does not realize that public health is only the sum-total of the individual healths, and that every avoidable injury to the public health means individual sufferings and losses which need not have been incurred. A few American States and cities have made some progress in the care of the public health; but the good work has been done chiefly by educated physicians and engineers serving gratuitously on boards of health. Such an organization is vastly better than none; but, as the results show, it is less efficient than the steady, paid service of such competent health-officers as all large European communities nowadays employ. Again, we see that this recently created but important municipal function requires experts for its satisfactory performance.

Another matter in which democratic government manifests, in comparison with aristocratic and autocratic governments, a curious neglect of the interests of the masses is the provision, or rather lack of provision, of parks, gardens, open-air parlors, and forests for the enjoyment of the populace. This subject is closely connected with the last to which I referred — the public health. One would have supposed that, before the urban populations began to feel keenly their deprivation of fresh air and rural beauty, liberal reservations of unoccupied land would have been made in our country for the use of the public. The fact is, however, that European towns and cities, both large and small, are much better provided with parks, gardens, small squares, and popular open-air resorts of all kinds, than American towns and cities. The gardens, parks, and game-preserves of royalty and nobility have there been converted, in many cases, to popular uses, with the happiest results. The largest and densest European cities — London, Vienna, Berlin, and Paris — are greatly better off in this respect than any American city. Even the least progressive parts of Europe, like Spain and Sicily, surpass the United States in making provision for the out-of-door enjoyments of crowded populations. All about our large cities and towns the building-up of neighborhoods once rural is going on with marvelous rapidity, and the city population is progressively excluded from private properties long unoccupied, but now converted into brick blocks and wooden villages, mostly offensive to the eye. Meantime the municipalities take no measures to provide either small squares or broad areas for the future use of the people.[1] Some of the smaller New England cities have actually hesitated to accept, or have even declined, the gift of valuable tracts which public-spirited citizens have offered them. A notion has been spread abroad by assessors and frugal citizens who prefer industrial or commercial values to spiritual and æsthetic or joy-giving values, that any area exempt from tax-

[1] It should be observed that this paper was written in 1891.

ation is an incubus on the community; the fact being that the exempted areas in most towns and cities represent, as a rule, just those things which make a dense community worth having at all, namely, the churches, museums, libraries, hospitals, colleges, schools, parks, squares, and commons. One would infer, from democratic practice, that in democratic theory public parks and gardens were made for the rich or the idle, whereas they are most needed by the laborious and the poor. The richer classes can provide their own enjoyments; they can go to the country or the sea when they please. It is the laboring masses that need the open-air parlor, the city boulevard, and the country park. The urban population in the United States have not yet grasped these principles; and herein lies one great difficulty in regard to good municipal administration in this matter. But there is another serious difficulty: the satisfactory construction and maintenance of public works of this nature require many years of steady work upon one plan, and they require both artistic and engineering skill in the officials who devise, execute, and maintain such works. Again, we see that good municipal administration must, in this department also, be in the hands of competent experts, and that not for a year at a time, but for long periods.

I have now touched, I believe, on the chief municipal functions which have a distinctly scientific quality. There remain the administration of justice, the protection of the city against fire, disorder, and crime, and the conduct of the public schools.

Experience has abundantly proved that independent and permanent tenures, after proper periods of probationary or subordinate service, are indispensable for the heads of all these departments of municipal administration; but these functions are less novel than those with which I have chiefly dealt, although even in these departments many new questions present themselves nowadays which never troubled at all the men of the last generation.

Of the judicial and legal departments of a great municipality it is perhaps unnecessary to say more than this — that their efficiency depends on the steady employment of learned, independent, and honorable lawyers and judges. Of the education department I can say, with confidence, that the welfare of the schools will always be best promoted by superintendents and teachers who have been selected by a professional appointing body, proved in actual service under the observation of competent inspectors, and then appointed to permanent places. Academies, endowed schools, and colleges often have better modes of selecting teachers than the public schools, and more secure tenures of office. Hence, in part, the greater comparative success of these institutions, their relative resources being considered. It is interesting to notice that, under stress of great disasters, the fire department has become the best-managed public organization in an American city. In that department are often found all the features of an efficient service — careful selection of the members of the force, steady employment, advancement for merit, compensation for injury, and a pension on retirement after faithful service.

I believe it is no exaggeration to say that good municipal administration has now become absolutely impossible without the employment, on permanent tenures, of a large number of highly trained and highly paid experts in various arts and sciences as directors of the chief city departments, and that the whole question of municipal reform is covered by the inquiry, How can a city government be organized so as to secure the services of these experts? Without attempting to go into the details of municipal organization, I venture to indicate the direction in which reform must be sought. Of late years the direction of reform movements has been toward increasing the responsibility of the mayor, by freeing him from the control of municipal elective bodies, and giving him larger rights of appointing and dismissing his subordinates. This method will succeed only so far as it procures for the city independent and highly trained expert service. I do not see that it tends to secure such service, unless the tenure of the mayoralty itself is prolonged and the heads of departments are made safe from arbitrary dismissal. On the whole, there is but slight tendency in the American cities to prolong the period of service of mayors. To give the mayor, who is himself a short-term official, larger powers of appointment and dismissal, does not tend to secure to the heads of departments long terms of service. Competent men will not leave their own business or the service of the numerous corporations which give useful men secure positions, to accept municipal positions the tenure of which is no longer, to say the least, than the tenure of the mayor. The inevitable result will be that the city will secure only second-, third-, or fourth-rate servants. As a rule, only incompetent people, or people out of work, or adventurers, will accept casual employment. I believe that all reform efforts ought to be primarily directed to the means of procuring, under democratic government as under aristocratic or autocratic government, honest, highly trained, and well-paid permanent officials. The intelligent American closely resembles the intelligent European in preferring an independent and permanent position. He will always accept lower pay for a steady job. He will always prefer, when he has passed the speculative and adventurous age, a moderately paid position with which go public consideration and a prospect of steady usefulness, to higher paid but insecure positions. The method of employing competent persons in permanent positions is also more economical than any other: it procures more service, and more faithful and interested service, than any other method. The experience of many American corporations illustrates this fact. In the service of banks, trust companies, insurance companies, railroads, factories, shops, colleges, and hospitals, it is the almost universal practice to retain as long as possible well-proved managers, trained clerks, and skilled workmen. This policy is, indeed, the only profitable policy. In many towns and counties, also, the tenure of elective offices is practically a tenure during efficiency. For a cure of the evils which now attend democratic government in cities, it is of the utmost consequence that the methods of municipal service should be assimilated to the methods of the great private and corporate services which require intelligence, high training, and long experience. The doctrine of rotation in office when applied to such functions as I have been describing is simply silly.

I adverted at the opening of this paper to the fact that town governments in the United States have remained good, down to the present day, through all the deterioration of city governments. The principal reason for this fact seems to be that the best men in a rural town can undertake the service of the town without interfering with their regular occupation or business, and may derive from that service a convenient addition to their ordinary earnings. A selectman, road commissioner, or school commissioner in a New England town has a position of respectability and local influence, with perhaps some small emolument; and he holds it without suffering any loss in his private business. In large cities, on the other hand, it is quite impossible for the chief officials to attend to their private business and at the same time fulfil their municipal functions. Moreover, city men of capacity and character are sure to be absorbed in their own affairs so completely that they give but a reluctant and spasmodic attention to the business of the public. Democratic freedom inevitably tends to produce this devotion to their own affairs on the part of intelligent and industrious citizens. An able professional man, merchant, or manufacturer cannot abandon his regular vocation to take municipal service, until his success in his profession or business has been so great that he can afford to impair, or dispense with, his ordinary annual earnings. Aside from persons of fortune and leisure, there are but two classes of competent and desirable men in this country who can, as a rule, enter the public service at all without sacrificing their individual and family interests. These two classes are lawyers, and business-men whose business is already so well organized that they can temporarily abandon it without incurring any loss which they care about. Of the Fifty-first Congress of the United States, nearly three quarters are lawyers—fully three quarters of the Senate, and nearly three quarters of the House. Of the other quarter, the majority are business-men of the kind I have described. A lawyer returning from public service to his profession generally finds, if he is a man of ability, that his private practice has been increased. A manufacturer or merchant who is already rich can of course run the risks of the public service. If the voters abandon him, or his superior discharge him, he can return to his private business. As a rule, no other persons in the American community can really afford to enter the public service, either municipal or national, as it is at present conducted.

Before municipal government can be set right in

the United States, municipal service must be made a life-career for intelligent and self-respecting young Americans; that is, it must be made attractive to well-trained young men to enter it,—as they enter any other profession or business,—meaning to stay in it, learn it thoroughly, and win advancement in it by fidelity and ability. To enforce this principle, to indicate this one necessary direction of all reform movements, has been my modest object in this paper. To say that this reform is impracticable is equivalent to saying that American cities cannot be well conducted; and that, again, is equivalent to saying that the democratic form of government is going to be a failure for more than half the total population. Free institutions themselves are valuable only as a means of public well-being. They will ultimately be judged by their fruits; and therefore they must be made to minister fairly well to the public comfort, health, and pleasure, and to conform in their administrative methods to the standards of intelligence and morality which are maintained by other trustees and large business agencies in the same communities.

WHEREIN POPULAR EDUCATION HAS FAILED

Published in the "Forum," December, 1892

WHEREIN POPULAR EDUCATION HAS FAILED

IT cannot be denied that there is serious and general disappointment at the results of popular education up to this date. Elementary instruction for all children and more advanced instruction for some children have been systematically provided in many countries for more than two generations at great cost and with a good deal of enthusiasm, though not always on wise plans. Many of the inventions of the same rich period of seventy years have greatly promoted the diffusion of education by cheapening the means of communicating knowledge. Cheap books, newspapers, and magazines, cheap postage, cheap means of transportation, and free libraries have all contributed to the general cultivation of intelligence, or at least to the wide use of reading matter and the spread of information. In spite, however, of all these efforts to make education universal, all classes complain more than ever before of the general conditions of society.

Now, if general education does not promote general contentment, it does not promote public happiness; for a rational contentment is an essential element in happiness, private or public. To this extent universal education must be admitted to have failed at the end of two generations of sincere and strenuous, if sometimes misdirected, effort. Perhaps it is too soon to expect from public education any visible increase of public contentment and happiness. It may be that general discontent is a necessary antecedent to social improvement and a preliminary manifestation of increased knowledge and wisdom in all classes of the community. Yet after two whole generations it seems as if some increase of genuine reasonableness of thought and action in all classes of the population ought to be discernible. Many persons, however, fail to see in the actual conduct of the various classes of society the evidence of increasing rationality. These sceptical observers complain that people in general, taken in masses with proper exclusion of exceptional individuals, are hardly more reasonable in the conduct of life than they were before free schools, popular colleges, and the cheap printing-press existed. They point out that when the vulgar learn to read they want to read trivial or degrading literature, such as the common newspapers and periodicals which are mainly devoted to accidents, crimes, criminal trials, scandals, gossip, sports, prize-fights, and low politics. Is it not the common school and the arts of cheap illustration, they say, that have made obscene books, photographs, and pictures, low novels, and all the literature which incites to vice and crime, profitable, and therefore abundant and dangerous to society? They complain that in spite of every effort to enlighten the whole body of the people, all sorts of quacks and impostors thrive, and that one popular delusion or sophism succeeds another, the best-educated classes contributing their full proportion of the deluded. Thus the astrologer in the Middle Ages was a rare personage and usually a dependent of princes; but now he advertises in the popular newspapers and flourishes as never before. Men and women of all classes, no matter what their education, seek advice on grave matters from clairvoyants, seers, Christian scientists, mind-cure practitioners, bone-setters, Indian doctors, and fortune-tellers. The ship of state barely escapes from one cyclone of popular folly, like the fiat-money delusion or the granger legislation of the seventies, when another blast of ill-informed opinion comes down on it, like the actual legislation which compels the buying and storing of silver by Government, or the projected legislation which would compel Government to buy cotton, wheat, or corn, and issue paper money against the stock.

The educated critics of the practical results of public education further complain that lawless violence continues to break out just as it did before common schools were thought of, that lynch law is familiar in the United States, riots common from Berlin to Seattle, and assassination an avowed means of social and industrial regeneration. Even religious persecution, these critics say, is rife. The Jews are ostracized in educated Germany and metropolitan New York, and in Russia are robbed and driven into exile by thousands. Furthermore, in spite of the constant inculcation of the principles of civil and religious liberty, new tyrannies are constantly arising. The tyrant, to be sure, is no longer an emperor, a king, or a feudal lord, but a contagious public opinion, a majority of voters inclined to despotism, or an oppressive combination of owners, contractors, or workmen. From time to time the walking delegate seems to be a formidable kind of tyrant, all the more formidable because his authority is but brief and his responsibility elusive. Popular elections and political conventions and caucuses provide another set of arguments for the sceptics about the results of universal education. Have these not been carried on with combined shoutings, prolonged, competitive howlings, banners, torches, uniforms, parades, misrepresentations, suppressions of truth, slanders and vituperation, rather than with arguments and appeals to enlightened self-interest, benevolence, patriotism, and the sense of public duty? Are votes less purchasable now than they were before the urban graded school and the State university were known? How irrational is the preparation made by the average voter for the exercise of the function of voting! He reads steadily one intensely partizan newspaper, closes his mind to all information and argument which proceed from political opponents, distrusts independent newspapers and independent men, and is afraid of joint debates. Such are some of the allegations and doubts of the educated critics with regard to the results of popular education.

On the other hand, the least-educated and most laborious classes complain that in spite of universal elementary education, society does not tend toward a greater equality of condition; that the distinctions between rich and poor are not diminished, but intensified; and that elementary education does not necessarily procure for the wage-earner any exemption from incessant and exhausting toil. They recognize indeed that machine labor has in many cases been substituted for hand labor; but they insist that the direction of machines is more exacting than old-fashioned hand work, and that the extreme division of labor in modern industries is apt to make the life of the operative or mechanic monotonous and narrowing. They complain that the rich, though elaborately instructed in school and church, accept no responsibilities with their wealth, but insist on being free to break up their domestic or industrial establishments at their pleasure, or in other words, to give or withhold employment as they find it most convenient or profitable. They allege that the rich man in modern society does not bear, either in peace or in war, the grave responsibilities which the rich man of former centuries, who was a great land-owner, a soldier, and a magistrate, was compelled to bear; and that education, whether simple or elaborate, has not made the modern rich man less selfish and luxurious than his predecessor in earlier centuries who could barely sign his name. They admit that the progress of science has made mankind safer from famine and pestilence than it used to be, but they point out that wars are more destructive than ever, this century being the bloodiest of all the centuries; that European armies are larger and more expensively equipped than ever before, and hence are more burdensome to the laboring populations which support them; while in the American republic the annual burden of paying the military and naval pensions which result from a single great war is heavier, twenty-seven years after the war ended, than the annual burden of maintaining the largest standing army in Europe. Clearly, the spread of education has not enabled the nations to avoid war or to diminish its cost either in blood or treasure. If universal education cannot abolish, or even abate, in seventy years, the horrible waste and cruelty of war, can anything great be hoped from it for the laboring classes?

They complain also that the education of the employer and the employed has not made the conditions of employment more humane and comfortable; that almost all services and industries — agricultural, domestic, and manufacturing — are organized on the brutal principle of dismissal on the instant or with briefest notice, and that assured employment during good behavior and efficiency, which is almost a prerequisite of happiness for a reasonable and provident person, remains the privilege of an insignificant minority of well-to-do people, like judges, professors, and officers of financial and industrial corporations. How much has all this boasted education increased the intelligence and insight of even the best-educated and most capable people, if they still cannot devise just and satisfying conditions of employment in their own households, shops, ships, and factories? It is much more important that fidelity, constancy, loyalty, and mutual respect and affection between employer and employed should be fostered by the prevailing terms of employment than that more yards of cotton cloth or more tons of steel should be produced, more miles of railroad maintained, or more bushels of wheat raised. Those fine human qualities are the ultimate product to be desired. Have they been developed and fostered during the two generations of popular education? Or have dishonesty in labor, disloyalty, mutual jealousy and distrust between employer and employed, and general discontent increased?

These indictments against universal education as a cure for ancient wrongs and evils are certainly formidable; but they exaggerate existing evils and leave out of sight great improvements in social conditions which the last two generations have seen. It is only necessary for us to call to mind a few of the beneficent changes which the past seventy years have wrought, to assure ourselves that some powerful influences for good have been at work in the best-educated nations. Consider, for example, the mitigation of human miseries which the reformation of penal codes and of prisons, the institution of reformatories, the building of hospitals, asylums, and infirmaries, and the abolition of piracy and slavery have brought about. Consider the positive influence toward the formation of habits of industry and frugality exerted by such institutions as savings-banks, mutual-benefit societies, and life-insurance corporations. Unanswerable statistics show that during the past seventy years there has been a steady improvement in the condition of the most laborious classes in modern society, the wage-earners, and this improvement touches their earnings, their hours of labor, their lodgings, their food and clothing, and the means of education for their children. Consider how step by step terrors have been disarmed, superstitions abolished, the average duration of human life lengthened, and civil order extended over regions once desolate or dangerous. Think how family and school discipline have been mitigated within two generations, and how all sorts of abuses and cruelties are checked and prevented by the publicity of modern life, a publicity which depends on the universal capacity to read.

Let us remember that almost all business is nowadays conducted on trust, trust that the seller will deliver his goods according to sample and promise, and trust that the buyer will pay at the time appointed. Now, this general trustworthiness is of course based on moral qualities which inhere in the race, but these qualities are effectively reinforced and protected by the publicity which general education has made possible. Consider how freedom of intercourse between man and man, tribe and tribe, nation and nation has been developed even within a single generation; how the United States have spread across the continent, how Italy has been made one nation, and Germany one, and the Austrian Empire confederated from three distinct nationalities. Every one of these great expansions or consolidations has resulted in greater freedom of intercourse, and in the removal of barriers and of causes of strife and ill-will. Moreover, on taking a broad view of the changes in civilized society since 1830, do we not see that there has been great progress toward unity,—not indeed toward uniformity, but toward a genuine unity? The different classes of society and the different nations are still far from realizing the literal truth of the New Testament saying, "We are members one of another"; but they have lately made some approach to realizing that truth. Now, unity of spirit with diversity of gifts is the real end to be attained in social organization. It would not be just to contend that popular education has brought to pass all these improvements and ameliorations; but it has undoubtedly contributed to them all. Moreover, we find on every hand evidences of increased intelligence in large masses of people. If war has not ceased, soldiers are certainly more intelligent than they used to be, else they could not use the arms of precision with which armies are now supplied. The same is true of all industries and trades—they require more intelligence than formerly in all the work-people. While, therefore, we must admit that education has not accomplished all that might fairly have been expected of it, we may believe that it has had some share in bringing about many of the ameliorations of the social state in the past two generations.

It is somewhat comforting to recall, as we confess to disappointment with the results of universal education, that modern society has had several disappointments before of a nature similar to that it now experiences. There was a time when it was held that a true and universally accepted religious belief would bring with it an ideal state of society; but this conviction resulted in sanguinary persecutions and desolating wars, for to attain the ideal state of society through one true religion was an end so lofty as to justify punishing, and even exterminating, all who did not accept the religion. Again, when modern representative institutions were first put into practice it seemed as if the millennium were near — popular government seemed of infinite promise for the happiness of mankind. Were not all despotisms to be done away with? Were not all men to enjoy liberty, equality, and fraternity? It was a painful surprise to discover that under a *régime* of general liberty a few could so use their freedom as to gain undue advantages over the many. It was a disappointment to find that superior shrewdness and alertness could secure, under public freedom and public law, a lordship such as superior force could hardly win when there were little freedom and little law. How high were the expectations based on universal suffrage—that exaltation of man as man without regard to his social condition, that strong expression of the equality of all men in political power! Yet all these successive hopes have proved in a measure delusive. On the whole, the most precious and stable result of the civilized world's experience during the past three hundred years is the doctrine of universal toleration, or liberty for all religious opinions under the protection of the state, there being as yet no such thing in Christian society as one true and universal religion. We have all had to learn that representative institutions do not at present necessarily produce good government,—in many American cities they coexist with bad government,—and that universal suffrage is not a panacea for social ills, but simply the most expedient way to enlist the interest and support of us all in the government of us all. Never yet has society succeeded in embodying in actual institutions a just liberty, a real equality, or a true fraternity.

It was reasonable, however, to expect more from universal education than from any of the other inventions to which I have alluded. Public education should mean the systematic training of all children for the duties of life; and it seems as if this systematic training could work almost a revolution in human society in two or three generations, if wisely and faithfully conducted. Why has it not? It seems to provide directly for a general increase of power to reason, and, therefore, of actual reasonableness in the conduct of life. Why is it possible to doubt whether any appreciable gain has thus far been made in these respects? I think I perceive in popular education, as generally conducted until recently, an inadequacy and a misdirection which supply a partial answer to these disquieting questions.

The right method of developing in the mass of the population the reasoning power and general rationality which are needed for the wise conduct of life must closely resemble the method by which the intelligence and reasoning power of an individual are developed. Let me next, therefore, present here in some detail the main processes or operations of the mind which systematic education should develop and improve in an individual in order to increase his general intelligence and train his reasoning power. The first of these processes or operations is observation; that is to say, the alert, intent, and accurate use of all the senses. Whoever wishes to ascertain a present fact must do it through the exercise of this power of observation, whether the fact lie in the animal, vegetable, or mineral kingdom; whether it be a fact of physics, physiology, sociology, or politics. Facts, diligently sought for and firmly established, are the only foundations of sound reasoning. The savage has abundant practice in observation; for he gets his daily food only by the keenest exercise of this power. The civilized man, whose food is brought to him by the railroad, is not forced by these elementary necessities to keep his observational powers keen and quick, and many of his occupations call for only a limited use of the observing organs; so that systematic education must provide in his case against the atrophy of these faculties. For the training of this power of observation it does not matter what subject the child studies, so that he study something thoroughly by an observational method. If the method be right, it does not matter, among the numerous subjects well fitted to develop this important faculty, which he choose, or which be chosen for him. The study of any branch of natural history, chemistry, or physics, any well-conducted work with tools or machines, and many of the sports of children and adults, such as sailing, fishing, and hunting, will develop this power, provided thorough exercise of the observational powers be secured. For the purpose we have now in view, it is vastly better that he study one subject thoroughly than several superficially. The field within which the power is exercised may be narrow or special; but these words do not apply to the power. During this training in accurate observation, the youth should learn how hard it is to determine with certainty even an apparently simple fact. He should learn to distrust the evidence of his own senses, to repeat, corroborate, and verify his observations, and to mark the profound distinction between the fact and any inference, however obvious, from the fact.

The next function, process, or operation which education should develop in the individual is the function of making a correct record of things observed. The record may be either mental only, that is, stamped on the memory, or it may be reduced to writing or print. The savage transmits orally to his children or his tribe such records as his brain contains of nature's lore and of his experience in war and the chase; but civilized man makes continuous and cumulative records of sifted, sorted, and grouped facts of observation and experience, and on these records the progress of the race depends. Hence the supreme importance that every child be instructed and drilled at every stage of his education in the art of making an accurate and vivid record of things seen, heard, felt, done, or suffered. This power of accurate description or recording is identical in all fields of inquiry. The child may describe what it sees in a columbine, or in the constellation of Orion, or on the wharves, or in the market, or in the Children's Hospital, and its power of description may be exercised in speech or in writing; but for the benefit of the community, as distinguished from the satisfaction of the individual and the benefit of his family or associates, the faculty should be abundantly exercised in writing as well as speech. In this constant drill the conscience cannot fail to be refined and instructed; for to make a scrupulously accurate statement of a fact observed, with all needed qualifications and limitations, is as good a training of the conscience as secular education can furnish.

The next mental function which education should develop, if it is to increase reasoning power and general intelligence, is the faculty of drawing correct inferences from recorded observations. This faculty is almost identical with the faculty of grouping or coördinating kindred facts, comparing one group with another or with all the others, and then drawing an inference which is sure, in proportion to the number of cases, instances, or experiences on which it is based. This power is developed by practice in induction. It is often a long way from the patent fact to the just inference. For centuries the Phenician and Roman navigators had seen the hulls of vessels disappearing below the blue horizon of the Mediterranean while their sails were visible; but they never drew the inference that the earth was round. On any particular subject it may take generations or centuries to accumulate facts enough to establish a just inference or generalization. The earlier accumulations may be insufficient, the first grouping wrong, the first samplings deceptive; and so the first general inference may be incorrect; but the method, rightly practised, leads straight to truth. It is the patient, candid, impartial, universal method of modern science.

Fourthly, education should cultivate the power of expressing one's thoughts clearly, concisely, and cogently. This power is to be procured only by much practice in the mother tongue, and this practice should make part of every child's education from beginning to end. So far as a good style can be said to be formed or created at all, it is ordinarily formed by constant practice under judicious criticism. If this practice and criticism are supplied, it is unimportant whether the student write an historical narrative, or a translation from

Xenophon, or a laboratory note-book, or an account of a case of hypnotism or typhoid fever, or a law-brief, or a thesis on comparative religion; the subject-matter is comparatively indifferent, so far as the cultivation of accurate and forcible speech or writing is concerned. In cultivating any field of knowledge this power of expression can be won if the right means be used, and if these means be neglected it will not be won in any field. For cultivating the habit of reasoning justly, however, there is one kind of practice in expressing one's thoughts which has special importance, namely, practice in argumentative composition — in the logical and persuasive development of an argument, starting from well-selected premises and brought to a just conclusion.

Let no one imagine that I am omitting poetry from systematic education. In that highest of all arts of expression, the art of poetry, the four mental functions or operations we have now considered — observing, recording, comparing and inferring, and expressing — may be seen in combination, each often exhibited to high degree. The poet's power of observation often supplies him with his most charming verses. Tennyson noticed that the ash put out its leaves in spring much later than the other trees, and this is the exquisite use he made of that botanical observation:

"Why lingereth she to clothe her heart with love,
Delaying, as the tender ash delays
To clothe herself, when all the woods are green?"

The poet's power of describing, and of stirring and inspiring by his descriptions, depends on the combination in him of keen observation, rare susceptibility to beauty and grandeur, spiritual insight, and faculty of inferential suggestion. In four lines Emerson puts before us the natural and spiritual scene at the Concord River on the 19th of April, 1775:

> "By the rude bridge that arched the flood,
> Their flag to April's breeze unfurled,
> Here once the embattl'd farmers stood,
> And fired the shot heard round the world."

In twenty-eight words here are the whole scene and all the essential circumstances — the place and season, the stout actors, their rustic social state, the heroic deed, and its infinite reverberation. What an accurate, moving, immortal description is this! Even for logical and convincing argument poetry is often the finest vehicle. If anybody doubts this let him read again the twenty-third Psalm, from its opening premise, "The Lord is my shepherd," to its happy conclusion, "Surely goodness and mercy shall follow me all the days of my life"; or let him follow the reasoning of God with Job, from the inquiry, "Where wast thou when I laid the foundations of the earth?" to Job's conclusion, "Wherefore I abhor myself and repent in dust and ashes."

These, then, are the four things in which the individual youth should be thoroughly trained, if his judgment and reasoning power are to be systematically developed: observing accurately; recording correctly; comparing, grouping, and inferring justly; and expressing cogently the results of these mental operations. These are the things in which the population as a mass must be trained in youth, if its judgment and reasoning power are to be systematically developed.

Let us now consider whether the bulk of the work done in free public schools for the mass of the children contributes materially to the development of the mental capacities just described. More than ninety per cent. of the school-children do not get beyond the "grades," or the grammar school, as we say in New England. Now, what are the staples of instruction in the "grades," or in the primary and grammar schools of New England? They are reading, spelling, writing, geography, and arithmetic. In very recent years there has been added to these subjects some practice in observation, through drawing, manual training, kindergarten work in general, and lessons in elementary science; but these additions to the staple subjects are all recent, and have not taken full effect on any generation now at work in the world. Moreover, it is but a small proportion of the total school-time which is even now devoted to these observational subjects. The acquisition of the art of reading is mostly a matter of memory. It is of course not without effect on the development of the intelligence; but it does not answer well any one of the four fundamental objects in an education directed to the development of reasoning power.

The same must be said of writing, which is in the main a manual exercise and one by no means so well adapted to cultivate the powers of observation, the sense of form, and the habit of accuracy as many other sorts of manual work, such as carpentering, turning, forging, and modeling. As to English spelling, it is altogether a matter of memory. We have heretofore put too much confidence in the mere acquisition of the arts of reading and writing. After these arts are acquired there is much to be done to make them effective for the development of the child's intelligence. If his reasoning power is to be developed through reading, he must be guided to the right sort of reading. The school must teach not only how to read, but what to read, and it must develop a taste for wholesome reading. Geography, as commonly taught, means committing to memory a mass of curiously uninteresting and unimportant facts.

There remains arithmetic, the school subject most relied on to train the reasoning faculty. From one sixth to one fourth, or even one third, of the whole school-time of American children is given to the subject of arithmetic — a subject which does not train a single one of the four faculties to develop which should be the fundamental object of education. It has nothing to do with observing correctly, or with recording accurately the results of observation, or with collating facts and drawing just inferences therefrom, or with expressing clearly and forcibly logical thought. Its reasoning has little application in the great sphere of the moral sciences, because it is necessary and not probable reasoning. In spite of the common impression that arithmetic is a practical subject, it is of very limited application in common life, except in its simplest elements — the addition, subtraction, multiplication, and division of small numbers. It indeed demands of the pupil mental effort; but all subjects that deserve any place in education do that. On the whole, therefore, it is the least remunerative subject in elementary education as now conducted.

But let us look somewhat higher in the hierarchy of educational institutions. It has been roughly computed that about five per cent. of the school-children in the United States go on to the secondary schools. In these schools is attention chiefly devoted to the development and training of the reasoning faculty? By no means. In most secondary schools of a high class a large part of the whole time is given to the study of languages. Thus in the Cambridge Public Latin School twenty-eight hundred and twenty lessons are devoted in the course of six years to the languages; to all other subjects ten hundred and seventy. At the Ann Arbor High School, in the seven distinct courses all taken together, there are twenty-seven hundred and forty-six lessons in languages, against forty-one hundred and eighty-four in all other subjects — and this although many options are allowed to the pupils of the school, and the variety of subjects not linguistic is large. In the Lawrenceville School, a well-endowed preparatory school in New

Jersey, twenty hundred and thirty-three lessons are devoted to languages, against nineteen hundred and seventeen devoted to all other subjects. Now, the teaching of a language may be made the vehicle of admirable discipline in discriminating thinking; but it is a rare language-teacher who makes it the vehicle of such thinking. The ordinary teaching of a foreign language, living or dead, cultivates in the pupil little besides memory and a curious faculty of assigning the formation of a word or the construction of a phrase to the right rule in the grammar — a rule which the pupil may or may not understand. The preponderance of language-lessons in many secondary schools presents, therefore, great dangers. Moreover, in most secondary schools, among the subjects other than languages, there will generally be found several which seem to be taught for the purpose of giving information rather than of imparting power. Such are the common high-school and academy topics in history, natural history, psychology, astronomy, political economy, civil government, mechanics, constitutional law, and commercial law. These subjects, as they are now taught, seldom train any power but that of memory. As a rule, the feebler a high school or academy is, the more these information subjects figure in its programme; and when a strong school offers several distinct courses, the shorter and weaker courses are sure to exhibit an undue number of these subjects. I need not say that these subjects are in themselves grand fields of knowledge, and that any one of them might furnish a solid mental training. It is the way they are used that condemns them. The pupil is practically required to commit to memory a primer or a small elementary manual for the sake of the information it contains. There can be no training of the reason in such a process.

If now we rise to the course which succeeds that of the high school or academy, the college course, we find essentially the same condition of things in most American institutions. The cultivation of the memory predominates; that of the observing, inferring, and reasoning faculties is subordinated. Strangest of all, from bottom to top of the educational system, the art of expressing one's thought clearly and vigorously in the mother tongue receives comparatively little attention.

When one reviews the course of instruction in schools and colleges with the intention of discovering how much of it contributes directly to the development of reasoning power, one cannot but be struck with the very small portion of time expressly devoted to this all-important object. No amount of *memoriter* study of languages or of the natural sciences, and no attainments in arithmetic, will protect a man or woman—except, imperfectly, through a certain indirect cultivation of general intelligence—from succumbing to the first plausible delusion or sophism he or she may encounter. No amount of such studies will protect one from believing in astrology, or theosophy, or free silver, or strikes, or boycotts, or in the persecution of Jews or of Mormons, or in the violent exclusion of non-union men from employment. One is fortified against the acceptance of unreasonable propositions only by skill in determining facts through observation and experience, by practice in comparing facts or groups of facts, and by the unvarying habit of questioning and verifying allegations, and of distinguishing between facts and inferences from facts, and between a true cause and an antecedent event. One must have direct training and practice in logical speech and writing before he can be quite safe against specious rhetoric and imaginative oratory. Many popular delusions are founded on the commonest of fallacies—this preceded that, therefore this caused that; or, in shorter phrase, what preceded, caused. For example: I was sick; I took such and such a medicine and became well; therefore the medicine cured me. During the civil war the Government issued many millions of paper-money, and some men became very rich; therefore the way to make all men richer must be to issue from the Government presses an indefinite amount of paper-money. The wages of American working-men are higher than those of English in the same trades; protection has been the policy of the United States and approximate free trade the policy of England; therefore high tariffs cause high wages. Bessemer steel is much cheaper now than it was twenty years ago; there has been a tariff tax on Bessemer steel in the United States for the past twenty years; therefore the tax cheapened the steel. England, France, and Germany are civilized and prosperous nations; they have enormous public debts; therefore a public debt is a public blessing. He must carry Ithuriel's spear and wear stout armor who can always expose and resist this fallacy. It is not only the uneducated or the little educated who are vanquished by it. There are many educated people who have little better protection against delusions and sophisms than the uneducated; for the simple reason that their education, though prolonged and elaborate, was still not of a kind to train their judgment and reasoning powers.

Again, very few persons scrutinize with sufficient care the premises on which a well-formed argument is constructed. Hence a plausible argument may have strong influence for many years with great bodies of people, when the facts on which alone the argument could be securely based have never been thoroughly and accurately determined. The great public discussion now going on throughout the country affords a convenient illustration. For generations it has been alleged that high tariffs are necessary in this country in order to protect American workmen from the competition of European workmen, whose scales of living and of wages are lower than those of the American; but until within four years no serious attempt has been made to ascertain precisely what the difference really is between the cost of English labor and of American labor on a given unit of manufactured product in the several protected industries. Such inquiries are complicated and difficult, and demand extensive and painstaking research, with all the advantages governmental authority can give.

The publication made in 1891 by the Commissioner of Labor at Washington concerning the cost of producing iron and steel is the first real attempt to determine the facts upon which the theory of a single group of important items in our tariff might have been based. One of Mr. Wright's carefully-stated conclusions in this huge, statistical volume is that the difference between the direct labor-cost of one ton of steel rails in the United States and in England is three dollars and seventy-eight cents. If we allow the large margin of fifty per cent. each way for possible error in these figures, we arrive at the conclusion that the excess of the direct labor-cost of producing from the assembled materials one ton of steel rails in this country lies somewhere between one dollar and eighty-nine cents and five dollars and sixty-seven cents, with the probability in favor of three dollars and seventy-eight cents. Now, the duty on one ton of steel rails is thirteen dollars and forty-four cents; so that it is obvious that the amount of this tax stands in no close relation to the difference between the cost of the American and English labor, and that some other motive than the protection of American *labor* determined the amount of the tax. Yet the argument that the high-tariff taxes exist for the protection of American wage-earners has long had great weight in the minds of millions of Americans who can read, write, and cipher. For my present purpose it is a matter of indifference whether the assumption which underlies this argument, namely, that workmen are not productive and valuable in proportion to their scale of wages and standard of living, be true or false. What I want to point out is that the argument has no right to much influence in determining the amount of taxes which burden the entire population, inasmuch as the facts on which alone it can be securely based are as yet wanting for a great majority of the protected industries. Is it not quite clear that the people, as a whole, have not been taught to scrutinize severely the premises of an argument to which they are inclined to give weight, and that popular education has never afforded, and does not now afford, any adequate defense against this kind of unreason?

Let me further observe that throughout all education, both public and private, both in the school and in the family, there has been too much reliance on the principle of authority, too little on the progressive and persistent appeal to reason. By commands, or by the authoritative imposition of opinions, it is possible for a time to protect a child, or a generation or nation of childish men, from some dangers and errors; but the habit of obedience to authority and of the passive reception of imposed opinions is almost inconsistent with an effective development of reasoning power and of independence of thought.

What, then, are the changes in the course of popular education which we must strive after if we would develop for the future more successfully than in the past the rationality of the population? In the first place, we must make practice in thinking, or in other words, the strengthening of reasoning power, the constant object of all teaching, from infancy to adult age, no matter what may be the subject of instruction. After the most necessary manual and mental arts have been acquired, those subjects should be taught most which each individual teacher is best fitted to utilize for making his pupils think, or which develop best in the individual pupil his own power to reason. For this purpose the same subject will not be equally good for all teachers or for all pupils. One teacher can make her pupils think most eagerly and consecutively in the subject of geography, another in zoölogy, and another in Latin. One pupil can be induced most easily to exercise strenuously his powers of observation and discrimination on the facts of a language new to him, another on the phenomena of plant life, and another on the events of some historical period. If only this training could be everywhere recognized in daily practice as the supreme and ultimate object in all teaching, a great improvement would soon be wrought in the results of public instruction.

Besides recognizing in practice this prime object of all education, we can make certain specific changes in the common subjects or methods of instruction which will greatly further this object, and we can promote such useful changes as have already been introduced. Thus we can give wise extension to the true observation studies already introduced into the earlier years of the school system. Again, we can give much more time than is now given to the practice of accurate description and argumentative composition in writing. This practice should begin in the kindergarten and be pursued through the university. We expect to teach children to write English with a very small part of the practice they get in speaking English. With all the practice and criticism of their speech that school-children get every day, correct speech is by no means common. Should we expect to get correct writing with much less attention than we give to speech?

We must also teach elaborately in schools those subjects which give practice in classification and induction. The natural sciences all lend themselves to this branch of school work; but they must be taught in such a way as to extract from them the peculiar discipline they are fitted to yield. It is of no use to commit to memory books on science. A little information may be gained in this way, but no power. They must be taught by the laboratory method, with constant use of the laboratory note-book, and with careful study of trains of experimentation and reasoning which in times past actually led to great discoveries. Yet to study the natural sciences is not a sure way to develop reasoning power. It is just as easy to teach natural science, even by laboratory methods, without ever making the pupils reason closely about their work, as to teach Latin or German without cultivating the pupils' powers of comparison and discrimination. Effective training of the reasoning powers cannot be secured simply by choosing this subject or that for study. The method of study and the aim in studying are the all-important things.

For the older pupils, the time devoted to historical studies ought to be much increased; not that they may learn the story of dynasties or of wars, but that they may learn how, as a matter of fact, arts came into being, commerce was developed by one city or nation after another, great literatures originated and grew up, new industries arose, fresh discoveries were made, and social conditions were ameliorated. They should discover through what imagining, desiring, contriving, and planning, whether of individual leaders or of masses of men, these great steps in human progress came to be taken. They should study the thinking and feeling of past generations for guidance to right thoughts and sentiments in the present and future. It is a disgrace to organized education that any nation should refuse, as our own people are so apt to do, to learn from the experience of other nations; the schools must have failed to teach history as they should have done. As Benjamin Franklin said, "Experience keeps a dear school; but fools will learn in no other, and scarce in that."

In the higher part of the system of public instruction two difficult subjects deserve to receive a much larger share of attention than they now obtain — political economy and sociology. They should be studied, however, not as information subjects, but as training or disciplinary subjects; for during the past thirty years the means of using them as disciplinary subjects have been accumulated in liberal measure. They can now be studied in their elements on broad foundations of fact, the results of scientific research; and many of their fundamental principles can be placed within the reach of minds not yet adult.

Finally, argumentation needs to be taught systematically in schools; not in the form of a theoretical logic, but in concrete form through the study of arguments which have had weight in determining the course of trade, industries, or public affairs, or have made epochs in discovery, invention, or the progress of science. The actual arguments used by the participants in great debates should be studied, and not the arguments attributed to or invented for the actors long after the event. Books preserve many such epoch-making arguments; and during the present century many which were only spoken have been preserved by stenography and the daily press. For these uses, arguments which can be compared with the ultimate event, and proved true or false by the issue, have great advantages. The issue actually establishes, or disproves, the conclusion the argument sought to establish. As examples of instructive arguments I may cite Burke's argument on conciliation with the American colonies, and Webster's, on the nature and value of the Federal Union; the debate between Lincoln and Douglas on the extension of slavery into the Territories; the demonstration by

Sir Charles Lyell that the ancient and the present systems of terrestrial changes are identical; the proofs contrived and set forth by Sir John Lubbock that the ant exhibits memory, affection, morality, and coöperative power; the prophetic argument of Mill that industries conducted on a great scale will ultimately make liberty of competition illusory, and will form extensive combinations to maintain or advance prices; and that well-reasoned prophecy of disturbance and disaster in the trade of the United States written by Cairnes in September, 1873, and so dramatically fulfilled in the commercial crisis of that month. Such arguments are treasuries of instruction for the rising generation, for they furnish safe materials for thorough instruction in sound reasoning. We have expected to teach sound reasoning incidentally and indirectly, just as we have expected to teach young people to write good English by teaching them foreign languages. It is high time that we taught the young by direct practice and high examples to reason justly and effectively.

Such are some of the measures which we may reasonably hope will make popular education in the future more successful than it has been in the past in developing universal reasonableness.

THREE RESULTS OF THE SCIENTIFIC STUDY OF NATURE

ADDRESS

At the Opening of the New Building of the American Museum of Natural History, New York, December 22, 1877.

THREE RESULTS OF THE SCIENTIFIC STUDY OF NATURE

IN whose honor are the chief personages of the nation, State, and city here assembled? Whose palace is this? What divinity is worshiped in this place? We are assembled here to own with gratitude the beneficent power of natural science; to praise and thank its votaries; and to dedicate this splendid structure to its service. The power to which we here do homage is the accumulated intelligence of our race applied, generation after generation, to the study of nature; and this palace is the storehouse of the elaborated materials which that intelligence has garnered, ordered, and illuminated. What has natural science done for mankind that it should be thus honored? In the brief moments allotted to me I can but mention three pregnant results of the scientific study of nature.

In the first place, natural science has engendered a peculiar kind of human mind — the searching, open, humble mind, which, knowing that it cannot attain unto all truth, or even to much new truth, is yet patiently and enthusiastically devoted to the pursuit of such little new truth as is within its grasp, having no other end than to learn, prizing above all things accuracy, thoroughness, and candor in research, proud and happy, not in its own single strength, but in the might of that host of students, whose past conquests make up the wondrous sum of present knowledge, whose sure future triumphs are shared in imagination by each humblest worker. Within the last four hundred years this typical scientific mind has gradually come to be the kind of philosophic mind most admired by the educated class; indeed, it has come to be the only kind of mind, except the poetic, which commands the respect of scholars, whatever their department of learning. In every field of study, in history, philosophy, and theology, as well as in natural history and physics, it is now the scientific spirit, the scientific method, which prevails. The substitution in the esteem of reasonable men of this receptive, forereaching mind for the dogmatic, overbearing, closed mind, which assumes that it already possesses all essential truth and is entitled to the exclusive interpretation of it, is a most beneficent result of the study of natural history and physics. It is an achievement which has had much to do with the modern increase of liberty in human society, liberty individual, political, and religious; it is an achievement of the highest promise for the future of the race.

The second result which I wish to specify is the stupendous doctrine of hereditary transmission, which, during the past thirty years, or within the lifetime of most of those who hear me, natural science has developed and enforced by observations and comparisons covering the whole field of organized life. This conception is far from being a new one. Our race has long practised, though fitfully and empirically, upon some crude and fragmentary forms of this idea. Tribes, clans, castes, orders of nobility, and reigning families, are familiar illustrations of the sway of this idea; in killing, banishing, and confining criminals, mankind has in all ages been defending itself — blindly, to be sure, but with effect — against evils which incidentally flow from hereditary transmission; but it has been reserved for natural science in this generation to demonstrate the universality of this principle, and its controlling influence upon the families, nations, and races of men, as well as upon all lower orders of animate beings. It is fitting that natural history should have given this demonstration to the world; for the basis of systematic natural history is the idea of species, and the idea of species is itself founded upon the sureness of hereditary transmission — upon the ultimate fact that individual characteristics are inheritable. As the knowledge of heredity, recently acquired by science, permeates society, it will profoundly affect social customs, public legislation, and governmental action. It will throw additional safeguards around the domestic relations; enhance the natural interest in vigorous family stocks; guide wisely the charitable action of the community; give a rational basis for penal legislation; and promote both the occasional production of illustrious men and the gradual improvement of the masses of mankind. These moral benefits will surely flow from our generation's study of heredity.

Finally, modern science has discovered and set forth the magnificent idea of the continuity of creation. It has proved that the development of the universe has been a progress from good to better — a progress not without reactions and catastrophes, but still a benign advance toward ever higher forms of life with ever greater capacities for ever finer enjoyments. It has laid a firm foundation for man's instinctive faith in his own future. From the sight and touch of what the eternal past has wrought, it deduces a sure trust in what the eternal future has in store.

And present gratitude
Insures the future's good;
And for the things I see
I trust the things to be.

It has thus exalted the idea of God — the greatest service which can be rendered to humanity. "Each age must worship its own thought of God," and each age may be judged by the worthiness of that thought. In displaying the uniform, continuous action of unrepenting nature in its march from good to better, science has inevitably directed the attention of men to the most glorious attributes of that divine intelligence which acts through nature with the patience of eternity and the fixity of all-foreseeing wisdom. Verily, the infinite, present Creator is worshiped in this place. A hundred lifetimes ago a Hebrew seer gave utterance to one of the grandest thoughts that ever mind of man conceived; but applied it only to his own little nation, and coupled it with barbarous denunciation of that nation's enemies. This thought, tender and consoling toward human weakness and insignificance as a mother's embrace, but sublime also as the starry heights, and majestic as the onward sweep of ages, science utters as the sum of all its teachings, as the supreme result of all its searching and its meditation, and applies alike to the whole universe and to its least atom: "The eternal God is thy refuge, and underneath are the everlasting arms."

THE HAPPY LIFE

ADDRESS

At the Woman's College of Baltimore, Nov. 7, 1895

THE HAPPY LIFE

MY subject is, "The Happy Life." I address here especially young people who have passed the period of childhood, with its unreflecting gaiety, passing shadows, gusty griefs, and brief despairs, and have entered, under conditions of singular privilege, upon rational and responsible living. For you, happiness must be conscious, considerate, and consistent with habits of observing, reading, and reflecting. Now reflecting has always been a grave business,

> "Where but to think is to be full of sorrow
> And leaden-eyed despairs,"

and it must be confessed that our times present some new obstacles to a life of considerate happiness for people who observe and read. A few generations ago the misery of the many did not much mar the happiness of the few; for wide diversities of human condition seemed natural not artificial, and fellow-feeling was comparatively undeveloped. Until this century the masses of mankind were almost dumb; but now their moans and complaints have become audible through telephone, telegraph, and rotary press. The millions are now saying what the moody poets have always said:

> "The flower that smiles to-day
> To-morrow dies.
> All that we wish to stay
> Tempts, and then flies.
> What is this world's delight?
> Lightning that mocks the night,
> Brief even as bright."

The gloomy moralist is still repeating, "I have seen all the works that are done under the sun, and behold! all is vanity and vexation of spirit."

The manual laborers of to-day, who are much better off than the same classes of laborers have been in any earlier times, are saying just what Shelley said to the men of England in 1819:

> "The seed ye sow another reaps,
> The wealth ye find another keeps,
> The robes ye weave another wears,
> The arms ye forge another bears."

They would adopt without change the words in which that eminent moralist, Robinson Crusoe, a century earlier, described the condition of the laboring classes: "The men of labor spent their strength in daily struggling for bread to maintain the vital strength they labored with; so living in a daily circulation of sorrow, living but to work, and working but to live, as if daily bread were the only end of wearisome life, and a wearisome life the only occasion of daily bread."

Matthew Arnold calls his love to come to the window and listen to the "melancholy, long-withdrawing roar" of the sea upon the moonlit beach at Dover; and these are his dismal words to her:

"Ah, love, let us be true
To one another! for the world, which seems
To lie before us like a land of dreams,
So various, so beautiful, so new,
Hath really neither joy, nor love, nor light,
Nor certitude, nor peace, nor help for pain;
And we are here as on a darkling plain,
Swept with confused alarms of struggle and flight,
Where ignorant armies clash by night."

The poets are by no means the only offenders; the novelists and scientists take their turn. The fiction of this century deals much with the lives of the wretched, dissolute, and vicious, and with the most unjust and disastrous conditions of modern society.

A fresh difficulty in the way of natural happiness is the highly speculative opinion lately put forward by men of science and promptly popularized, to the effect that external nature offsets every good with an evil, and that the visible universe is unmoral, or indifferent as regards right and wrong, revealing no high purpose or intelligent trend. This is indeed a melancholy notion; but that it should find acceptance at this day, and really make people miserable, only illustrates the curious liability of the human intelligence to sudden collapse. The great solid conviction, which science within the past three centuries has enabled thinking men and women to settle down on, is that all discovered and systematized knowledge is as nothing compared with the undiscovered, and that a boundless universe of unimagined facts and forces interpenetrates and encompasses what seems the universe to us. In spite of this impregnable conviction, people distress themselves because, forsooth, they cannot discern the moral purpose, or complete spiritual intent, of this dimly seen, fractional universe which is all we know. Why should they discern it?

It is, then, in spite of many old and some new discouragements that we are all seeking the happy life. We know that education spreads, knowledge grows, and public liberty develops; but can we be sure that public and private happiness increase? What the means and sources of happiness are in this actual world, with our present surroundings, and with no reference to joys or sorrows in any other world, is a natural, timely, and wholesome inquiry. We may be sure that one principle will hold throughout the whole pursuit of considerate happiness — the principle that the best way to secure future happiness is to be as happy as is rightfully possible to-day. To secure any desirable capacity for the future, near or remote, cultivate it to-day. What is the use of immortality for a person who cannot use well half an hour? asks Emerson.

In trying to enumerate the positive satisfactions which an average man may reasonably expect to enjoy in this world, I, of course, take no account of those too common objects of human pursuit, wealth, power, and fame; first, because they do not, as a rule, contribute to happiness; and secondly, because they are unattainable by mankind in general. I invite you to consider only those means of happiness which the humble and obscure millions may possess. The rich and famous are too few to affect appreciably the sum of human happiness. I begin with the satisfactions of sense.

Sensuous pleasures, like eating and drinking, are sometimes described as animal, and therefore unworthy. It must be confessed, however, that men are, in this life, animals all through,—whatever else they may be,—and that they have a right to enjoy without reproach those pleasures of animal existence which maintain health, strength, and life itself. Familiar ascetic and pessimistic dogmas to the contrary notwithstanding, these pleasures, taken naturally and in moderation, are all pure, honorable, and wholesome. Moreover, all attempts to draw a line between bodily satisfactions on the one hand, and mental or spiritual satisfactions on the other, and to distinguish the first as beastly indulgences and the second as the only pleasures worthy of a rational being, have failed and must fail; for it is manifestly impossible to draw a sharp line of division between pleasures, and to say that these are bodily, and those are intellectual or moral. Are the pleasures of sight and hearing bodily or mental? Is delight in harmony, or in color, a pleasure of the sense, or of the imagination? What sort of a joy is a thing of beauty? Is it an animal or a spiritual joy? Is the delight of a mother in fondling her smiling baby a physical or a moral delight? But though we cannot divide pleasures into animal and moral, unworthy and worthy, we can nevertheless divide them into lower and higher pleasures; the lower those which, like eating and drinking, prompt to the maintenance and reproduction of life, and which can be impaired or destroyed by prolongation or repetition; the higher those which, like the pleasures of the eye or ear, seem to be ends in themselves; in the lower there can be destructive excess, in the higher excess is impossible.

Recognizing then that there are higher pleasures than eating and drinking, let us clearly perceive that three meals a day all one's life not only give in themselves a constantly renewed innocent satisfaction, but provide the necessary foundation for all other satisfactions. Taking food and drink is a great enjoyment for healthy people, and those who do not enjoy eating seldom have much capacity for enjoyment or usefulness of any sort. Under ordinary circumstances it is by no means a purely bodily pleasure. We do not eat alone, but in families, or sets of friends and comrades, and the table is the best center of friendships and of the domestic affections. When, therefore, a workingman says that he has worked all his life to procure a subsistence for himself and his family, he states that he has secured some fundamental satisfactions, namely, food, productive employment, and family life. The satisfaction of eating is so completely a matter of appetite that such distinction as there is between the luxurious and the hardy in regard to this enjoyment is altogether in favor of the hardy. Who does not remember some rough and perhaps scanty meal in camp, or on the march, or at sea, or in the woods, which was infinitely more delicious than the most luxurious dinner during indoor or sedentary life? But that appetite depends on health. Take good care, then, of your teeth and your stomachs, and be ashamed, not of enjoying your food, but of not enjoying it. There was a good deal of sound human nature in the unexpected reply of the dying old woman to her minister's leading question: "Here at the end of a long life, which of the Lord's mercies are you most thankful for?" Her eye brightened as she answered, after a moment's consideration: "My victuals."

Let us count next pleasures through the eye. Unlike the other senses, the eye is always at work except when we sleep, and may consequently be the vehicle of far more enjoyment than any other organ of sense. It has given our race its ideas of infinity, symmetry, grace, and splendor; it is a chief source of childhood's joys, and throughout life the guide to almost all pleasurable activities. The pleasure it gives us, however, depends largely upon the amount of attention we pay to the pictures which it incessantly sets before the brain. Two men walk along the same road — one notices the blue depths of the sky, the floating clouds, the opening leaves upon the trees, the green grass, the yellow buttercups, and the far stretch of the open fields — the other has precisely the same pictures on his retina, but pays no attention to them. One sees, and the other does not see; one enjoys an unspeakable pleasure, and the other loses that pleasure which is as free to him as the air. The beauties which the eye reveals are infinitely various in quality and scale; one mind prefers the minute, another the vast; one the delicate and tender, another the coarse and rough; one the inanimate things, another the animate creation. The whole outward world is the kingdom of the observant eye. He who enters into any part of that kingdom to possess it has a store of pure enjoyment in life which is literally inexhaustible and immeasurable. His eyes alone will give him a life worth living.

Next comes the ear as a minister of enjoyment, but next at a great interval. The average man probably does not recognize that he gets much pleasure through hearing. He thinks that his ears are to him chiefly a convenient means of human intercourse. But let him experience a temporary deafness, and he will learn that many a keen delight came to him through the ear. He will miss the beloved voice, the merry laugh, the hum of the city, the distant chime, the song of birds, the running brook, the breeze in the trees, the lapping wavelets, and the thundering beach; and he will learn that familiar sounds have been to him sources of pure delight — an important element in his well-being.

Old Isaac Walton found in the lovely sounds of earth a hint of heaven —

> How joyed my heart in the rich melodies
> That overhead and round me did arise!
> The moving leaves — the water's gentle flow —
> Delicious music hung on every bough.
> Then said I in my heart, If that the Lord
> Such lovely music on the earth accord;
> If to weak, sinful man such sounds are given,
> Oh! what must be the melody of Heaven!

A high degree of that fine pleasure which music gives is not within the reach of all; yet there are few to whom the pleasure is wholly denied. To take part in producing harmony, as in part-singing, gives the singers an intense pleasure which is, doubtless, partly physical and partly mental. I am told that to play good music at sight, as one of several performers playing different instruments, is as keen a sensuous and intellectual enjoyment as the world affords. These pleasures through the eye and ear are open in civilized society to all who have the will to seek them, and the intelligence to cultivate the faculties through which they are enjoyed. They are quite as likely to bless him who works with hand or brain all day for a living, as him who lives inactive on his own savings or on those of other people. The outward world yields them spontaneously to every healthy body and alert mind; but the active mind is as essential to the winning of them as the sound body.

There is one great field of knowledge, too much neglected in our schools and colleges, which offers to the student endless pleasures and occupations through the trained and quickened senses of sight, hearing, and touch — I mean the wide field called natural history, which comprehends geography, meteorology, botany, zoölogy, mineralogy, and geology. Charles Darwin, the greatest naturalist of this century, said that with natural history and the domestic affections a man might be truly happy. Not long ago I was urging a young naturalist of twenty-six to spend the next summer in Europe. He thought it was hardly right for him to allow himself that indulgence; and when I urged that the journey would be very enjoyable as well as profitable, he replied, "Yes, but you know I can be happy anywhere in the months when things are growing." He meant that the pleasures of observation were enough for him, when he could be out of doors. That young man was poor, delicate in health, and of a retiring and diffident disposition, yet life was full of keenest interest to him.

Our century is distinguished by an ardent return of civilized man to that love of nature from which books and urban life had temporarily diverted him. The poetry and the science of our times alike foster this love, and add to the delights which come to lovers of Nature through the senses the delights of the soaring imagination, and the far-reaching reason. In many of our mental moods the contemplation of Nature brings peace and joy. Her patient ways shame hasty little man; her vastnesses calm and elevate his troubled mind; her terrors fill him with awe; her inexplicable and infinite beauties with delight. Her equal care for the least things and the greatest corrects his scale of values. He cannot but believe that the vast material frame of things is informed and directed by an infinite Intelligence and Will, just as his little animal body is informed by his own conscious mind and will.

It is apparent from what I have said of pleasures through the eye and ear, and from contact with nature, that a good measure of out-of-door life is desirable for him who would secure the elements of a happy life. The urban tendency of our population militates against free access to out-of-door delights. The farmer works all day in the fields, and his children wander at will in the open air; the sailor can see at any moment the whole hemisphere of the heavens and the broad plain of the sea; but the city resident may not see a tree or a shrub for weeks together, and can barely discern a narrow strip of sky, as he walks at the bottom of the deep ditches we call streets. The wise man, whose work is in the city and in-doors at that, will take every possible opportunity to escape into the fresh air and the open country. Certain good tendencies in this respect have appeared within recent years. Hundreds of thousands of people, who must work daily in compact cities, now live in open suburbs; cities provide parks and decorated avenues of approach to parks; out-of-door sports and exercises become popular; safe country boarding-schools for city children are multiplied; and public holidays and half-holidays increase in number. These are appreciable compensations for the disadvantages of city life. The urban population which really utilizes these facilities may win a keener enjoyment from nature than the rural population, to whom natural beauty is at every moment accessible. The cultivation of mind and the increased sensibility which city life develops heighten the delight in natural beauty. Moreover, though man destroys much natural loveliness in occupying any territory for purposes of residence or business, he also creates much loveliness of grassy fields and banks, mirroring waters, perfectly developed trees, graceful shrubs, and brilliant flowers. In these days no intelligent city population need lack the means and opportunities of frequent out-of-door enjoyment. Our climate is indeed rough and changeable, but on the whole produces scenes of much more various beauty than any monotonous climate; while against the occasional severity of our weather artificial protection is more and more provided. What we may wisely ask of our tailors and our landscape architects is protection in the open air from the extremes of heat, cold, and wind. The provision of an equable climate in-doors is by no means sufficient to secure either the health or the happiness of the people.

From the love of nature we turn to family love. The domestic affections are the principal source of human happiness and well-being. The mutual loves of husband and wife, of parents and children, of brothers and sisters, are not only the chief sources of happiness, but the chief springs of action, and the chief safeguards from evil. The young man and the young woman work and save in order that they may be married and have a home of their own; once married, they work and save that they may bring up well a family. The supreme object of the struggling and striving of most men is the family. One might almost say that the security and elevation of the family and of family life are the prime objects of civilization, and the ultimate ends of all industry and trade. In respect to this principal source of happiness, the young mechanic, operative, clerk, or laborer is generally better off than the young professional man, inasmuch as he can marry earlier. He goes from the parental roof to his own roof with only a short interval, if any, between. The workingman is often a grandfather before he is fifty years old; the professional man but seldom. Love before marriage, being the most attractive theme of poetry and fiction, gets a very disproportionate amount of attention in literature, as compared with the domestic affections after marriage.

Concerning these normal domestic joys, any discerning person who has experienced them, and has been intimate with four or five generations, will be likely to make three observations: In the first place, the realization of the natural and legitimate enjoyments in domestic life depends upon the possession of physical and moral health. Whatever impairs bodily vigor, animal spirits, and good temper, lessens the chance of attaining to the natural, domestic joys — joys which by themselves, without any additions whatever except food and steady work, make earthly life worth living. In the second place, they endure, and increase with lapse of years; the satisfactions of normal married life do not decline, but mount. Children are more and more interesting as they grow older; at all stages, from babyhood to manhood and womanhood they are to be daily enjoyed. People who think they shall enjoy their children to-morrow, or year after next, will never enjoy them. The greatest pleasure in them comes late; for as Hamerton mentions in his "Human Intercourse," the most exquisite satisfaction of the parent is to come to respect and admire the powers and character of the child. Thirdly, the family affections and joys are the ultimate source of civilized man's idea of a loving God — an idea which is a deep root of happiness when it becomes an abiding conviction. They have supplied all the conceptions of which this idea is the supreme essence, or infinite product. It deserves mention here, that these supreme enjoyments of the normal, natural life — the domestic joys — are woman's more than man's; because his function of bread-winning necessarily separates him from his home during a good part of his time, particularly since domestic or house industries have been superseded by factory methods.

I turn now to the satisfaction which comes from physical exertion, including brain-work. Everybody knows some form of activity which gives him satisfaction. Perhaps it is riding on a horse, or rowing a boat, or tramping all day through woods or along beaches with a gun on the shoulder, or climbing a mountain, or massing into a ball or bloom a paste of sticky iron in a puddling-furnace (that heaviest of labor), or wrestling with the handles of the plunging, staggering plough, or tugging at a boat's tiller when the breeze is fresh, or getting in hay before the shower. There is real pleasure and exhilaration in bodily exertion, particularly with companionship (of men or animals) and competition. There is pleasure in the exertion even when it is pushed to the point of fatigue, as many a sportsman knows, and this pleasure is, in good measure, independent of the attainment of any practical end. There is pleasure in mere struggle, so it be not hopeless, and in overcoming resistance, obstacles, and hardships. When to the pleasure of exertion is added the satisfaction of producing a new value, and the further satisfaction of earning a livelihood through that new value, we have the common pleasurable conditions of productive labor. Every working man who is worth his salt (I care not whether he works with his hands and brains, or with his brains alone) takes satisfaction first in the working; secondly, in the product of his work; and thirdly, in what that product yields to him. The carpenter who takes no pleasure in the mantel he has made, the farm-laborer who does not care for the crops he has cultivated, the weaver who takes no pride in the cloth he has woven, the engineer who takes no interest in the working of the engine he directs, is a monstrosity. It is an objection to many forms of intellectual labor that their immediate product is intangible and often imperceptible. The fruit of mental labor is often diffused, remote, or subtile. It eludes measurement, and even observation. On the other hand, mental labor is more enjoyable than manual labor in the process. The essence of the joy lies in the doing, rather than in the result of the doing. There is a life-long and solid satisfaction in any productive labor, manual or mental, which is not pushed beyond the limit of strength. The difference between the various occupations of man in respect to yielding this satisfaction is much less than people suppose; for occupations become habitual in time, and the daily work in every calling gets to be so familiar that it may fairly be called monotonous. My occupation, for instance, offers, I believe, more variety than that of most professional men; yet I should say that nine tenths of my work, from day to day, was routine work, presenting no more novelty, or fresh interest, to me than the work of a carpenter or blacksmith who is always making new things on old types presents to him. The Oriental, hot-climate figment that labor is a curse is contradicted by the experience of all the progressive nations. The Teutonic stock owes everything that is great and inspiring in its destiny to its faculty of overcoming difficulties by hard work, and of taking heartfelt satisfaction in this victorious work. It is not the dawdlers and triflers who find life worth living; it is the steady, strenuous, robust workers.

Once, when I was talking with Dr. Oliver Wendell Holmes about the best pleasures in life, he mentioned, as one of the most precious, frequent contact with quick and well-stored minds in large variety; he valued highly the number, frequency, and variety of quickening, intellectual encounters. We were thinking of contact in conversation; but this pleasure, if only to be procured by personal meetings, would obviously be within the reach, as a rule, of only a very limited number of persons. Fortunately for us and for posterity, the cheap printing-press has put within easy reach of every man who can read, all the best minds both of the past and the present. For one tenth part of a year's wages a young mechanic can buy, before he marries, a library of famous books which, if he masters it, will make him a well-read man. For half-a-day's wages a clerk can provide himself with a weekly paper which will keep him informed for a year of all important current events. Public libraries, circulating libraries, Sunday-school libraries, and book-clubs nowadays bring much reading to the door of every household and every solitary creature that wants to read. This is a new privilege for the mass of mankind; and it is an inexhaustible source of intellectual and spiritual nutriment. It seems as if this new privilege alone must alter the whole aspect of society in a few generations. Books are the quietest and most constant of friends; they are the most accessible and wisest of counsellors, and the most patient of teachers. With his daily work and his books, many a man, whom the world thought forlorn, has found life worth living. It is a mistake to suppose that a great deal of leisure is necessary for this happy intercourse with books. Ten minutes a day devoted affectionately to good books — indeed to one book of the first order, like the English Bible or Shakspere, or to two or three books of the second order, like Homer, Virgil, Milton, or Bacon — will in thirty years make all the difference between a cultivated and an uncultivated man, between a man mentally rich and a man mentally poor. The pleasures of reading are of course in good part pleasures of the imagination; but they are just as natural and actual as pleasures of sense, and are often more accessible and more lasting.

In the next place, I call your attention to the fact that man is a part of outward nature, and that the men and women among whom our lot is cast are an important part of our actual environment. In some relation or other to these human beings we perforce must stand. The question, in what relation we had better stand to them, is a practical, this-world question, and not a sentimental or next-world question. Further, our sympathetic feelings, over which we have hardly more control than we have over the beating of our hearts, go out to our fellow-men more and more widely, as better means of communication bring home to us thè joys and sorrows of wide-spread multitudes. In what relation is it for our satisfaction to stand in this world toward our fellow-men? Shall we love or hate them, bless or curse them, help or hinder them? These are not theoretical questions which arise out of religious speculation, or some abstract philosophy. They are earthly, every-day, concrete questions, as intensely practical as the question, How are we to get our daily bread? or, Where are we to find shelter from the snowstorm? Human beings are all about us; we and they are mutually dependent in ways so complex and intricate that no wisdom can unravel them. It is in vain for us or them to say, "Let us alone," for that is a downright impossibility. To the question, How do reasonable men, under these circumstances, naturally and inevitably incline to act toward their fellow-beings? there is but one common-sense, matter-of-fact answer — namely, They incline to serve, and coöperate with, them. That civilized society exists at all, is a demonstration that this inclination in the main governs human relations. Every great city is dependent for food, drink, and fuel upon a few bridges, dams, canals, or aqueducts, which a dozen intelligent human devils, armed with suitable explosives and fire-bombs, could destroy in a night. If the doctrine of total depravity were anything but the invention of a morbid human imagination, the massing of people by hundreds of thousands would be too dangerous to be attempted. Civilized society assumes that the great majority of men will combine to procure advantages, resist evils, defend rights, and remedy wrongs. Following this general and inevitable inclination, the individual finds that by serving others he best serves himself, because he thus conforms to the promptings of his own and their best nature. The most satisfactory thing in all this earthly life is to be able to serve our fellow-beings — first, those who are bound to us by ties of love, then the wider circle of fellow-townsmen, fellow-countrymen, or fellow-men. To be of service is a solid foundation for contentment in this world. For our present purpose, it does not matter where we got these ideas about our own better nature and its best satisfaction; it is enough that our generation, as a matter of fact, has these ideas, and is ruled by them.

The amount of service is no measure of the satisfaction or happiness which he who renders the service derives from it. One man founds an academy or a hospital; another sends one boy to be educated at the academy, or one sick man to be treated at the hospital. The second is the smaller service, but may yield the greater satisfaction. Sir Samuel Romilly attacked the monstrous English laws which affixed the death penalty to a large number of petty offenses against property, like poaching, sheep-stealing, and pocket-picking. In the dawn of a February morning, when the wind was blowing a gale and the thermometer was below zero, Captain Smith of the Cuttyhunk lighthouse took three men off a wreck which the heavy sea was fast pounding to pieces on a reef close below the light. Sir Samuel Romilly's labors ultimately did an amount of good quite beyond computation; but he lived to see accomplished only a small part of the beneficent changes he had advocated. The chances are that Captain Smith got more satisfaction for the rest of his life out of that rescue, done in an hour, than Sir Samuel out of his years of labor for a much-needed reform in the English penal code. There was another person who took satisfaction in that rescue ever after, and was entitled to. When day dawned on that wintry morning, Captain Smith's wife, who had been listening restlessly to the roar of the sea and the wind, could lie still no longer. She got up and looked out of the window. To her horror there was a small schooner on the reef, in plain sight, one mast fallen over the side, and three men lashed to the other mast. Her husband was still fast asleep. Must she rouse him? If she did, she knew he would go out there into that furious sea and freezing wind. If she waited only a little while, the men would be dead, and it would be of no use to go. Should she speak to him? She did. Oh! it is not the amount of good done which measures the love or heroism which prompted the serviceable deed, or the happiness which the doer gets from it. It is the spirit of service which creates both the merit and the satisfaction.

One of the purest and most enduring of human pleasures is to be found in the possession of a good name among one's neighbors and acquaintances. As Shakspere puts it

> The purest treasure mortal times afford
> Is spotless reputation.

This is not fame, or even distinction; it is local reputation among the few scores or hundreds of persons who really know one. It is a satisfaction quite of this world, and one attained by large numbers of quiet men and women whose names are never mentioned beyond the limits of their respective sets of acquaintance. Such reputation regards, not mental power or manual skill, but character; it is slowly built upon purity, integrity, courage, and sincerity. To possess it is a crowning satisfaction which is oftenest experienced to the full rather late in life, when some other pleasures begin to fade away.

Lastly, I shall venture to call your attention to the importance — with a view to a happy life — of making a judicious selection of beliefs. Here we are living on a little islet of sense and fact in the midst of a boundless ocean of the unknown and mysterious. From year to year and century to century the islet expands as new districts are successively lifted from out the encompassing sea of ignorance, but it still remains encircled by this prodigious sea. In this state of things, every inquisitive truth-seeking human being is solicited by innumerable beliefs, old and new. The past generations, out of which we spring, have been believing many undemonstrated and undemonstrable things, and we inherit their beliefs. Every year new beliefs appeal to us for acceptance, some of them clashing with the old. Everybody holds numerous beliefs on subjects outside the realm of knowledge, and, moreover, everybody has to act on these beliefs from hour to hour. All men of science walk by faith and not by sight in exploring and experimenting, the peculiarity of their walk being that they generally take but one step at a time, and that a short one. All business proceeds on beliefs, or judgments of probabilities, and not on certainties.

The very essence of heroism is that it takes adverse chances; so that full foreknowledge of the issue would subtract from the heroic quality. Beliefs, then, we must have and must act on, and they are sure to affect profoundly our happiness in this world. How to treat our old beliefs and choose our new ones, with a view to happiness, is in these days a serious problem for every reflective person.

The first steps toward making a calm choice are to observe strictly the line of demarcation between facts on the one hand and beliefs on the other, and to hold facts as facts, and beliefs as nothing more than beliefs. Next we need a criterion or touchstone for beliefs, old and new. The surest touchstone is the ethical standard which through inheritance, education, and the experience of daily life has, as a matter of fact, become our standard. It is not for our happiness to believe any proposition about the nature of man, the universe, or God, which is really at war with our fundamental instincts of honor and justice, or with our ideals of gentleness and love, no matter how those instincts and ideals have been implanted or arrived at. The man or woman who hopes to attain reflective happiness, as he works his strenuous way through the world, must bring all beliefs, old and new, to this critical test, and must reject, or refuse to entertain, beliefs which do not stand the test.

One obvious fact of observation seems to contradict this correlation of beliefs with ethical content, and therefore with happiness. Millions of comfortable men and women do, as a matter of fact, believe various long-transmitted doctrines which are clearly repulsive to the moral sense of the entire present generation. How can this be? Simply because these millions accept also antidotal doctrines which neutralize the natural effect of the first beliefs. This process may persist for generations without affecting much the happiness of mankind, but nevertheless it has its dangers; for if faith in the antidotes be lost first, a moral chaos may set in.

Sudden and solitary changes of belief are seldom happy. A gentle, gradual transformation of beliefs, in company with kindred, neighbors, and friends, is the happiest. Men have always been gregarious in beliefs; if they cannot remain with their own herd, it will be for their happiness to join a more congenial herd as quickly as possible.

Of the two would-be despots in beliefs — the despot who authoritatively commands men to believe as he says, and the despot who forbids men to believe at all — the first is the more tolerable to the immense majority of mankind. Under the first despot millions of people have lived and now live in contented faith; but nobody can live happily under the other. To curious, truth-seeking, pioneering minds one seems as bad as the other, and neither in any way endurable.

A certain deliberation in accepting new beliefs is conducive to happiness, particularly if the new ideas are destructive rather than constructive. Emerson recommends us, as a measure of intellectual economy, not to read a book until it is at least one year old, so many books disappear in a year. In like manner, of novel speculative opinions all but the best-built and most buoyant will go under within ten years of their launching.

We may be sure that cheerful beliefs about the unseen world, framed in full harmony with the beauty of the visible universe, and with the sweetness of domestic affections and joys, and held in company with kindred and friends, will illuminate the dark places on the pathway of earthly life and brighten all the road.

Having thus surveyed the various joys and satisfactions which may make civilized life happy for multitudes of our race, I hasten to admit that there are physical and moral evils in this world which impair or interrupt earthly happiness. The worst of the physical evils are lingering diseases and untimely deaths. I admit, too, that not a few men do, as a matter of fact, lead lives not worth living. I admit, also, that there are dreadful as well as pleasing sights and sounds in this world, and that many seemingly cruel catastrophes and destructions mark the course of nature. Biological science has lately impressed many people with the prevalence of cruelty and mutual destruction in the animal and vegetable world. From man down, the creatures live by preying on each other. Insidious parasites infest all kinds of plants and animals. Every living thing seems to have its mortal foe. The very ants go to war, for all the world like men; and Venus's Flytrap (Dionæa) is as cruel as a spider. So, human society is riddled with mischiefs and wrongs, some, like Armenian massacres, due to surviving savagery, and some, like slums, to sickly civilization. It would seem impossible to wring satisfaction and considerate happiness from such evils. Yet that is just what men of noble nature are constantly doing. They fight evil, and from the contest win content, and even joy. Nobody has any right to find life uninteresting, or unrewarding, who sees within the sphere of his own activity a wrong which he can help to remedy, or within himself an evil which he can hope to overcome. It should be observed that the inanimate creation does not lend itself, like the animate creation, to the theory that for every good in nature there is an equivalent evil, and for every beautiful thing an ugly offset. There is no direct offset to the constant splendor of the heavens by night or to the transient glories of the sunset, no drawback on the beauty of perfect form and various hue in crystalline minerals, and no implicated evil counterbalancing the serenity of the mountains or the sublimity of the ocean. Even the lightning and the storm are wondrously beautiful.

Again, the existence of evils and mysteries must not blind us to the abounding and intelligible good. We must remember that the misfortunes hardest to bear are those which never come, as Lowell said. We must clear our minds, as far as possible, of cruel imaginings about the invisible world and its rulers; and, on the other hand, we must never allow imagined consolations, or compensatory delights, in some other world to reconcile us to the endurance of resistible evils in this. We must never distress ourselves because we cannot fully understand the moral principles on which the universe is conducted. It would be vastly more reasonable in an ant to expect to understand the constitution of the sun.

We must be sure to give due weight, in our minds, to the good side of every event which has two sides. A fierce northeaster drives some vessels out of their course, and others upon the ruthless rocks. Property and life are lost. But that same storm watered the crops upon ten thousand farms, or filled the springs which later will yield to men and animals their necessary drink. A tiger springs upon an antelope, picks out the daintiest bits from the carcass, and leaves the rest to the jackals. We say, Poor little antelope! We forget to say, Happy tiger! fortunate jackals! who were seeking their meat from God, and found it. A house which stands in open ground must have a sunny side as well as a shady. Be sure to live on the sunny side, and even then do not expect the world to look bright, if you habitually wear gray-brown glasses.

We must assiduously cultivate a just sense of the proportion between right and wrong, good and evil in this world. The modern newspaper press is a serious obstacle to habitual cheerfulness, because it draws constant attention to abnormal evils and crimes, and makes no account of the normal successes, joys, and well-doings. We read in the morning paper that five houses, two barns, three shops, and a factory have burned up in the night, and we do not say to ourselves that within the same territory five hundred thousand houses, three hundred thousand barns, as many shops, and a thousand factories have stood in safety. We observe that ten persons have been injured on railways within twenty-four hours, and we forget that two million have traveled in safety. Out of every thousand persons in the city of Cambridge twenty die in the course of a year, but the other nine hundred and eighty live; and of the twenty who die some have filled out the natural span of life, and others are obviously unfit to live. Sometimes our individual lives seem to be full of troubles and miseries — our own, or those of others. Then we must fall back on this abiding sense of the real proportion between the lives sorrowful and the lives glad at any one moment, and of the preponderance of gain over loss, health over sickness, joy over sorrow, good over evil, and life over death.

I shall not have succeeded in treating my subject clearly if I have not convinced you that earthly happiness is not dependent on the amount of one's possessions or the nature of one's employment. The enjoyments and satisfactions which I have described are accessible to poor and rich, to humble and high alike, if only they cultivate the physical, mental, and moral faculties through which the natural joys are won. Any man may win them who, by his daily labor, can earn a wholesome living for himself and his family. I have not mentioned a single pleasure which involves unusual expense, or the possession of any uncommon mental gifts. It follows that the happiness of the entire community is to be most surely promoted, not by increasing its total wealth or even by distributing that wealth more evenly, but by improving its physical and moral health. A poorer population may easily be happier than a richer, if it be of sounder health and morality.

In conclusion, let me ask you to consider whether the rational conduct of life on the this-world principles here laid down would differ in any important respect from the right conduct of life on the principles of the Christian gospels. It does not seem to me that it would.

A HAPPY LIFE

A TRIBUTE TO ASA GRAY

READ AT THE AMERICAN ACADEMY OF ARTS AND SCIENCES, JUNE 13, 1888

A HAPPY LIFE

THE life of Asa Gray always seemed to me a singularly happy one. His disposition was eminently cheerful, and his circumstances and occupations gave fortunate play to his natural capacity for enjoyment. From opening manhood he studied with keenest interest in a department of natural history which abounds in beauty, fragrance, and exquisite adaptation of means to ends, and opens inexhaustible opportunities for original observing, experimenting, and philosophizing. For sixty years he enjoyed to the full this elevating and rewarding pursuit. These years fell at a most fortunate period; for the continent was just being thoroughly explored and its botanical treasures brought to light. Dr. Gray's labors therefore cover the principal period of discovery and of accurate classification in American botany. Merely to have one's intellectual life-work make part of a structure so fair and lasting is in itself a substantial happiness.

His pursuit was one which took him out-of-doors,

and made him intimate with nature in all her moods. It required him to travel often, and so enabled him to see with delight different lands, skies, and peoples. It gave him intellectual contact with many scholars of various nationalities, whose pursuits were akin to his own. Intellectual sympathy and coöperation led to strong friendships founded securely upon common tastes and mutual services. All these are elements of happiness—love of nature, acquaintance with the wide earth, congenial intercourse with superior minds, and abiding friendships.

Although Dr. Gray had no children, his domestic experience was unusually happy. His life illustrated a remark of his friend Darwin—that with natural history and the domestic affections a man can be perfectly happy. His way of living was that most agreeable to a philosopher; for it was independent, comfortable, and free alike from the restrictions of poverty and the incumbrances of luxury. With simplicity and regularity of life went health and a remarkable capacity for labor.

All appropriate honors came in due course to Dr. Gray from academies, scientific associations, and universities at home and abroad. The stream began to flow as early as 1844, and continued to the end of his life. With these honors came the respect and affection of hundreds of persons who were devoted to the pursuit in which he was a leader. His reputation was larger than that of a specialist; he was recognized as a clear thinker on philosophical and religious themes, a just and sagacious critic, and a skilful and vigorous writer. It is the greatest of human rewards to be thus enfolded, as years advance, in an atmosphere of honor, gratitude, and love.

Finally, Dr. Gray enjoyed the conscious satisfaction of having rendered, during his long and industrious life, a great and lasting service to his kind. For many years past he could not but know that he had made the largest and most durable contribution to American botanical science which had ever been made, and that he had done more than any other man to diffuse among his countrymen a knowledge of botany and a love for it. He knew, moreover, that by his own work, and by the interest which his labors inspired in others, he had placed on a firm foundation the botanical department of the university which he served for forty-six years, and that the collections he had created there would have for generations a great historical importance. To have rendered such services was solid foundation indeed for heartfelt content.

A REPUBLICAN GENTLEMAN

A TRIBUTE TO MARTIN BRIMMER

READ AT THE MASSACHUSETTS HISTORICAL SOCIETY, FEBRUARY 13, 1896

A REPUBLICAN GENTLEMAN

MARTIN BRIMMER, the fourth and last of the name in this country, was born on the 9th of December, 1829. As a boy he was carefully educated at the best schools and by the best tutors of the day; and, like his father and two uncles, he graduated at Harvard College. His health was somewhat delicate, and lameness cut him off from many of the active sports of boyhood and manhood. He never had a robust body; but it was serviceable for the main objects of living, and it must have had a certain toughness of fiber, for in middle life he recovered from two severe illnesses, and three years ago from a heavy fall which made him seriously ill for many weeks. In spite of this delicacy of body, no comrade of his youth and no witness of his maturer life ever accused Martin Brimmer of lack of courage, decision, or persistence. He was always gentle, but always firm.

His education was prolonged by foreign travel, which he greatly enjoyed and profited by throughout life. His reading was extensive, and the language he used, whether in conversation or in writing, was pure and accurate. He had a clear English style which gave effect to thoughts inspired by good sense and good feeling. He read aloud well; and this useful faculty gave weight to any opinions or proposals for which he desired to procure the consent of others.

His father died before he graduated at Harvard, and from each parent he inherited a considerable fortune. To the making of money he never had occasion to give any thought, and not much to the keeping of money. The pursuit of wealth had no attractions for him, and that winning of a livelihood which occupies almost exclusively the time and energy of most men did not enter at all into his experience. He was rich and "knew how to abound." His houses contained many precious things — particularly the books and pictures he loved. He was an intelligent and discriminating patron of art, and therefore was surrounded at home by many objects delightful to the eye; but in his personal habits he was always simple, refined, and manly. Enervating luxuries had no allurements for him. He was not tempted to accumulate money; on the contrary, he dispensed it with extraordinary generosity and judgment. His rich material surroundings were only an incidental environment of his pure, lofty, and self-forgetting life.

He was always ready to render any public service for which he considered himself fit. At thirty years of age he was a representative in the Massachusetts Legislature; at thirty-four he was first elected a Fellow of the Corporation of Harvard University, and at thirty-five he was a member of the State Senate. In 1878 he was a candidate for Congress, but was defeated at the election. Perfectly disinterested himself in all public functions, he was absolutely incapable of appealing to interested or corrupt motives in others.

Of the numerous public trusts with which he was connected, the most important were Harvard University and the Boston Museum of Fine Arts. He was a Fellow of the University Corporation from 1864 to 1868, a Member of the Board of Overseers from 1870 to 1877, and again a Fellow of the Corporation from 1877 to his death. He was president of the Museum of Fine Arts from the organization of the corporation in 1870 to his death. He was a director in numerous charitable organizations, and a member of innumerable committees organized for temporary public service; and in all such labors his singular fairness, good temper, and good judgment made him a leader among his associates. In contentious meetings, his influence was invaluable. He soothed irritations, moderated fanaticisms, and made men and women of the most incompatible temperaments unite contentedly in good works.

Of all his public services, his labors on behalf of the Museum of Fine Arts were the most fortunate, congenial, and productive. Through much study and observation he had acquired a real knowledge of the fine arts, and an accurate and discriminating judgment in regard to pictures, statuary, and all other artistic objects. He believed ardently in the refining and uplifting power of the fine arts, and was as well prepared as he was eager to devote himself to the building up in Boston of a worthy museum. For twenty-five years he inspired and directed the work of that institution, and to him is chiefly due the large measure of success which the Museum of Fine Arts has already attained.

It is apparent from this brief outline of his labors that Martin Brimmer was generous indeed in giving his time to the public. He was one of the most industrious of men; but his industry was manifested in the discharge of public and semi-public trusts. He did not work thus strenuously for himself—it was always for others. Generous in giving his time to others, he was equally generous in giving his money. He never withheld his name from any Boston subscription-paper in a good cause. His gifts had the most varied character, and, like his sympathies, embraced all the agencies of education, religion, and charity within his knowledge. His benefactions were distributed all over our country. Under a calm manner, there burned steady enthusiasms which inspired many of his habitual or occasional activities. When the struggle to make Kansas a slave State was going on, Martin Brimmer contributed freely to the support of the men who were determined to make it a free State, by force if necessary; but perceiving the gravity of the situation, he went to Kansas to satisfy himself on the spot of the real conditions of the struggle. In the efforts to aid and protect the Freedmen after the Civil War, he took a spontaneous and hearty interest.

He was warmly attached to the principles of religious toleration; and in active defense of those principles he exerted himself repeatedly — Huguenot though he was by descent — to defeat fanatical attempts to exclude all Catholics from the Boston School Committee. He was a regular attendant at the services of the Protestant Episcopal Church, a generous contributor in every sense to its support, and interested in its legislation and its policy; but in his noble nature there was nothing of the partizan or the fanatic, and in all public affairs, and in all the trusts with which he was connected, he was a consistent supporter of an undenominational policy. In the largest sense he was a man of liberal mind.

In spite of some grievous disappointments and bereavements, Mr. Brimmer had an unusually happy life. His contemporaries thought him quiet and serious in youth; but as life advanced he grew gayer, until, in his later years, he visibly enjoyed all cheerful and improving human intercourse. His marriage was one of rare felicity; the coming into his home of four orphaned children of his wife's brother brought him somewhat late in life new domestic joys, if also new cares; and, as he grew older, he could not but be sensible of the respect and confidence with which all classes of people regarded him.

With his death his family name becomes extinct.

All the more, it is the duty of the friends who survive him to tell and enforce the lesson of his life for the benefit of the rising generation. Here was a rich man who was neither indolent nor self-indulgent; a man who had the means of giving himself to the lower pleasures of life, and who sought only the higher; a man of leisure who was always laborious and serviceable; a man of delicate body who was as brave and resolute as he was gentle; a man who, living, illustrated all the virtues and graces of friend, husband, counselor, citizen, and public servant, and, dying, left behind him no memory of look, thought, or deed that is not fragrant and blessed.

PRESENT DISADVANTAGES OF RICH MEN

SPEECH

AT THE UNITARIAN CLUB, BOSTON, JANUARY 5, 1893

PRESENT DISADVANTAGES OF RICH MEN

I OFTEN feel sorry for rich men in our day. They deserve a great deal of commiseration in our community; for they have lost a good many of the favoring chances that rich men had in other times. The rich men of former centuries and other countries were soldiers, magistrates, great land-owners, and great stockowners; they could not be rich on any other terms. They were necessarily called to the discharge of great public duties. They had to take their lives in their hands when frequent war came upon their country. They shared with their tenants, or clansmen, or retainers the dangers of battle. They always bore great charges in the maintenance of estates, only a part of which they privately enjoyed. They always had severe labors as magistrates.

All these chances of commending themselves to the community the rich men of to-day have lost. It is a change in the organization of society which has deprived them of these privileges. It has deprived the young rich—the young men who inherit riches—of a great many of the opportunities of service which, on the whole, endeared their like to the feudal societies. Even now, when we see the English dandies parading on Piccadilly, or riding in Rotten Row, in the middle of the working day, we have to remember that a fair proportion of those young fellows are liable at any hour to be ordered off on her Majesty's service, with sword by the side, risking their lives for the honor of England. There are no such chances for the rich American youth to-day. They are in danger of leading soft, luxurious lives.

Again, I observe that the life of the rich man who has made his money, and is a little out of the struggle to get more, becomes dull, monotonous, and uninteresting; and that the young men who inherit money often find life a terrible bore. It is that very class of people that oftenest ask Mallock's question, "Is life worth living?" It is the people who do not have to work for their own livelihood and that of their families who most frequently ask that question. I remember that Mallock's book was lying on the transom in a yacht I used to sail, when we cabin folks went ashore one afternoon to take a walk; and the steward picked up the red-covered book, read its title, "Is Life Worth Living?" and turned its pages. That man was away from his family nine months in the year. Three months he spent in what he considered a state of great ease and enjoyment on board the yacht; six months he went as mate in a coaster—a very hard life. Only three months, in mid-winter, did he spend at home. He did not earn more than six hundred dollars a year. His people were poor — all of them. But when we cabin folks came on board again, he took one of my sons aside, and asked, "What sort of a man wrote this book?" My son tried to explain what sort of a person Mr. Mallock was. "Well," said the steward, "he must be 'loony'! No man in his senses could ask that question." That is the state of mind of most men who work hard for their living. It is your young fellow who has much money in the bank and more in bonds who doubts the worth of living. It is a miserable question to ask: the man who asks it is in a wretched, unnatural state of mind.

It seems to me, too, that our rich men have lost great pleasures which the rich men of other times used to enjoy. It is a great pleasure, for instance, and a very honorable pleasure, in my opinion, to maintain generously and handsomely a fine family estate in the country, with all the old trees and noble animals that should adorn it — an estate which has been, and is to be, transmitted in the same family from generation to generation. How many men have that satisfaction in this country, the richest country in the world? Very few. I believe I know two men who live on their grandfather's places in the country — only two. We cut up our great estates, and sell them for house-lots if we can. We part with them; we move away from them; we give up the care of them. We do not maintain and beautify them, either for our children or for the public enjoyment. You and I never can own great estates; and we miss that lesser enjoyment, which is common in Europe, namely, the sight of great estates which rich men maintain,—the splendid parks, the beautiful lawns, the rich gardens, and noble mansions which rich men in feudal societies maintained for the enjoyment of their fellow-men, as well as for their own. I wish we might see some of these customs develop in our own land. If I cannot own a pair of handsome horses myself, I want to see somebody else owning and driving them. The sight of appropriate and durable splendor is a great enjoyment for all who look on it. But these things must be of very slow growth in our democratic society.

Yet we are going to have rich men, I believe, and richer men than ever. The continuous development of very rich men is a necessary consequence of the freedom and equality before the law that we all propose to enjoy. I do not believe that any legislative body, or any social philosopher, can prevent the coming up of rich men, unless we all agree that we will no longer attempt to enjoy entire freedom and perfect equality before the law. Given the freedom, the natural money-getters will make fortunes. Therefore I do not believe that any method of distribution, or even dissipation, of wealth will succeed in preventing, in this country, the constant rise of very rich men. Moreover, do we not all see a new condition of things which tends to the preservation of a rich class? When I was a boy, it was not the custom, among the generation preceding mine, to secure property to women when they were married; it was not the custom to settle estates on women and minors. The agencies to secure the faithful execution of such trusts were hardly created. But now there are many agencies for the execution of just such trusts—mostly created within sixty years. In consequence, it is a great deal easier than it used to be to keep safe money once made, or money which the creator of a great property desires to transmit to his children. And this safety in keeping is going to increase—for it is one of the results of a more perfect civilization. This means a great deal morally: it means fidelity and carefulness, and the power to procure this fidelity and careful ability in the interest of persons themselves incompetent to preserve great estates. That is going to be more and more possible in our country; and therefore we are going to see, in my judgment, more and more families in which wealth is transmitted. I look, therefore, for no decrease in the rich class, but rather for an increase.

The remedy for the difficulties which encompass this whole problem of great wealth, it seems to me, has been already indicated. It was indicated by the essayist of the evening: it is contained in the word *service*—in the desire and purpose to be of service. It was indicated, also, by Professor Giddings when he said that the cure is in setting up true ideals—in the recognition of wealth as a means, and not an end. This remedy must be procured through education—home education, school and college education, and church education. The main doctrine of the New Testament, as a whole, is that loving service leads to happiness and safety — for the individual, to what we call heaven; for society, to what we call the kingdom of God.

THE EXEMPTION FROM TAXATION

OF CHURCH PROPERTY, AND THE PROPERTY OF EDUCATIONAL, LITERARY, AND CHARITABLE INSTITUTIONS

THE EXEMPTION FROM TAXATION[1]

THE property which has been set apart for religious, educational, and charitable uses is not to be thought of or dealt with as if it were private property; for it is completely unavailable for all the ordinary purposes of property, so long as the trusts endure. It is like property of a city or State which is essential for carrying on the work of the city or State, and so cannot be reckoned among the public assets; it is irrecoverable and completely unproductive. The capital is sunk, so to speak, just as the cost of a sewer or a highway is capital sunk. There is a return, both from a church or a college,

[1] CAMBRIDGE, December 12, 1874.

To the Commissioners of the Commonwealth, appointed "to inquire into the expediency of revising and amending the laws of the State relating to taxation and the exemptions therefrom":—

GENTLEMEN:—In accordance with a request contained in a letter of October 14, 1874, from Prof. J. H. Seelye, that I lay before your Commission my "views respecting the present exemption from taxation of property used for religious, educational, and charitable purposes," I respectfully present for your consideration the following paper. Your obedient servant,

CHARLES W. ELIOT.

and from a sewer or a highway, in the benefit secured to the community; but the money which built them is no longer to be counted as property, in the common sense. It can never again be productive, except for the purposes of the trust for which it was set apart.

When a new road is made where there was none, the State, or some individual, sacrifices the value of the land it covers, and the money spent in building the road. It also sacrifices the opportunity to tax, in the future, the improvements which might have been put upon that land if it had not been converted into a road, and all the indirect taxable benefits which might have been derived from the use for productive purposes of the land, and of the money which the road cost. When a church, or a college, or a hospital, buys land, and erects buildings thereon, the State does not sacrifice the value of the land, or the money spent upon the buildings; private persons make these sacrifices; but the State does sacrifice, by the exemption statute, the opportunity to tax, in the future, the improvements which might have been put upon that land if it had not been converted to religious, educational, or charitable uses, and all the indirect taxable benefits which might have been derived from the use for productive purposes of the land, and of the money which the buildings cost.

This is the precise burden of the exemption upon the State. Why does the State assume it? For a reason similar to, though much stronger than, its reason for building a new road and losing that area forever for taxation. The State believes that the new road will be such a convenience to the community, that the indirect gain from making it will be greater than the direct and indirect loss. In the same way the State believes, or at least believed when the exemption statute was adopted, that the indirect gain to its treasury which results from the establishment of the exempted institutions is greater than the loss which the exemption involves. If this belief is correct, in the main, though not perhaps universally and always, the exemption can hardly be described as a burden to the State at large.

The parallel between a sewer or a highway, on the one hand, and land and buildings of exempted institutions, on the other, may be carried a little farther with advantage. The abutters often pay a part of the cost of the sewer or the highway which passes their doors, because it is of more use to them than to the rest of the inhabitants, and the members of the religious, educational, or charitable society erect their necessary buildings and pay for their land themselves. If it be granted that the religious, educational, or charitable use is a public use, like the use of a sewer or a highway, there is no more reason for taxing the church, the academy, or the hospital, than for annually taxing the abutters on a sewer or a highway on the cost of that sewer or on the cost of the highway and its value considered as so many feet of land, worth, like the adjoining lots, so many dollars a foot. The community is repaid for the loss of the taxable capital sunk in the sewer by the benefit to the public health, and the resulting enhancement of the value of all its territory. In like manner, it is repaid for the loss of the capital set apart for religious, educational, and charitable uses, by the increase of morality, spirituality, intelligence, and virtue, and the general well-being which results therefrom. To tax lands, buildings, or funds which have been devoted to religious or educational purposes would be to divert money from the highest public use — the promotion of learning and virtue — to some lower public use, like the maintenance of roads, prisons or courts, an operation which cannot be expedient until too large an amount of property has been devoted to the superior use. This is certainly not the case in Massachusetts to-day. The simple reasons for the exemption of churches, colleges, and hospitals from taxation are these: first, that the State needs those institutions; and secondly, that experience has shown that by far the cheapest and best way in which the State can get them is to encourage benevolent and public-spirited people to provide them by promising not to divert to inferior public uses any part of the income of the money which these benefactors devote to this noblest public use. The statute which provides for the exemption is that promise.

Exemption from taxation is not then a form of State aid, in the usual sense of those words; it is an inducement or encouragement held out by the State to private persons, or private corporations, to establish or maintain institutions which are of benefit to the State. The answer to the question,

—Why should the State give encouragement, in any form, to private corporations which support churches, academies, colleges, hospitals, asylums, and similar institutions of learning, advanced education, and public charity?—involves, therefore, an exposition of the public usefulness of these corporations. I say advanced education, because the lower grades of education are already provided for at the public charge, and there seems to be little disposition to question the expediency and rightfulness of this provision.

The reason for treating these institutions in an exceptional manner is, that having no selfish object in view, or purpose of personal gain, they contribute to the welfare of the State. Their function is largely a public function; their work is done primarily, indeed, for individuals, but ultimately for the public good. It is not enough to say of churches and colleges that they contribute to the welfare of a State; they are necessary to the existence of a free State. They form and mold the public character; and that public character is the foundation of everything which is precious in the State, including even its material prosperity. To develop noble human character is the end for which States themselves exist, and civil liberty is not a good in itself, but only a means to that good end. The work of churches and institutions of education is a direct work upon human character. The material prosperity of every improving community is a fruit of character; for it is energetic, honest, and sensible men that make prosperous business, and not prosperous business that makes men. Who have built up the manufactures and trade of this bleak and sterile Massachusetts? A few men of singular sagacity, integrity and courage, backed by hundreds of thousands of men and women of common intelligence and honesty. The roots of the prosperity are in the intelligence, courage and honesty. Massachusetts to-day owes its mental and moral characteristics, and its wealth, to eight generations of people who have loved and cherished Church, School, and College.

The public services of these institutions can hardly need to be enlarged upon. A single sentence may be given to the utility of that class of institutions which I may be supposed to speak for —the institutions of advanced education—the academies, colleges, scientific and technical schools, professional schools and seminaries, art collections and museums of natural history. All the professions called learned or scientific are fed by these institutions; the whole school-system depends upon them, and could not be maintained in efficiency without them; they foster piety, art, literature, and poetry; they gather in and preserve the intellectual capital of the race, and are the storehouses of the acquired knowledge on which invention and progress depend; they enlarge the boundaries of knowledge; they maintain the standards of honor, public duty, and public spirit, and diffuse the refinement, culture, and spirituality without which added wealth would only be added grossness and corruption.

Such is the absolute necessity of the public work which the institutions of religion, education, and charity do, that if the work were not done by these private societies, the State would be compelled to carry it on through its own agents, and at its own charge. In all the civilized world, there are but two known ways of supporting the great institutions of religion, high education, and public charity. The first and commonest way is by direct annual subsidies or appropriations by government; the second way is by means of endowments. These two methods may of course be combined. An endowment, in this sense, is property, once private, which has been consecrated forever to public uses. If, in one generation, a group of people subscribe to buy a piece of land, and build a church thereon, that church is an inalienable endowment for the benefit of succeeding generations. It cannot be diverted from religious uses, or ever again become private property. If a private person bequeath $50,000 with which to maintain six free beds for Boston sick or wounded in the Massachusetts General Hospital, which is an institution supported by endowments, that beneficent act obviates forever the necessity of maintaining six beds at the Boston City Hospital, which is an institution supported by direct taxation. If, by the sacrifices of generous and public-spirited people in seven generations, Harvard University has gradually gathered property which might now be valued at five or six millions of dollars, the State of Massachusetts is thereby saved from an annual expenditure of three or four hundred thousand dollars for the purpose of maintaining the liberal arts and professions; unless, indeed, the people of the State should be willing to leave the work of the university undone. To the precise extent of the work done by the income of endowments is the State relieved of what would otherwise be its charge. If some benevolent private citizen had built with his own money the State Lunatic Hospitals, the State would have been relieved of a very considerable charge. To tax such endowments is to reduce the good work done by them, and therefore to increase the work to be done by direct appropriation of government money, unless the people are willing to accept the alternative of having less work of the kind done. If the State wants the work done, it has but two alternatives — it can do it itself, or it can encourage and help benevolent and public-spirited individuals to do it. There is no third way.

The above argument in favor of the exemption of institutions of religion, education, and charity from taxation being conclusive unless it can be rebutted, I propose to consider successively the various attempts which have been made to repel or evade it.

The first objection which I propose to consider would be expressed somewhat in this fashion by one who felt it: "I admit that churches, colleges, and hospitals are useful, and I do not wish to see their good work diminished; but these institutions get the benefit of schools, police, roads, street lamps, prisons, and courts, and should help to support them; their friends and supporters are generous, and will more than make good what the institutions contribute to the city or town expenses." The meaning of this suggestion is just this: The body of taxpayers in a given community having, through the public spirit and generosity of a few of their number, got rid of one of their principal charges, — namely, the support of the institutions of religion, high education, and charity,— propose to avoid paying their full proportion of the remaining charges for public purposes, such as schools, roads, prisons, and police. They propose, by taxing the institutions which the benevolent few established for the benefit of the whole body, to throw upon these same public-spirited and generous men an undue share of the other public charges. To state the same thing in another form: there are in the community common charges, A, B, C, D, and E; A has been provided for by a few private persons at their own cost, and the burden of other taxpayers has been to that extent lightened; thereupon the taxpayers say, Let us take part of the money which these men have given for A, and use it for meeting charges B, C, D, and E. Our friends who provided for A will give some more money for that purpose, and we shall escape a part of our share of the cost of providing for B, C, D, and E. It is at once apparent that this objection is both illogical and mean: illogical, because if churches, colleges, and hospitals subserve the highest public ends, there is no reason for making them contribute to the inferior public charges; and mean, because it deliberately proposes to use the benevolent affections of the best part of the community as means of getting out of them a very disproportionate share of the taxes.

The next objection to the exemption which I propose to consider is formulated as follows: Churches, colleges, and hospitals do indeed render public service; they are useful to the State; but let them be established because the people feel the need of them, just as people feel the need of houses, and food, and clothes, and by all means let them support themselves; they ought not to be favored or artificially fostered. Railroads, factories, and steamship lines do service to the State; but it does not follow that they ought to be fostered by direct grants of public money, or be exempt from taxation. This objection is a plausible one at first sight; but there is a gap in the argument wide enough for whole communities to fall through into ignorance and misery. For the building of railroads, factories, and steamships there exists an all-sufficient motive — namely, the motive of private gain; and they ought not to be built unless there be a genuine motive of that sort. A few men can combine together to build a cotton mill whenever there seems to be a good chance to make money by so doing; and they will thus supply the community with mills. The benefit they might confer upon the State would not be a legitimate motive for building a mill in the absence of the probability of private gain. Now this motive of private gain is not only absent from the minds of men who found or endow churches, colleges, or hospitals, but would be absolutely ineffective to the end of procuring such institutions. It would be impossible for three or four men to establish and carry on a university simply for the education of their own sons. Those who found and maintain hospitals have, as a rule, no personal use of them. It is an unworthy idea that a church exists for the personal profit and pleasure of its members, or a college for the private advantage of those who are educated there. A church or a college is a sacred trust, to be used and improved by its members of to-day, and to be by them transmitted to its members of to-morrow. A modern church is an active center of diffused charity, and of public exhortation to duty. The press has enlarged the public influence of the pulpit by adding the multitude who read the printed sermon to the congregation who listen to it. The orators, poets, artists, physicians, architects, preachers, and statesmen do not exercise their trained faculties simply for their own pleasure and advantage, but for the improvement and delight, or the consolation and relief, of the community. In short, they do not live for themselves, and could not if they would. To increase virtue and piety, to diffuse knowledge and foster learning, and to alleviate suffering, are the real motives for founding and maintaining churches, colleges and hospitals. The work must be done through the individuals on whom the institutions spend their efforts, but the motive of those who promote the work is the public good and the advancement of humanity. Mills, hotels, railroads, and steamships, moreover, though they benefit the public, benefit them only in a material way; they provide clothing, shelter, easy transportation, and, in general, increase material well-being. People may be relied on to make themselves comfortable or wealthy, if they can; but they need every possible aid in making themselves good, or learned. The self-interest of no man, and of no association of men, would lead to the establishment of a university. The motive of private gain or benefit being wholly lacking in most cases, and feeble in all, it is to be expected that institutions of religion, high education, and public charity would not be founded and maintained, except by the direct action of the State, on the one hand, or, on the other, by the benefactions of private persons encouraged by fostering legislation. This is precisely the experience of all the modern nations. The American States now do less for the institutions of religion directly than any civilized nation, and they have done wisely in completely avoiding an establishment of religion; but from the time when they ceased to support religious institutions directly they fostered them by exempting them from taxation. Institutions of high education never have been self-supporting in any country; and there is no reason whatever to suppose that they ever can be. If they were made self-supporting, they would be inaccessible to the poor, and be maintained exclusively for the benefit of the rich. The higher the plane of teaching, the more the teaching costs, and the fewer the pupils, from the nature of the case, As to the charitable corporations whose whole income is used upon the sick, blind, or insane poor, the notion that they could ever be self-supporting is of course an absurdity. Hospitals and asylums which are wholly devoted to taking care of men and women of the laboring classes who have lost their health, their reason, or some of their senses, cannot be self-supporting in the nature of the case. It is an abuse of language to apply the word to them; they are inevitably supported by private benevolence, or from the government treasury, or by the combination of these two resources.

The opinion, then, that churches, colleges, and charitable institutions would be established in sufficient numbers without fostering legislation, and be as well maintained taxed as untaxed, has no warrant either in sound reason or in experience. Not a bit of practical experience can be found in the civilized world to support it; and the analogy set up between these institutions of religion, education, and charity, on the one hand, and establishments of trade, manufactures, and transportation, on the other, is wholly inapplicable and deceptive.

I come now to the consideration of an objection to the exemption, which is local in its nature, but not on that account less worthy of careful examination. Those who urge this objection admit that the public receive great benefits from churches, colleges, and hospitals; but, as these institutions necessarily have local habitations, and taxes under our laws are locally levied, they allege that the particular cities or towns in which the institutions happen to be situated bear, in loss of taxable property, the so-called burden of their exemption, while the whole State, or perhaps the whole country, shares the public benefits which accrue from them. The public burdened, it is alleged, is not the same public as the public benefited. This objection assumes, in the first place, that it is a burden to a city or town to have a lot of land within its borders occupied by an institution exempted from taxation; and this assumption is based upon the belief that, if the exempted institution did not occupy the lot, the taxable houses, or factories, or stores within the limits of the city or town would be increased by the number of houses or stores which might stand upon the exempted lot. This is a proposition which is generally quite incapable of proof, and is intrinsically improbable, but which nevertheless has, in some cases, a small basis of unimportant fact. It implies that there is an unsatisfied demand for eligible land on which to build houses, or factories, or stores, within the city or town limits; but this can be the case only in very few exceptionally situated cities, and not all the time in them, but only spasmodically in seasons of speculation or unusual activity, and even then not over their whole area, but only in very limited portions of it. Of course the cost of the buildings which might be erected upon a lot rescued from an exempted institution is not to be counted as an additional resource for the tax-gatherer; for that amount was, under our laws, taxable somewhere before as personal property. If, in any town or city, there are houses, or factories, or stores enough to meet the demand for such accommodations, the town or city will gain nothing by having more buildings erected. There may be more houses or more stores, but each house or each store will be worth less. In a large city there will always be a few streets, and perhaps wharves, which are absolutely needed for business purposes. Thus, for example, it might not be expedient to have an exempted institution, which had no need of water-front, occupy a portion of a limited water-front, every yard of which was needed for commerce. It might not be expedient that a church should occupy a street corner, or an open square, in the heart of the business quarter of a growing city — though London has not felt obliged to move St. Paul's into the country, or build upon Trafalgar Square. But such peculiar cases are to be wisely treated as the exceptions which they really are; at any rate, they cannot be made the basis of a great State's policy toward its most precious institutions—its institutions of religion, learning, and charity. As a rule, the amount of taxed property, real and personal, in a town or city is in no way diminished by the fact that a portion of its territory is exempted from taxation; and in many cases it is obvious that the taxable property is actually increased by reservations, whether natural — like small sheets of water, or artificial—like parks, squares, or open grounds about churches and public buildings. It is well known that in many new towns and cities of the

Western States it was a well-recognized and, in some cases, very successful device for raising the price of house-lots, and stimulating the speculation in land, to make a large reservation in the center of the town for an academy or college. This is one of the reasons why there are such a multitude of colleges in the West. It is but a few years since several towns were bidding against each other to get the Massachusetts Agricultural College planted within their borders. The town of Amherst paid $50,000 for this privilege. In Boston itself, the block of land on which the buildings of the Natural History Society and the Institute of Technology stand was given to those corporations on the condition that, if the lands surrounding the reserved area did not rise in value, in consequence of the grant, enough to cover the estimated value of the reservation itself, then the two corporations should pay the deficiency. These corporations never had to pay anything for their land. The city had just as much value in land available for taxation after the gift was made to these two exempted societies as it would have had if no such gift had been made. It cannot be maintained that the exemption of the church lots in a country town is in any possible sense a burden to the town, or that it diminishes in any way the valuation or amount of the property in the town which is available for taxation. On the contrary, every estate in the town is worth more to the occupant and to the assessor, because of the presence of those churches. The proposition that the presence, in a town or city, of exempted institutions diminishes the amount of taxable property therein is, therefore, not only incapable of proof, but is manifestly untrue in the vast majority of cases.

There are, nevertheless, some cases in which a new exemption involves a real loss, though not without compensations, to the town or city from which the property was abstracted; and there are also cases in which the restoration of an exempted piece of property to taxation might be a real gain, in spite of considerable losses. When a benevolent citizen of one town gives $100,000 of personal property to an exempted institution situated in another town, the first town loses so much property which was there taxable, and the second town has the local benefit of the institution, if there be any. On the other hand, the town which loses in this case has similar chances of gaining local benefits by gifts to institutions situated within its limits from citizens of other towns. Again, it by no means follows that the citizen who gave this $100,000 would have kept it in a taxable form at his place of residence, if he had not given it to an exempted institution. Such gifts are often — perhaps generally — made out of annual earnings or sudden profits; and if the $100,000 had not been given to an exempted institution, it might have been unprofitably consumed, or lost, or given away to individuals resident elsewhere. A good deal of the personal property which now goes to churches, colleges, and hospitals would be consumed outright if it were not so saved. If the gift is made by will, instead of during life, there are more chances that the $100,000 would, in the distribution of the property, have been carried away from the testator's place of residence, at any rate. When a piece of estate is transferred to an exempted institution for its own proper use, the local benefits of the institution, if there be any, are for the same town which gives up the taxes on the piece of real estate, and the withdrawal of that piece from productive uses probably brings some other piece into use at once, or at least sooner than would otherwise have happened. It would seem, at first sight, as if it would be clear gain to get a piece of land, once exempted, taxed again, and covered with taxable houses or stores; but there are always drawbacks on the gain. If Boston Common should be cut up and built upon, the conveniently situated houses and stores built there would cause other houses and stores, less well placed, to be vacated or to fall in value; and the improvement of real estate in the outskirts would be arrested or checked for a time. The estates which face the Common would also fall in value. It would be a permanent gain that the business of the city would probably be more conveniently done thereafter; and this indirect gain, whatever it might be, would ultimately be represented in the taxable property of the city. In this particular instance the productiveness of Boston would doubtless be diminished by the loss of health, vigor, and spirits, on the part of the inhabitants, consequent upon the loss of the healthful open area. It is, then, quite impossible to maintain that any exemption is a clear loss to the place in which it exists. With every loss there come chances of advantage. Sometimes the loss is great and the compensation small, and sometimes the advantages quite outweigh the loss. We have seen that, in the long run, there is no real loss to the State at large; and, in all probability, the local gains and losses of the various towns and cities of the Commonwealth would be found to be distributed with tolerable fairness, if the averaging period were long enough. Absolute equality in matters of taxation is unattainable.

It is important to demonstrate satisfactorily the statement just made, that great advantages often accrue to a town or city from the presence of institutions exempted from taxation, advantages which much more than offset any losses which are real. A concrete instance will best illustrate this proposition; and no better instance can be chosen than that of Harvard University, an exempted institution occupying about seventy acres of land in the city of Cambridge, which land, with the buildings thereon and their contents, is alleged by the assessors to be worth from three to four millions of dollars. This case is perhaps as strong as any on the side of the objectors to the exemption, because the exempted area is large and its value is high, and on this very account it is a case well adapted to my present purpose. In the first place, all the land which faces or adjoins the university's inclosures is enhanced in value in consequence of that position. The open grounds of the university have the same effect on the surrounding lands which open spaces of an ornamental character always have in cities. They improve the quality and value of the whole neighborhood. Secondly, the university brings to Cambridge a large amount of personal property, which becomes taxable there. The fifty families of which the heads are teachers in the university possess, on the average, an amount of personal property which much exceeds the property of the average family throughout the city. A considerable number of families are always living near the university for the sake of educating their children. They come to Cambridge for this express purpose, and stay there from four to seven years, or sometimes indefinitely. Many of these families have large means; in fact, few others could afford such a temporary change of residence. Again, families of former officers and teachers in the university continue to live in Cambridge; and it is notorious that some of the largest properties taxed in the city are of this sort. Finally, families come to Cambridge to live because of the society which has gathered about the university. The amount of taxable personal property brought into Ward One of Cambridge by the university in these several ways counts by millions. Accordingly, this ward is the richest ward in Cambridge, and has always been the most desirable part of the city to live in, as the character of its houses and of its population abundantly testifies. It has eighteen per cent. of the houses in Cambridge and sixteen per cent. of the polls, while it has thirty per cent. of the taxable property. The ward had no natural advantage over the rest of the city, having, to this day, its fair share of bogs, salt marshes, and sandy barrens. The greater part of its surface is but a few feet above high-water mark, and nothing but the presence of the university during two hundred and forty years has made it the desirable place of residence it is.

In still another way does the university bring taxable money to Cambridge. It collects from its students in Cambridge about $150,000 a year, adds thereto about $50,000 of the income of its personal property, and pays this large sum out as salaries and wages to people who live in Cambridge. A large portion of this sum is annually taxed by the city as the income of individuals in excess of $2,000 a year.

It is well understood that the building of a new factory in a village, or the introduction of some new industry into a town, which gives employment to a large number of respectable people, is a gain to that village or town. Whatever brings into a town a large body of respectable consumers benefits that town. Now, the university brings into Cambridge a large body of respectable consumers: there are fifty families of teachers, about fifty more unmarried officers, about one thousand students, and about one hundred janitors, mechanics, laborers, bedmakers and waiters, a fair proportion of whom have families. As the great part of these persons belong to the refined and intelligent and well-to-do class, they consume very much more than the average of the community. The money thus spent in Cambridge is mainly brought from without, for the greater part of it is either derived from the personal property of the university, or it is money brought from home by the students. If it were not for the presence of this body of consumers, the land, houses, and shops of that part of Cambridge would all be worth less than they are, and the assessors would find so much less to tax.

It is a great advantage to a city to have a place of high education at its doors, just as it adds to the attractiveness and prosperity of a city to maintain good schools. Nearly one hundred Cambridge young men are now members of the university.

The grounds of the university adorn the city, and serve as protection against spreading conflagrations. They give light and air, trees, shrubs, grass, and birds to a part of the city which must soon become densely populated. In the future they will serve many of the purposes of a public park, while they will be maintained without expense to the city. The buildings and collections of the university, which are becoming more and more attractive, are a source of interest and pleasure to all the people of the neighborhood. It is a curious illustration of the incidental advantages which Cambridge has reaped from the presence of the university, that printing and binding are still principal industries in the city, industries which give employment to hundreds of work-people and a large taxable capital. The business of printing was planted in Cambridge by the college, and was maintained there by the college, in spite of great difficulties, for many years.

Finally the presence of the university gives distinction to the city. Cambridge is one of the famous spots of the country, and its citizens take pride and pleasure in its eminence.

I have taken a single notable example through which to exhibit the various advantages which a town or city may derive from the presence of one of the exempted institutions. *Mutatis mutandis*, the principles just laid down apply to almost all of them, with a force which varies with the locality, the nature of the institution, and the stage of its development. The benefits of many of the exempted charitable institutions are almost exclusively local. The direct benefits of a town's churches are largely, though not exclusively, local, and if the church buildings are beautiful, or interesting from historical associations, this indirect benefit is local too. It may not be impossible to pick out some exceptional institution of education or charity, or some single peculiarly placed church, to which these principles concerning the bearing of the exemption upon the interests of localities may not apply in their full force, or may not apply at all at a given moment; but the legislator should never be much influenced by the exceptions to general rules, or by momentary abnormal phenomena, or by the back eddies in a strong current of opinion.

We have seen that exempted institutions are considered by towns desirable acquisitions, in spite of the exemption. There is competition among them even for the State prison and the lunatic asylums; and they doubtless understand their own interests. But if the towns were allowed to tax the institutions now exempted, what a treasure would a college, or a hospital, with a large amount of personal property, be to a town! The town would have all the indirect local benefits of the institution, and the taxes on its property besides; and this unmerited addition to the property taxable in the town would correspond to no service performed, sacrifice made, or burden borne by the town.

It has been often asserted that to exempt an institution from taxation is the same thing as to grant it money directly from the public treasury. This statement is sophistical and fallacious. It is true that the immediate effect on the public treasury is in dollars and cents the same, whether Harvard University be taxed $50,000, and then get a grant of $50,000, or be exempted from taxes to the amount of $50,000, and get no grant. The immediate effect on the budget of the university would also be the same. The proximate effects of these two methods of State action in favor of religion, education, and charity are however unlike — so unlike, indeed, that one is a safe method, while the other is an unsafe method in the long run, though it may be justifiable under exceptional circumstances. The exemption method is comprehensive, simple, and automatic; the grant method, as it has been exhibited in this country, requires special legislation of a peculiarly dangerous sort, a legislation which inflames religious quarrels, gives occasion for acrimonious debates, and tempts to jobbery. The exemption method leaves the trustees of the fostered institutions untrammeled in their action, and untempted to unworthy acts or mean compliances. The grant method, as practised here, puts them in the position of importunate suitors for the public bounty, or, worse, converts them into ingenious and unscrupulous assailants of the public treasury. Finally and chiefly,—and to this point I ask special attention,—the exemption method fosters public spirit, while the grant method, persevered in, annihilates it. The State says to the public-spirited benefactor, "You devote a part of your private property forever to certain public uses; you subscribe to build a church, for example, or you endow an academy; we agree not to take a portion of the income of that property every year for other public uses, such as the maintenance of schools, prisons, and highways." That is the whole significance of the exemption of any endowment from taxation. The State agrees that no part of the income of property, once private, which a former generation, or the present generation, has devoted forever to some particular public use, shall be diverted by the State to other public uses. The exemption method is emphatically an encouragement to public benefactors. On the contrary, the grant method extinguishes public spirit. No private person thinks of contributing to the support of an institution which has once got firmly saddled on the public treasury. The exemption method fosters the public virtues of self-respect and reliance; the grant method leads straight to an abject dependence upon that superior power — Government. The proximate effects of the two methods of State action are as different as well-being from pauperism, as republicanism from communism. It depends upon the form which the action of the State takes, and upon the means which must be used to secure its favor, whether the action of the State be on the whole wholesome or pernicious. The exemption is wholesome, while the direct grant is, in the long run, pernicious.

There has been, of late years, a good deal of vague declamation against endowments. We have heard much of the follies and whimsies of testators, and fearful pictures have been painted of dead hands stretched out from the cold grave to chill and oppress the living. We frequently read sneers and flings at those benefactors of the public who, living or dying, consecrate their money to religious, educational, or charitable uses. In urging the abolition of the exemption, much use has been made of this sort of appeal. What is its basis? Are there any grounds whatever for jealousy of endowments? Millions of private property in this State have been devoted to public uses of religion, education, and charity. These endowments are all doing good work for the present generation, and are likely to do good to many generations to come. To how many injurious or useless endowments can any one point in Massachusetts? There are persons who too hastily say that they hold Catholic churches to be injurious endowments; but it must be a very bigoted Protestant that does not admit that a Catholic church is better for a Catholic population than no church at all. Catholics would doubtless, in these days, grant as much as that for a Protestant population. The judicious legislator, when he speaks of the church, does not mean any particular church, or the churches of any particular sect; he means the sum of all the churches, the aggregate of all religious institutions, Christian, Israelite and Greek, Roman and Protestant, Congregational, Baptist, Anglican and Quaker. To legislate, directly or indirectly, either for or against any particular religious belief or worship would be utterly repugnant to all sound American opinion and practice.

What silly fancy or absurd whim of a testator can be instanced in Massachusetts? Is anybody in this country obstructed, as to his rights, duties, or enjoyments, by any endowment or foundation provided by the living or the dead? The suggestion is to the last degree ungrateful and absurd. Because there have been found in England a few endowments six or seven centuries old, which, in the changed condition of society, had come to do more harm than good, shall we on this fresh continent, in this newly organized society, distrust all endowments? Let us at least wait to be hurt before we cry out. If the time ever comes in this country when certain endowments, or classes of endowments, are found to do more harm than good to the community, legislation must then reform them, so as to prevent the harm and increase the good. We may be sure that our descendants of five centuries hence will have the sense to treat the endowments which we are establishing as England has treated some of her medieval endowments — reconstruct them, when they need it, without destroying them. Taxation would not only be no remedy for the folly of endowments, if there were foolish endowments; but it would actually abridge the moral right of the State to interfere with mischievous endowments. Institutions which are fostered by the State through exemption from taxation must admit the ultimate right of the State to inquire into the administration of their affairs. An institution, on the other hand, which got no help from the State, and was taxed like a private person, would have a right to claim all the immunity from State inquiry into its affairs which an individual may claim. Thus the State may and should demand from every exempted institution an annual statement of its affairs which could be given to the public; but no such statement for public use could properly be demanded of an institution which paid taxes like any private citizen. Such an institution would have a moral right to the privacy to which an individual is entitled in a free country.

In this country, when one wishes to scoff at endowments, he must draw on his imagination for his facts. There is but one well-founded charge to bring against our countrymen in this matter of setting apart private property for public uses of religion, education, and charity. They scatter their gifts too widely; so that a greater number of institutions are started than can be well maintained. But the remedy for this evil is to consolidate endowments — not to tax them. This consolidation has already begun, and will be brought about by the gradual enlightenment of public opinion on this subject. To draw a vivid picture of alleged scandals and abuses, and then propose some action of an irrelevant nature, desired for other reasons, as if it were a remedy for those scandals and abuses, is a well-known device of ingenious disputants; but it is a device which ought not to impose on clear-headed people. To prejudice the mass of the people against endowments is the part of a demagogue, for it is to induce them to act ignorantly in direct opposition to their own real interests; since endowments exist for the benefit of the great mass of the people, while they are a matter of but slight concern to the rich. The rich man does not care whether education be dear or cheap; he does not want the scholarships of a college; he does not need to send his children to a hospital; he could afford to keep a clergyman in his own family, if he cared to. It is the poor man who needs the church which others have built; the college which, because it has endowments, is able to offer his ambitious son a liberal education; the hospital which will give him, when disabled, attendance as skilful and careful as the rich man can buy. Moreover, the poor man has no direct interest in this proposed taxation of the institutions now exempted; it will not help him pay his poll-tax, nor lessen the amount of it; it will help no one but the property-holders. It is natural enough that a property-holder who has no public spirit should desire to escape his share of the charge of supporting institutions of public utility, on the ground that he feels no personal need of them. But that a man of property feels no want of institutions which are necessary to the security of the community, and does not believe in them, are no reasons for excusing him from his share in the support of these institutions. The doctrine that a citizen can justly be called upon to contribute to the support of those things only which he approves, or which are of direct benefit to him, would cripple our public schools as well as our colleges, and, in fact, would destroy the basis of almost all taxation.

The Massachusetts statute about the exemption, as it is administered, guards effectually against all the real evils described by the law term "mortmain" — a word the translation of which seems to be such an irresistible rhetorical titbit for many who advocate taxing churches and carrying on universities by legislative grants. It is, indeed, inexpedient that religious, educational, or charitable corporations should hold large quantities of real estate for purposes of revenue; first, because experience shows that such corporate bodies do not, as a rule, improve real estate as steadily and promptly as individuals; and secondly, because the accumulation of large quantities of land in single hands, although permissible, and often rather beneficial than hurtful to the community, is an operation which needs the natural check of death and distribution among heirs. This check is wanting in the case of permanent corporations. Now, the Massachusetts statute does not exempt from taxation real estate held by religious, educational, and charitable institutions for purposes of revenue. On the contrary, all such property so held by these institutions pays taxes precisely as if the pieces of property belonged to private individuals. If the Old South Church corporation owns stores from which it derives income applicable to the purposes of its trust, those stores are taxed precisely as if they were the property of individuals. Harvard University owns a number of stores in the business part of Boston; with one exception (a store included in the exemption given by the charter of 1650), these stores are taxed just as if they belonged to an individual. If the Catholic Church undertakes to hold real estate for income, or as an investment, it has to pay taxes on such property, under the existing statute, like any private citizen. No exempted institution can hold real estate free of taxes except that which is fairly necessary for the purposes of the religious, educational, or charitable trust. It would be a dishonorable evasion of the real intent of the statute to claim exemption on real estate which was bought with the intention of selling it again at a profit; and if any addition could be made to the statute which would make such a practice impossible, or would subject to penalties any institution which should be guilty of it, such an addition would be an improvement; although it is altogether likely that the offense contemplated has never, as a matter of fact, been committed. Of course, the mere fact that an institution has made a sale of exempted land is not in itself evidence of an evasion of the statute; for poverty may compel an institution to part with land which it ought, in the real interest of the trust, to keep. It is also a perfectly legitimate transaction for an exempted institution to sell one site in order to occupy another. One cause of the agitation for the abolition of the exemption has been the distrust awakened by sales of church property at large profit in the older parts of our growing cities. But these sales are perfectly legitimate. Those who believe in the public utility of churches need only to be assured that the proceeds of these advantageous sales must be invested in new churches — that none of the property can relapse into the condition of private property. This assurance the action of the Massachusetts courts indisputably gives. It is hard to see why these transfers of churches from more valuable to less valuable city lots should seem a grievance to anybody. Whenever a city church sells its old site for a large sum, buys a new site for a much smaller sum, and with the balance erects a handsome church, the amount of property exempted from taxation remains precisely what it was before, and the city gains an ornamental building. There is less value in the exempted land than before, but more in the building. On the whole, considering the nature of American legislation concerning testamentary dispositions and the holding and transfer of land, considering the nature and history of our ecclesiastical bodies and the mobility of our whole social fabric, there is probably no economical evil from which an American State is so little likely to suffer as the medieval evil of mortmain. To live in apprehension of it would be as little reasonable as for the people of Boston to live in constant dread of being overwhelmed by an eruption of lava from Blue Hill.

It has been suggested by persons who apprehend that the institutions of religion, education and charity, or some of them, will get a disproportionate and injurious development, that only a limited exemption should be allowed them, the limit to be fixed by legislation. If, however, the property of these corporations is really held and used for a high public purpose, it is hard to understand how it can be for the interest of the public to pass any laws which tend to limit the amount of that property — at least until more property has been set aside for that purpose than can be well used. If it is inexpedient for the State to use for its common purposes — not religious or educational — any portion of the income of a church or an academy up to $5000, why is it not also inexpedient to divert from religious or educational uses any portion of the income above $5000? If the legislature could tell with certainty just how much property it was expedient for a church, or a college, or a hospital to have, then a limit for exempted property in each case would be natural and right; but the legislature cannot have this knowledge; and if they could acquire it for to-day, it would be outgrown to-morrow. Moreover, the circumstances and functions of the various exempted institutions are so widely different and so changeable, that each institution would necessarily have its own limit prescribed by law, and would be incessantly besieging the legislature for a change in its limit. The legislature would be forced to keep removing the limit of exemption, because in most cases there would be no logic in the limit. The more books there are in a library the better; it would be absurd to exempt the first hundred thousand, and tax the second hundred thousand. The more good pictures, statues, and engravings there are in an art museum, the better; it would be absurd to exempt a museum while it had few of these precious objects, and tax it when it got more, and so became more useful to the public. A sumptuary law to prevent the erection of beautiful churches, by taxing the excess of the value of a church above a certain moderate sum, would be singular legislation for Massachusetts. Who can tell how much money Harvard, or Amherst, or Williams could use legitimately to-day for the advantage of the State in advanced education? If one knew to-day, the knowledge would be worthless next year. The one perfectly plain fact is that no one of the institutions of advanced education in this State has one half the property which it could use to advantage. It would be cruel mockery to enact that a woman who can hardly buy calico and flannel shall not wear velvet and sable. The amount of exempted real estate which any of the exempted institutions can hold is limited by natural causes. As such real estate is, as a rule, completely unproductive, the institution will not be likely to tie up any more of its property in that form than it can help. A limit to exempted real estate has seemed desirable to some persons, because it has sometimes happened in large cities that institutions of religion, education, or charity have changed their sites with great profit; but in such cases the community gets the whole advantage of the profit in the increased work of the church, college, or hospital. Moreover, such transactions imply a growing population, likely to make increasing demands upon the institutions of religion, education, and charity, which, therefore, need all the new resources which the growth of population fairly brings them.

Those who advocate limiting the amount of the exempted property which may be held for a religious, educational, or charitable trust seem to forget that it is the public which is the real enjoyer of all such property, and that it is the public only which is really interested in its increase, except as gratitude, affection, or public spirit may prompt individuals to share this public interest. All such trusts are gifts "to a general public use, which extends to the poor as well as the rich," to quote Lord Camden's definition of a charity in the legal sense. They are gifts for the benefit of an indefinite number of persons, by bringing their minds under the influence of religion or education, or by relieving their bodies from disease. They are trusts in the support and execution of which the whole public is concerned, on which account they are allowed, unlike private trusts, to be perpetual. Now, for the public to make laws which tend to discourage private persons from giving property to the public for its own uses is as unwise as for the natural heir to put difficulties in the way of a well-disposed relative who is making his will. The fact that the property of these public trusts is administered by persons who are not immediately chosen or appointed by the public obscures to some minds the essential principle that the property is really held and used for the public benefit; but the mode of administration does not alter the uses, or make the property any less property held for the public. Experience has shown that many of the religious, educational and charitable works of the community can be peacefully, frugally, and wisely carried on by boards of trustees; and that method has been preferred in England and the United States. On the continent of Europe these functions are discharged by government; but, under both methods of administration, the functions are public functions. The fact that nobody has any permanent interest in the property of such trusts, except the public, is well brought out by imagining what would occur if a church, or an academy, or an insane asylum should be taxed, and nobody should come forward to pay the taxes. It is nobody's private interest to pay such taxes. The city or town could proceed to sell the church or other building belonging to the trust; but if it did so, the effect would be that a piece of property which had been set apart for public uses would become private property again, unless some benevolent persons should, for the love of God or the love of their neighbors, buy the property over again for its original public uses. A city might as well levy taxes on its city hall, and sell it for taxes in default of payment.

It remains to consider the effect of abolishing the exemption. No church could be maintained upon ground which would be very valuable for other purposes, and costly church edifices would be out of the question. A society whose land and building were worth $300,000 would have to pay $4,500 a year in taxes, besides all the proper expenses of a church. The burden would be intolerable. The loss to the community, in that pure pleasure which familiar objects of beauty give, would be unspeakable. The village could spare its spired wooden church as ill as the city its cathedral. Cities have learned that fine architecture in their own buildings is a justifiable luxury. On the same betterment principle handsome churches are profitable to the public as well as delightful. I say nothing of the grievous moral loss to the whole people which would result from crippling the existing churches, and making it harder to build the new ones which our growing population should have. That loss would be deep and wide-spread and lasting; but other pens than mine can better depict it. Educational institutions would be obliged to take the taxes out of the income of their personal property or out of their tuition fees. The fifty or sixty thousand dollars which the city of Cambridge would take next year from Harvard University would be deducted from the money now available for salaries of teachers. This sum represents the pay of from twelve to fifteen professors, or of a much larger number of teachers of the lower grades. Moreover, the sum thus withdrawn from teaching would annually increase with the rising value of land in Cambridge; while it can by no means be assumed that the personal property and tuition fees of the University would increase proportionally. The burden might easily become wholly unbearable. The barbarous character of the proposition to tax property devoted to educational purposes may be well brought home by specifying a few of the items of what would be the tax on Harvard University. Memorial Hall, with the two acres of land in which it stands, would be taxable for not less than $550,000 next year, and there is no telling the price per foot to which the land may rise, for it is well situated between three good streets. Eight thousand dollars would be next year's tax on that monument of pure devotion to the public good; and every year the tax would increase. Charlestown might as well be allowed to tax Bunker Hill Monument, as Cambridge to tax Memorial Hall. To commemorate the virtue of its one hundred and forty graduates and students who died for their country in the war of the Rebellion would cost the University the salaries of at least two professorships every year, in addition to the original cost of the land and buildings and the maintenance of the buildings. Moreover, every added picture or bust would entail an additional contribution on the part of the University to the ordinary expenses of the city of Cambridge. To place Charles Sumner's bust in the Hall would increase the annual taxes by $7.50, and to hang there the portrait of Col. Robert G. Shaw, who was killed at Fort Wagner, would give $15 a year to the city. The College Library may be freely consulted by all persons, whether connected with the University or not. With the building which contains it, this collection of books could hardly be valued at less than $300,000 — a sum very far short of its cost. There would, therefore, be a tax upon that library of perhaps $4,500 a year now; and, as about $10,000 worth of books are bought each year, the annual increase of the tax would be sure. If it is inexpedient that such a library should be exempt from taxation, how wrong it must be that cities and towns should pay all the expenses of public libraries, besides exempting them from taxation. The Observatory, an institution maintained solely for the advancement of knowledge, and having no regular income except from its endowments, is necessarily surrounded by open grounds, embracing several acres, and it must remain so protected, if good work is to be done there. The taxes on this land would eat up half the income of the Observatory now, and in a few years the whole income. The richer and more populous Cambridge became, the heavier would be the charges upon the University, for the higher would be the price of land throughout the city. It is to be observed that the facts and illustrations used to support the proposition that institutions of religion, education, and charity must be taxed are mostly drawn from the rich towns and cities of the Commonwealth — not from the country villages. The advisability of taxing churches, colleges, and hospitals does not seem to suggest itself until a community gets very rich — until its territory is at a great price per square foot. When Cambridge was a country village, she was glad to give the College a site for its first building.

The abolition of the exemption would reduce the service of all the institutions of advanced education in the State from 20 to 25 per cent. at present, and this diminution of efficiency would grow greater year by year. All the academies, colleges, professional schools, and scientific or technical schools, all the libraries not town libraries, all the museums of art or natural history, would see from one fifth to one quarter of their income diverted from education, and applied to ordinary city and town expenditures. An extravagant city or town government might at any time demand much more than one fourth of their income. Precious institutions, which render great services to the whole State, or perhaps to the nation, would be at the mercy of a single local government.

It is impossible that a Massachusetts legislature should consent to so great a reduction in the work of the institutions of advanced education all over the State; that work is none too great now. Considering the place which Massachusetts has always claimed among her sister States in all matters of education, and which she must hold if her influence is to be maintained, it is incredible that she should seriously contemplate putting all her best institutions at such a terrible disadvantage in the race for excellence with similar institutions in the other States, where high education would remain untaxed. Of course, the direct aid of the State would be urgently invoked, and, indeed, it is obvious that the State would be compelled to assume the charges which the crippled endowments for religion, education, and charity could no longer sustain; the State tax would thereby be largely increased, and the taxpayers would lose rather than gain by the change. There is but small chance that local taxes would be diminished by abolishing the exemption. Give the cities and towns of Massachusetts new resources, and instantly they will make new expenditures which will more than absorb those resources. It is the excessive expenditure of towns and cities which has been the principal cause of this extraordinary proposition to tax religion, education, and charity. The assessors are driven to desperate devices for increasing the public revenue. The one real remedy for the evils, which cause the eager search for something new to tax, is reduction of expenditure; and this reduction can only be accomplished through the election of independent and courageous legislators and administrators in towns, cities, and the State at large. Whenever the people find themselves in serious difficulty, they instinctively show their fundamental reliance upon men of character by calling upon them to bring the State out of trouble. The proposition under discussion is a proposition to cripple or crush the institutions which breed men of character. It should be called a proposition to get rid of churches, to cripple colleges, to impair charities, and to extinguish public spirit. The direct intervention of the State might indeed avert some of these evils, but only at the great cost of adding to the already too numerous and too complex functions of the State, and of strengthening the vicious tendency to centralization of powers in government.

The two nations in which endowments for public uses have long existed are the two free nations of the world. In England and the United States, the method of doing public work by means of endowments managed by private corporations has been domesticated for several centuries; and these are the only two nations which have succeeded on a great scale in combining liberty with stability in free institutions. The connection of these two facts is not accidental. The citizens of a free State must be accustomed to associated action in a great variety of forms; they must have many local centers of common action, and many agencies and administrations for public objects, besides the central agency of government. France perfectly illustrates the deplorable consequences of concentrating all powers in the hands of government. Her people have no experience in associated action, and no means of getting any. To abandon the method of fostering endowments, in favor of the method of direct government action, is to forego one of the great securities of public liberty.

The sudden abolition of the exemption would work great hardship, because of the nature of the contracts and undertakings into which the exempted institutions are accustomed to enter. Churches and colleges have been planted or built up, life salaries have been promised, wills have been made, gifts received, trusts accepted, and investments made, all on the faith of this exemption. In all the institutions of advanced instruction, for example, professors are appointed for life, and great hardships would result from the violation of that implied contract. It would have been impossible for Amherst College to accept the gift of its new Chapel, or Harvard University the gift of its Memorial Hall, except under the exemption statute. Several active churches in our cities have built chapels for the benefit of the poorer classes; they did this good work under the exemption statute, and neither would nor could otherwise have done it.

In case the legislature should see fit to abolish the exemption, equity would require that taxation should fall, not on property acquired during the existence of the exemption, but only on that acquired after the exemption was repealed. The legislature of a civilized State should always set an example of scrupulous respect for every acquired right or vested interest, particularly when it is endeavoring to enact justice and equality in the distribution of public burdens.

But I trust that it is not necessary to discuss how or by what stages this exemption should be abolished. The American States, rough and rude communities as they are in some respects, still lacking many of the finer fruits of civilization, nevertheless possess in an extraordinary degree the main elements of national strength. Churches, schools, and colleges were their historical foundations, and are to-day their main reliance. The general respect for religion and education, the prevalence of public spirit, the diffusion of knowledge, the common maintenance of high standards of character—these, and not growing wealth and increasing luxury, are the things which guarantee free institutions. Massachusetts has grown to be what she is under legislation which fostered institutions of religion, high education, and charity, and these institutions, with the public schools, are the very foundations of her social fabric. We must not undermine the foundations of the solid old house which our fathers so wisely built.

If abuses have crept in, let them be reformed. If institutions which are really not of a public character get exempted, cut them off; if greater publicity is desirable in regard to the condition and affairs of the institutions exempted, provide for annual published returns; if there be fear of improper sales of land, long exempted, to the private advantage of the trustees or proprietors of the moment, enact that all sales of such property shall be by order of a court, and that the court shall take cognizance of the investment of the proceeds. But while we reform the abuses, let us carefully preserve the precious uses of the exemption statute. That statute is an essential part of our existing system of taxation. It may be expedient that the whole system should be reconstructed; but the exemption of religious, educational, and charitable property is certainly not the point at which the reconstruction should begin.

Let us transmit to our descendants, in long generations, the invaluable institutions of religion, education, and charity which we inherited from our fathers, and transmit them, not merely as strong and ample as ever, but multiplied, beautified, and enriched by our loving care.

THE FUTURE OF THE NEW ENGLAND CHURCHES

ADDRESS

Delivered at the 250th Anniversary of the First Church, Boston, 1880

THE FUTURE OF THE NEW ENGLAND CHURCHES

LOOKING back with grave satisfaction over the long, continuous life of this church, and of its kindred churches, do we not survey the very springs and sources of the peculiar character of the New England people? Do we not clearly see whence this people has come? Only the more instant becomes that question which of late years has been much in all our hearts — whither is this people going? There cannot be many persons in this company who have not already said to themselves at this two hundred and fiftieth anniversary, Will the First Church of Boston have a five hundredth anniversary, or a four hundredth? I invite your attention very briefly to three reasons for indulging the confident expectation that it will.

I remark, first, that the instinct of worship is a universal instinct of the race, an instinct which civilization refines and exalts, but has no tendency to extinguish. The religious sentiment has always been, and still is, the strongest power in the world, making war and peace, resisting vice, establishing and overthrowing governments, fostering democracy, destroying slavery, preserving knowledge, building cathedrals, creating literature, and inspiring oratory, music, and art. Unless we can count on the permanence of this religious quality or faculty in man, we cannot count upon the permanence of any of his attributes. Yet modern science teaches that race qualities change so slowly that the ordinary division of time into years and centuries is not fitted to express the rate of change. It is hardly necessary to say that rapid change of theological opinion may, and often does, go on from generation to generation without producing any effect upon the sentiments of religion, or upon the real functions of a religious organization. The doctrines or dogmas taught now in this church bear but a faint resemblance to those of the seventeenth century; but the main objects of the church are, and ever will be, the same that they were in 1630, namely, to worship God with prayer and praise, to teach men their duty and urge them to do it, and to carry their thoughts out of the monotonous round of their daily lives, beyond the sea, above the sky, to the dwelling-place of the Most High. Benjamin Wadsworth, who left the pastorate of this church to encounter many hardships and trials as president of Harvard College, held some theological opinions which are not current in these days. Thus, in a sermon preached just after the First Church was burned in 1711, he says very simply, " 'T is of the mere undeserved mercy of God that we have not all of us been roaring in the unquenchable flames of hell long ago, for 't is no more than our sins have justly deserved." And again, in a sermon entitled "The Gospel not Opposed but by the Devil and Men's Lusts," he gravely remarks that "nothing is more grating, cutting, and enraging to the Devil than to have the gospel faithfully preached to men." Doubtless this hearty belief in the unpleasantness of the sensations which faithful preaching inflicted upon the enemy of mankind was an effective incentive to many a worthy minister. But when Dr. Wadsworth, holding these now obsolete notions, came to the practical matter of advising parents how to bring up their children, as he did in his sermon entitled "The Saint's Prayer to Escape Temptations," he gave good advice for all time, which the latest president of Harvard College will gladly adopt as his own; as, for example, "Teach them the Scriptures; charge them to live soberly, righteously, and godlily; endeavor the preventing of idleness, pride, envy, malice, or any vice whatsoever; teach them good manners (a civil, kind, handsome, and courteous behaviour); render them truly serviceable in this world, and so dispose of them in trade or business, and in marriage, as they may be least liable to temptations, and may probably be most furthered in virtue and piety." Let us, then, settle down upon an abiding faith that the instinct of worship is an indestructible element in man's nature, and that the religious and ethical sentiments of mankind, which have survived all the physiological, psychological, social, and political changes to which the race has been subjected, will exhibit no less vitality in the future than they have in the past.

In the second place, I wish to point out that the principle of associated action for the promotion of a common object has been wonderfully developed in this country and in England during the present century. Manufactures are carried on, goods and passengers are transported, money is lent, colonies are founded, hospitals, schools, and libraries are maintained by associations of men who combine for one defined object, and employ paid servants to do the common work. There is hardly a conceivable philanthropic enterprise which is not already the field of some benevolent society. This facility of association being one of the chief characteristics of our time, and a church having become, under the laws, only an association of like-minded men and women for the satisfaction of their religious needs and the furtherance of good works, it is inconceivable that the principle of association, which is proving so valuable in every other field of human activity, should fail to work well when applied, as it is in every American Protestant church, to the promotion of worship, charity, and piety. To our faith in the permanence of the religious needs and aspirations, let us then add the conviction that never, in the history of the world, has it been so natural and easy, as it is now, to satisfy those cravings by the fruitful method of voluntary association.

Thirdly, let us gain confidence in the future of the New England churches by contemplating the prodigious changes of legal condition and external circumstance through which they have already passed in safety. To appreciate the magnitude of these changes, we must recall the facts that suffrage in Massachusetts was long conditioned upon church membership; that towns could be fined for neglecting to support the gospel; that for two centuries attendance at meeting on the Sabbath could be enforced by fine; that all corporations holding lands within a parish were taxable down to 1831 for the support of public worship, and that down to 1835 the property of individual parishioners was held liable for the debts of the parish. Never was there a closer union of Church with State than that which existed in Massachusetts in 1630, and never has there been more complete separation of Church from State than that which exists in Massachusetts to-day. Churches and ministers have gradually been stripped of every peculiar privilege and every adventitious support, until they now stand upon this firm ground — that they partly satisfy an imperious need and ineffable longing of the human soul. Time to come can hardly have in store for the New England churches changes comparable in gravity with those which they have already experienced. Their present legal condition is healthier, freer, more natural, and more likely to be stable than any previous condition. The minister is judged, like other men, by his gifts, attainments, and character; and the church is valued for the services which it renders to the community.

It would have been happier for the cause of religion if the disestablishment of churches had proceeded as rapidly in Europe as it has in Massachusetts. History, then, might not have had to record that millions of educated and liberal-minded men have been alienated from religion by the habitual political attitude of the established churches.

Two hundred and fifty years is a long life for anything of human creation. There is not a written political constitution in the world which has even half that age. Empires and republics have come and gone, old dynasties have disappeared, and new ones risen to power within that period. In our own little Commonwealth, not only the external form of government has changed, but the whole theory of the political constitution. Every industry, manufacture, and human occupation has undergone fundamental changes in its processes and its results. But all these years this venerable church has maintained its original organization and held stoutly on its way through gladness and gloom, through sunshine and storm. Solemnly, resolutely, and hopefully, may it move on for centuries to come.

Does any one ask why universities, which must inevitably be occupied chiefly with secular knowledge, should feel any great concern for the permanence of religious institutions? I answer, that universities exist to advance science, to keep alive philosophy and poetry, and to draw out and cultivate the highest powers of the human mind. Now science is always face to face with God, philosophy brings all its issues into the one word duty, poetry has its culmination in a hymn of praise, and a prayer is the transcendent effort of intelligence.

WHY WE HONOR THE PURITANS

ADDRESS

At the Celebration of the 250th Anniversary of the First Parish Church in Cambridge, February 12th, 1886

WHY WE HONOR THE PURITANS

I WISH to confess, in the first place, that I made a grave error when I advocated in the Committee of Arrangements a morning celebration of this anniversary. To this proposal Dr. McKenzie objected that the men of his congregation could not well attend in the forenoon, and that it would be a serious charge and trouble to provide a mid-day meal for so large a number of people as might assemble. How much the better Puritan he was, I discovered a few days later, when I came, in the records of the Great and General Court, upon the following enactment, passed October 1, 1633: "And whereas it is found by common experience that the keeping of lectures at the ordinary hours now observed in the forenoon to be divers ways prejudicial to the common good, both in the loss of a whole day, and bringing other charges and troubles to the place where the lecture was kept; it is therefore ordered that hereafter no lecture shall begin before one o'clock in the afternoon." Fortunately my unhistorical recommendation did not prevail.

It is proper that a representative of Harvard College should take part in these commemorative exercises. The college owed its foundation to the nonconformist ministers who came hither with the first emigration. It was founded, as Thomas Shepard said, that "the Commonwealth may be furnished with knowing and understanding men, and the churches with an able ministry." For the first ten years of the life of the College three fifths of its graduates became ministers in the established Congregational Church of the colony, and for a whole generation more than half of its graduates entered that ministry. Two hundred and fifty years have wrought a great change in this respect. Instead of more than half of the graduates becoming Congregational ministers, not more than six per cent. become ministers at all; and this small contingent is scattered among a great variety of denominations. In 1654, Henry Dunster, the first President of the College, was indicted by the grand jury and turned out of office because he had become a Baptist; now the two oldest professorships of Divinity are held in peace by Baptist ministers. When I came hither to the collation this afternoon, there walked beside me a birthright Quaker who is the Dean of the College Faculty. I fear that Governors Dudley, Endicott, and Winthrop, and Ministers John Wilson and John Norton would not have been pleased to see a Quaker in charge of the College. I fear that if the young minister John Harvard should now visit his posthumous child, the College, with his ideas of 1636 undeveloped, he would wish at first sight that the institution bore some other name.

There has been a tone of exultation and triumph in our celebration, as if we thought that the Puritans exulted and triumphed. I do not think they did. They were terribly straitened, and were full of fear and anxiety. They saw nothing of the great and happy future. What they knew was that their lives were full of hardship and suffering, of toil and dread. Even their own precious liberty, for which they had made such sacrifices, seemed to them in perpetual danger from oppressors without and heretics within. How crushing must have been the constant sense of their isolation upon the border of a vast and mysterious wilderness! The Puritans were a poor and humble folk. Thomas Shepard was the son of a grocer in a small English village. John Harvard was the son of a butcher in one of the most obscure parishes of London. There were very few men among them of birth or station. In the early years they were often pinched for food. What must they not have suffered from this bitter climate! They lived at first in such shanties as laborers build along the line of new railroads in construction, or in such cabins as the pioneers in Western Kansas or Dakota build to shelter them from the rigors of their first winter. They had nothing which we should call roads or bridges or mails. Snow, ice, and mud, and the numerous creeks and streams isolated the scattered villages and farms, and made even the least communication difficult for half of the year. We are apt to think of the men who bore these hardships as stout and tough, and to waste no pity on them, because we cannot help imagining that they knew they were founding a mighty nation. But what of the tenderer women? Generations of them cooked, carried water, washed and made clothes, bore children in lonely peril, and tried to bring them up safely through all sorts of physical exposures without medical or surgical help, lived themselves in terror of savages, in terror of the wilderness, and under the burden of a sad and cruel creed, and sank at last into nameless graves, without any vision of the grateful days when millions of their descendants should rise up and called them blessed. What a piteous story is that of Margaret Shepard, married young to nonconforming Thomas, braver than he, confirming his faltering resolution to emigrate, sailing with him for these inhospitable shores, although very ill herself, and dying here within a fortnight of the gathering of the church over which her husband was to preside! Let us bear her memory in our hearts to-night.

But I dwell too much on physical hardships. The Puritans had other fears and anxieties. They dreaded the exercise here of English royal power. They watched with apprehension the prolonged struggle of the Catholics with the Protestant powers in Germany, giving thanks for mercies vouchsafed to the churches of God whenever the Protestants obtained a substantial success. But worst of all, they did not feel sure of themselves. They were not always confident that they could hold to their own ideals of life. Within ten years they had serious doubts about the success of their civil and religious polity in the few settlements they had made. In 1639 "the 4th day of the second month was thought meet for a day of humiliation, to seek the face of God, and reconciliation with him by our Lord Jesus Christ, in all the churches. Novelties, oppression, atheism, excess, superfluity, idleness, contempt of authority, and troubles in other parts to be remembered." John Pratt, of Newtown, must have given expression to a very common feeling when he wrote in an apologetic letter to the Court of Assistants these words: "Whereas I did express the danger of decaying here in our first love, I did it only in regard of the manifold occasions and businesses which here at first we meet withal, by which I find in my own experience (and so, I think, do others also) how hard it is to keep our hearts in that holy frame which sometimes they were in where we had less to do in our outward things."

The Puritans did not know from day to day what should be on the morrow; and this uncertainty only makes their heroism seem greater. Examine the list of evils against which they prayed on the fourth of the second month in 1639, and consider what they would think of the state of our generation in regard to the same subjects. "Novelties!" Is there any people on earth fonder of novelties than we? The American people is the only people I have ever lived among which takes the statement that a thing or a project is new as a recommendation. We like and welcome novelties. "Oppression!" They were in constant fear of oppression exercised by King and Church. That form of oppression we have escaped from, only to find ourselves compelled to be on our guard against another form,—the oppression, namely, of bewildered and misled majorities. "Atheism!" There are many excellent persons within these walls to whom the word atheists would have been applied by the men who ordered this fast. I do not believe that Governor Dudley or Governor Endicott would have tolerated the opinions of the most orthodox person here present. We all know that to-day there are millions of men of the Puritan stock whom the Puritans would have called atheists and treated as such. "Excess! Superfluity!" Think what they meant by these words. To their minds these evils had already invaded their society. This order was passed only nine years after the landing of the Winthrop colony. They had been through great sufferings from hunger, cold, and disease. They tried to regulate prices and consumption. They prohibited slashed clothes, large sleeves, laces whether of gold, silver, or thread, embroideries, long hair, and cakes and buns in markets and victualling-houses. They laid heavy taxes upon sugar, spice, wine, and strong waters, because they held these things to be unnecessary indulgences. What would they think of our way of living, our women's apparel, our church decorations, and our houses full of bric-à-brac? We who are in danger of having our intellectual and spiritual life buried under the weight of our luxuries and trivial possessions may well reflect upon the Puritans' idea of excess and superfluity. "Idleness!" They prayed against idleness; yet it is said of them that they worked sixteen hours a day, and for recreation laid stone walls. The notion that eight hours make a working day they would probably have accounted a mischievous whimsy. "Contempt of authority!" Our social system would seem to them full of dangerous license and pestilent toleration.

Neither the civil nor the religious polity of the Puritans succeeded. It was impossible to constitute a state on the basis of church membership; it was impossible to make life all duty without beauty. The society which they strove to found was an impossible one; for in their social aims they ignored essential and ineradicable elements in human nature. The Crusaders did not succeed, and the infidels still hold Jerusalem. The Puritans did not succeed, with all their sacrifices and struggles, in realizing the ideals they had at heart. Why, then, do we so honor them? It is not simply because they were stout-hearted. Many a soldier of fortune, many a freebooter or robber chieftain, has been stout-hearted too. It is because they were stout-hearted for an ideal,—not our ideal, but theirs,—their ideal of civil and religious liberty. Wherever and whenever resolute men and women devote their lives and fortunes not to material but to spiritual ends, there and then heroes are made, and, thank God, are made to be remembered. The Puritans thought to establish a theocracy; they stand in history as heroes of democracy.

We cannot help asking ourselves if we, their descendants, may possibly be remembered two hundred and fifty years hence for any like devotion to our own ideals. Have we ideals for which we would toil, and suffer, and if need be, die? The Civil War gave one answer to that question. But I believe that in peace as well as in war our nation has shown that it has ideals for which it is ready to bear labor, pain, and loss. I believe that no people ever sees clearly those steps in its own progress, those events in its own life, which future generations will count glorious. Yet I think we can discern some moral ideals toward which our generation strives. We strive toward a progressive improvement of human condition, an amelioration of the average lot. We begin to get a realizing sense of that perfect democratic ideal—"We are all members one of another." The gradual diminution of the exercise of arbitrary authority in the family, in education, and in government is another ideal toward which we press. We have come at last to really believe that he that would be greatest among us must be our servant. Finally, I think that we are working upward toward a truer and more beautiful idea of God, and that these very times may be remembered in later generations for the furthering of that better conception. We no longer think of God as a remotely enthroned monarch who occasionally intervenes in the affairs of men, or even as the Lord of Hosts. More and more we think of him as the transcendent intelligence and love in whom we and all things, from instant to instant, "live and move and have our being."

HEROES OF THE CIVIL WAR

ADDRESS

In Memorial Hall, Harvard University, May 30, 1896

HEROES OF THE CIVIL WAR

THE personal heroism of the men we commemorate here — of those who survived as well as of those who fell — had two elements which are especially affecting and worthy of remembrance.

In the first place, these men went through all the squalor, wretchedness, and carnage of war without having any clear vision of their country's future. They did not know that victory was to crown the Union cause; they did not know that the nation was to come out of the four years' struggle delivered from slavery, united as never before, and confident as never before in its resources and its stability. One of the worst horrors in 1860–61, before the war opened, was the sickening doubt whether we really had any country.

Civil war is immeasurably worse than any other war, because it inevitably creates just this terrible doubt about the national future. It was not till 1864–65 that it became plain that the North would ultimately win military success, and even then all men saw that after military success would come immense civil difficulties. The heroism of the soldiers on both sides, and the pathos of their sufferings and sacrifices, are greatly heightened by their inability to forecast the future. Like all devoted souls, they walked by faith, and not by sight. Most of the men whose names are written on these walls died with no shout of victory in their ears, or prospect of ultimate triumph before their glazing eyes. To console them in their mortal agony, in their supreme sacrifice, they had nothing but their own hope and faith.

Secondly, the service these men rendered to their country was absolutely disinterested. No professional interest in war influenced them. No pay, or prize money, or prospect of pension had the least attraction for them. They offered their services and lives to the country, just for love, and out of the determination that, if they could help it, the cause of freedom should take no harm. On the spur of the moment they abandoned promising civil careers, dear homes, and the natural occupations of men who had received collegiate training, for the savage destructions and butcheries of war. No mercenary motive can be attributed to any of them. This disinterestedness is essential to their heroic quality. The world has long since determined the limits of its occasional respect for mercenary soldiers. It admires in such only the faithful fulfilment of an immoral contract. The friends we commemorate here had in view no outward rewards near or remote.

To these heroes of ours, and to all soldiers of like

spirit in the Civil War, we owe debts which can never be paid except in respect, admiration and loving remembrance. We owe to them the demonstration that out of the hideous losses and horrors of war, as out of pestilences, famines, shipwrecks, conflagrations and the blastings of the tornado, noble souls can pluck glorious fruits of self-sacrifice and moral sublimity. And further, we owe them a great uplifting of our country in dignity, strength and security.

INTERNATIONAL ARBITRATION

SPEECH

At the American Conference on International Arbitration held in Washington, April 22 and 23, 1896

INTERNATIONAL ARBITRATION

I CANNOT bring you a learned essay on international law, such as that we have just listened to with so much pleasure from an authoritative voice.[1] I must speak to you without preparation, as a plain American citizen, who thinks about public problems, who has read some history of his own and other lands, and who loves his country.

You remind me, Sir, in your introduction, that I cannot help speaking in some sense for an ancient institution of our land — Harvard University. I will say, in the first place, that Harvard University has as little reason as any institution in our country to feel an irrational or exaggerated dread of war. It has survived many wars — Indian, French, and English. Ever since the early days, when the Puritan meeting-houses had to be fortified, and all males over sixteen were required to carry their guns and ammunition to meeting, the graduates of Harvard University have been taking part in war after war, till we come down to the twelve hundred grad-

[1] John Randolph Tucker, of Washington and Lee University.

uates and students who entered the army and navy of the United States in the Civil War. The chief building of the University commemorates one hundred and fifty Harvard men who laid down their lives for the country in that war alone. When Lord Percy marched to reinforce Major Pitcairn, retreating from Lexington, his column passed right by the college gate. When the little band of raw militia, who were to throw up intrenchments on Bunker Hill, were paraded on the green in front of the University on the evening before the battle, the President of Harvard College offered prayer before them, as for men going into deadly peril in a righteous cause. The British army was within three miles. The leading patriots of that day in Boston and Cambridge literally took in their hands "their lives, their fortunes, and their sacred honor." All the buildings of Harvard College were occupied for months by the patriot army besieging Boston. The Corporation of the College, which is working to-day under the charter given in 1650, has been through crisis after crisis, industrial, financial, and agricultural, always trying to preserve the precious funds given for the promotion of learning. Panics, crises, or periods of financial and industrial disturbance, supervene invariably upon war. Many and many a one has the College passed through. In two hundred and sixty years we have had full experience of war and its consequences to the institutions of education and religion; and yet, Harvard University knows full well, by its own observation and experience, that, as the last speaker has just said, heroic virtue may be plucked by noble souls from out the desolation, carnage, and agony of war. We know, too, that even from an unjust war, like that with Mexico, a nation may win advantages real and permanent, though undeserved. Therefore, when we plead for arbitration, we do not necessarily deny that war has a greatness of its own, and that out of it may sometimes come permanent gain for the moral forces of human society; but we do maintain that the deliberate bringing about of war through a belligerent public policy can be compared only to the deliberate and intentional introduction of a pestilence into a crowded city, in order, forsooth, that thousands of victims may have opportunity to suffer and die with patience, and that some noble souls — nurses, doctors, and mothers — may have opportunity to develop and display heroic qualities. The one operation would be just as reasonable as the other. Never, never let us hear it maintained in our country that war should be deliberately provoked and brought about, in order that there may be developed in a few souls the noble qualities which give victory over loss, pain, and death.

And what shall we say about careless inattention to those insidious or hidden sources of national exasperation which, in their development, may produce war? I believe, Mr. President, that it is just apprehension about such carelessness, such inattention to the tendencies of a public policy that may lead to war, which has brought this conference together. We have lately seen in a public print some remarks, presumably by a graduate of Harvard University—for every possible shade of opinion is developed among the graduates of that populous institution—about the inopportuneness of this assembly. I shall venture to say some words on that subject.

Why have we come together at this time? It is, I believe, because we, like other thoughtful American citizens, have been surprised and shocked at the risk of war which the country has lately incurred. Only four months ago, a message of the President of the United States seemed to thousands of sober-minded men, in this and other countries, to contain a grave threat of war in case a boundary question between two other nations should fail of settlement by arbitration, and our own uninvited decision of it should be rejected. Shortly after, we learnt with astonishment that, months before, the Secretary of State had issued from this capital papers of a tenor which, in a contest between two individuals, would fairly have been called exasperating. All men know that the peaceful settlement of a controversy between two self-confident and strong men is not promoted if one says to the other, "My fiat shall be law between us." Such views, conveyed in public documents, took thousands of thoughtful Americans by surprise. The surprise and the shock to public opinion were, I dare say, unforeseen and unintended; but they were inevitable from the tone of the papers.

Then we had another surprise. We have thought that the separation of the executive and legislative functions in our republic had one great advantage on which we might rely — namely, that when executive propositions of a serious nature were laid before the legislative branches, the legislature might be depended on to take time for consideration, and so to procure delay. We have been painfully surprised to learn by the actual event that that reliance is not well founded.

Moreover, there has been brought forcibly to our notice a phenomenon new in our country, and perhaps in the world — namely, the formidable inflammability of our multitudinous population, in consequence of the recent development of telegraph, telephone, and bi-daily press. I think that fairly describes the phenomenon of four months ago — our population is more inflammable than it used to be, because of the increased use in comparatively recent years of these great inventions.

Still another disquieting fact has been forced on our attention. Quite within recent years it has become the practice to employ as cabinet officers men who have not had legislative experience, or experience with any branch of the Government, before assuming these important functions. One reason for this new practice is that senatorships are much more attractive than cabinet offices. But, be the reason what it may, this recent practice has introduced into our governmental system a new and serious danger — the danger of inexperience in high place, the danger of bringing into great public functions men suddenly taken from business, or from the controversial profession of the law.

Besides these revelations of the last four months, there is another inducement for thoughtful Americans to interest themselves in all the means of interposing obstacles to sudden movements toward war. We have heard during the last eight or ten years from both political parties, and perhaps as much from the one as from the other, the advocacy of a policy entirely new among us, absolutely repugnant to all American diplomatic doctrines, and imported straight from the aristocratic and military nations of Europe. I refer, of course, to this recent doctrine called jingoism — a detestable word for a detestable thing. I should be at a loss to decide which party in this country has been most guilty of this monstrous teaching; and if inquired of by some observant person in this audience, I should be obliged in honesty to confess, that among the worst offenders in this respect are to be found several graduates of Harvard University. What can be clearer than that this doctrine is an offensive foreign importation, against which, unfortunately, our protective legislation has proved an inadequate defense. The very term is of English origin, and is taken, not from the best side of English politics, but from the worst, from the politics of Palmerston and Disraeli, and not of Bright, Gladstone, Hartington, and Balfour. It is the most abject copy conceivable of a pernicious foreign idea; and yet some of our public men endeavor to pass it off among our people as American patriotism. A more complete delusion, a falser representation, cannot be imagined. The whole history of the

American people runs directly counter to this European notion. Our nation has always advocated the rights of neutrals, arbitration, and the peaceful settlement of international disputes. It has contributed more than any other nation to the development of successful methods of arbitration. It has contributed more than any other nation to the promotion of peace and the avoidance of great armaments. What other powerful nation has dispensed with a standing army? What other nation with an immense seaboard has maintained but an insignificant fleet? It has been our glory to be safe, though without fortresses, fleets, or armies. Can anything be more offensive to the sober-minded, industrious, laborious classes of American society than this doctrine of jingoism, this chip-on-the-shoulder attitude, this language of the ruffian and the bully? That is just what jingoism means in its native soil, where it is coupled with a brutal and insolent militarism, natural enough to countries where the government has been despotic or aristocratic, and the military class has been enormous, but absolutely foreign to American society.

The teaching of this doctrine by our press and some of our public men is one of the reasons why this conference is gathered now. We want to teach just the opposite doctrine. We want to set forth in the daily and periodical press, and by publications of our own, what the true American doctrine on international relations really is. As one of the speakers said this afternoon, we want to have the children of this country — the young men who are rising up into places of authority and influence—taught what the true American doctrine of peace has been, what the true reliance of a great, strong, free nation should be—not the force of arms, but the force of righteousness. The moment is opportune for the inculcation of these doctrines. We have escaped a serious danger; but thoughtful men should say, "We will now make such preparation as will give us a new security for peace—namely, the preconcerted, prearranged security of a treaty of arbitration." That it is which this meeting has come together to support, maintain, and inculcate as the duty and privilege of the American people.

I can hardly conceive that any person who has read the history of our country should arrive at any other conclusion with regard to its natural mission; and yet, in this very conference, one gentleman arose to say that we had a mission to carry our political ideas over the world, to spread the knowledge of our free institutions and our methods of self-government among the peoples of the earth; and that, like England, we should execute this mission by ships and guns, and like her, should fortify our seaboard to resist aggression. A propaganda of armed force was recommended, to carry over the world the public principles of liberty for which our nation stands.

Now I, too, believe that this nation has a mission in the world, a noble mission; but it is not that one. It is not by force of arms that we may best commend to the peoples of the earth the blessings of liberty and self-government, but rather by taking millions from various peoples into our own land, and here giving them experience of the advantages of freedom. Have we not done that? Eighteen millions strong they have come since 1850. All of us have come within three hundred years; and this great nation has grown up on this continental territory, believing in and practising the principles of self-government, freedom, and peace. There is only one other means by which we should teach these principles to men. It is by example — by giving persuasive example of happiness and prosperity arrived at through living in freedom and at peace. Never should we advocate the extension of our institutions by force of arms, either on sea or on land; never should we attempt to force another nation to adopt arbitration or any other doctrine of peace.

I naturally think of the educational object of this meeting. I trust that in all our public schools these principles which I have just stated may be taught as the true American doctrine on this subject. One speaker, this afternoon, mentioned a special subject in which he thought instruction should be given throughout our land. He said: "We have been taught in our schools about the battles of the nation. We have not been taught about the arbitrations of our nation." Let us teach the children what is the rational, sober, righteous mode of settling international difficulties. Let us teach them that war does not often settle disputes, while arbitration always does; that what is reasonable and righteous between man and man should be made reasonable and righteous between nation and nation.

[The following inscriptions were prepared for the Water-Gate at the World's Fair, Chicago, in 1893, by request of Director Burnham. The shapes and sizes of the several tablets, and therefore the approximate number of letters which could be used on each, had been already determined. My plan was to commemorate on the side toward the lake the explorers and pioneers in the literal sense, and on the side toward the Court of Honor the pioneers of civil and religious liberty.

The inscription beginning "To the bold men," on the side toward the lake, prepared the way for Lowell's splendid verse on the other side, "But bolder they, etc." That verse, the two Bible texts, Lowell's lines on the left lower panel toward the Court of Honor, and Lincoln's sentence on the right lower panel I selected; the rest I wrote.—C. W. E.]

INSCRIPTIONS ON THE WATER-GATE AT THE WORLD'S FAIR, CHICAGO.

TOWARD THE LAKE.

A FEW
DARED TOILED
AND SUFFERED
MYRIADS ENJOY
THE FRUITS.

TO THE BOLD MEN
THEIR NAMES REMEMBERED OR FORGOTTEN
WHO FIRST EXPLORED THROUGH PERILS MANIFOLD
THE SHORES LAKES RIVERS MOUNTAINS VALLEYS AND PLAINS
OF THIS NEW WORLD.

OF MANY RACES
TONGUES CREEDS
AND AIMS
BUT ALL HEROES
OF DISCOVERY.

THE WILDERNESS AND THE SOLITARY PLACE SHALL BE GLAD FOR THEM.

TO THE
BRAVE SETTLERS
WHO LEVELED
FORESTS
CLEARED FIELDS
MADE PATHS BY
LAND AND WATER
AND PLANTED
COMMONWEALTHS.

TO THE
BRAVE WOMEN
WHO IN
SOLITUDES
AMID STRANGE
DANGERS AND
HEAVY TOIL
REARED FAMILIES
AND MADE HOMES.

INSCRIPTIONS ON THE WATER-GATE AT THE WORLD'S FAIR, CHICAGO.

TOWARD THE COURT OF HONOR.

CIVIL LIBERTY
THE MEANS
OF BUILDING UP
PERSONAL AND
NATIONAL CHARACTER.

TO THE PIONEERS OF CIVIL AND RELIGIOUS LIBERTY.
BUT BOLDER THEY WHO FIRST OFF-CAST
THEIR MOORINGS FROM THE HABITABLE PAST
AND VENTURED CHARTLESS ON THE SEA
OF STORM-ENGENDERING LIBERTY.

TOLERATION
IN RELIGION
THE BEST FRUIT
OF THE LAST
FOUR CENTURIES.

YE SHALL KNOW THE TRUTH AND THE TRUTH SHALL MAKE YOU FREE.

I FREEDOM DWELL
WITH KNOWLEDGE:
I ABIDE
WITH MEN BY
CULTURE TRAINED
AND FORTIFIED.
CONSCIENCE
MY SCEPTRE IS
AND LAW MY SWORD.

WE HERE
HIGHLY RESOLVE
THAT GOVERNMENT
OF THE PEOPLE
BY THE PEOPLE
FOR THE
PEOPLE
SHALL NOT PERISH
FROM THE EARTH.

INSCRIPTION WRITTEN IN 1877 FOR THE MONUMENT ON BOSTON COMMON

TO THE MEN OF BOSTON
WHO DIED FOR THEIR COUNTRY
ON LAND AND SEA IN THE WAR
WHICH KEPT THE UNION WHOLE
DESTROYED SLAVERY
AND MAINTAINED THE CONSTITUTION
THE GRATEFUL CITY
HAS BUILT THIS MONUMENT
THAT THEIR EXAMPLE MAY SPEAK
TO COMING GENERATIONS

ON THE ROBERT GOULD SHAW MONUMENT, ON BOSTON COMMON

TO THE FIFTY-FOURTH REGIMENT OF MASSACHUSETTS INFANTRY

THE WHITE OFFICERS
TAKING LIFE AND HONOR IN THEIR HANDS
CAST IN THEIR LOT WITH MEN OF A DESPISED RACE UNPROVED IN WAR
AND RISKED DEATH AS INCITERS OF SERVILE INSURRECTION IF TAKEN PRISONERS
BESIDES ENCOUNTERING ALL THE COMMON PERILS
OF CAMP, MARCH, AND BATTLE

THE BLACK RANK AND FILE
VOLUNTEERED WHEN DISASTER CLOUDED THE UNION CAUSE
SERVED WITHOUT PAY FOR EIGHTEEN MONTHS TILL GIVEN THAT OF WHITE TROOPS
FACED THREATENED ENSLAVEMENT IF CAPTURED
WERE BRAVE IN ACTION, PATIENT UNDER HEAVY AND DANGEROUS LABORS
AND CHEERFUL AMID HARDSHIPS AND PRIVATIONS

TOGETHER
THEY GAVE TO THE NATION AND THE WORLD UNDYING PROOF
THAT AMERICANS OF AFRICAN DESCENT POSSESS
THE PRIDE, COURAGE, AND DEVOTION OF THE PATRIOT SOLDIER
ONE HUNDRED AND EIGHTY THOUSAND SUCH AMERICANS
ENLISTED UNDER THE FLAG IN 1863–65

www.ingramcontent.com/pod-product-compliance
Lightning Source LLC
Chambersburg PA
CBHW030856270326
41929CB00008B/450

* 9 7 8 3 3 3 7 7 1 7 0 5 6 *